A DELICATE MATTER

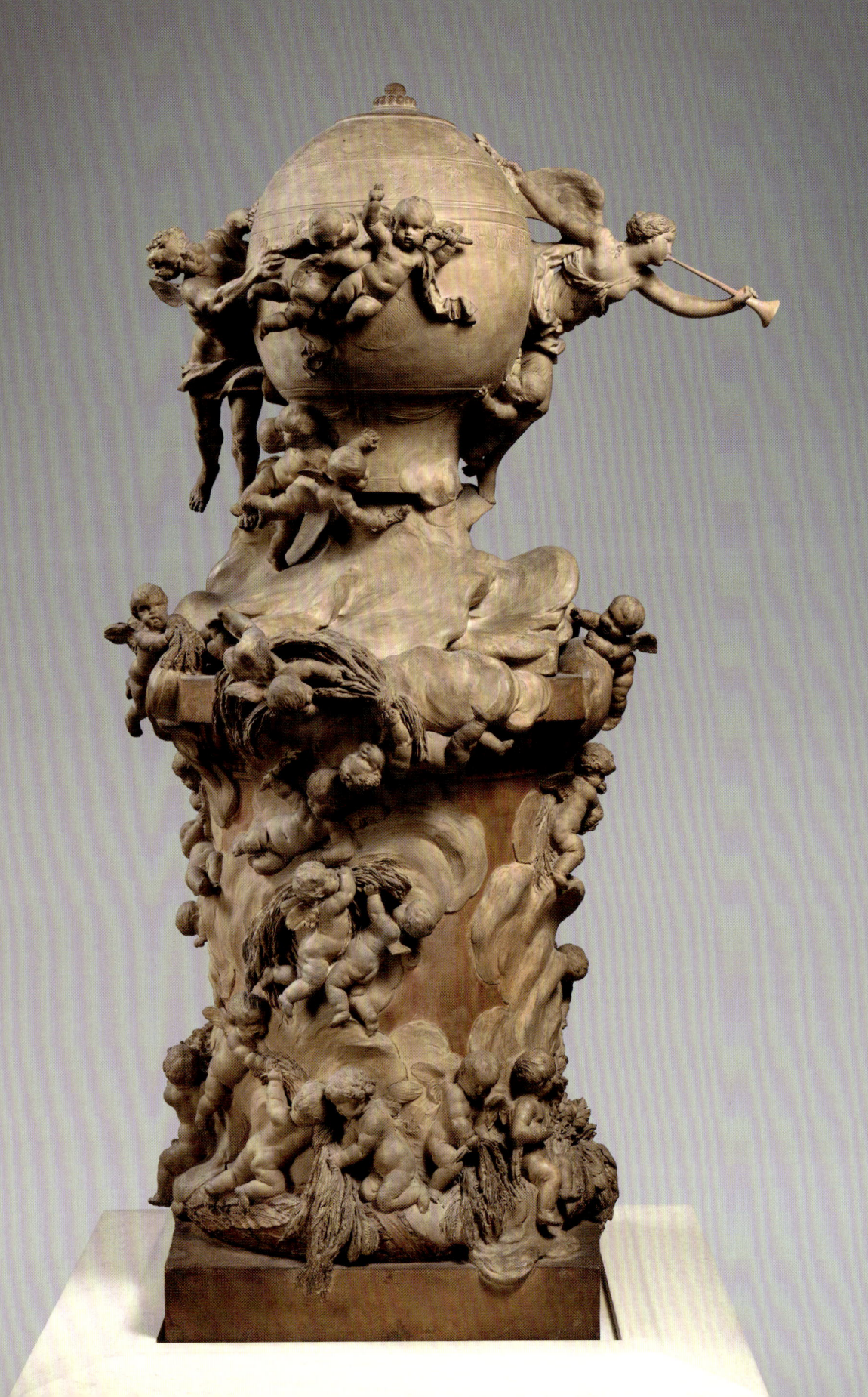

A DELICATE MATTER

*Art, Fragility, and Consumption
in Eighteenth-Century France*

OLIVER WUNSCH

The Pennsylvania State University Press
University Park, Pennsylvania

Publication of this book is supported by the Lise Meitner Group on Decay, Loss and Conservation in Art History at the Bibliotheca Hertziana, Max-Planck-Institut für Kunstgeschichte, BH-P-22-34.

Names: Wunsch, Oliver, author.
Title: A delicate matter : art, fragility, and consumption in eighteenth-century France / Oliver Wunsch.
Description: University Park, Pennsylvania : The Pennsylvania State University Press, [2024] | Includes bibliographical references and index.
Summary: "Examines how fragile and decaying artworks transformed the relation between art, time, and value in eighteenth-century France"— Provided by publisher.
Identifiers: LCCN 2023014757 | ISBN 9780271095288 (hardback)
Subjects: LCSH: Art, French—18th century. | Art—Economic aspects—France—History—18th century. | Artists' materials—France—History—18th century. | Art—Collectors and collecting—France—History—18th century. | Art and society—France—History—18th century. | Fragile art works Delicate art works
Classification: LCC N6846 .W86 2024 | DDC 709.44/09033—dc23/eng/20230522
LC record available at https://lccn.loc.gov/2023014757

Copyright © 2024 Oliver Wunsch
All rights reserved
Printed in China
Published by
The Pennsylvania State University Press,
University Park, PA 16802–1003

The Pennsylvania State University Press is a member of the Association of University Presses.

It is the policy of The Pennsylvania State University Press to use acid-free paper. Publications on uncoated stock satisfy the minimum requirements of American National Standard for Information Sciences—Permanence of Paper for Printed Library Material, ANSI Z39.48–1992.

Additional images: frontispiece, Clodion (Claude Michel), *Model for a Proposed Monument to Commemorate the Invention of the Balloon*, ca. 1784; page vi, Antoine Watteau, *Gersaint's Shop Sign*, 1720.

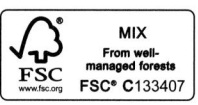

For Aaron Wunsch

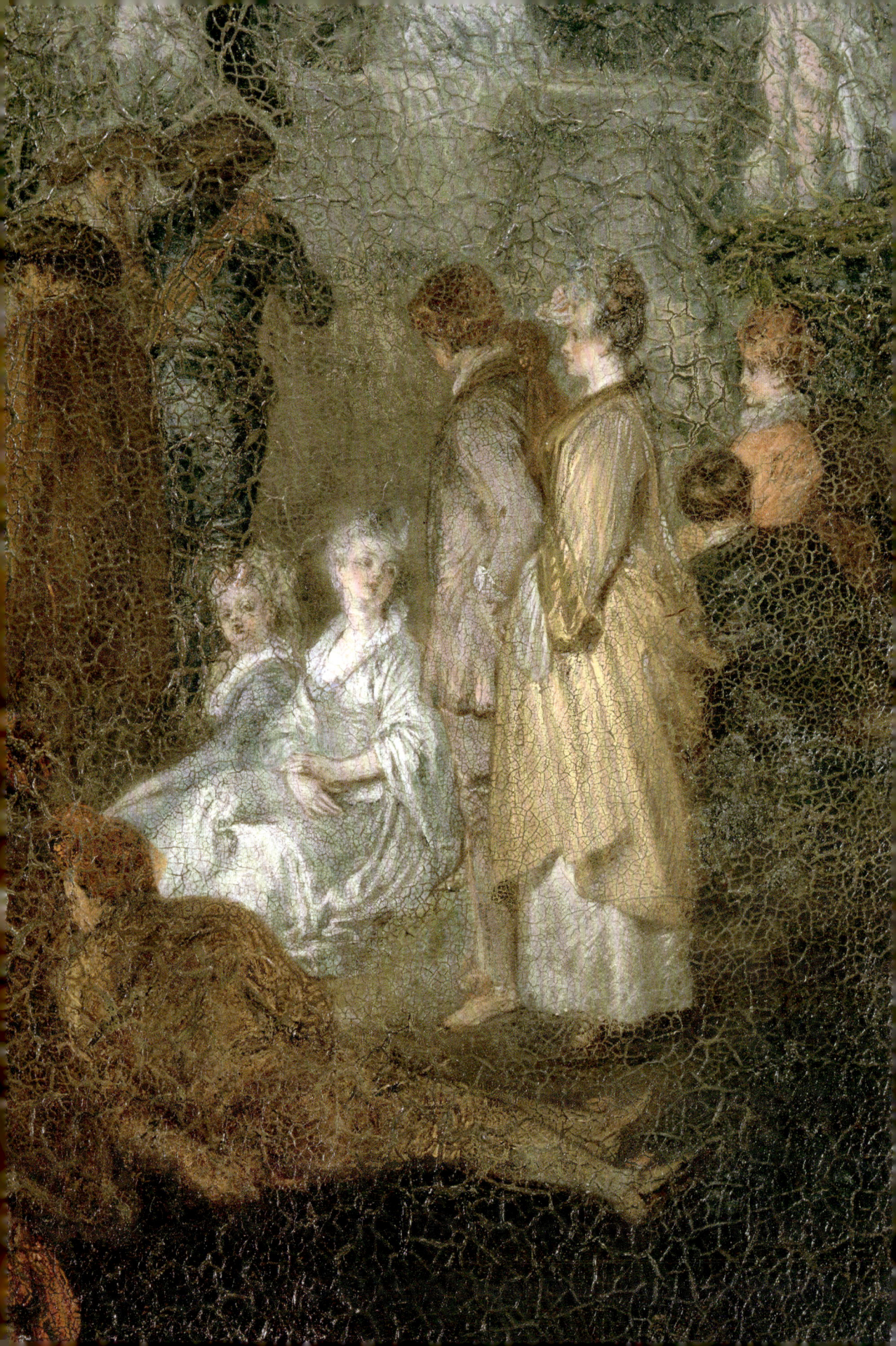

Contents

List of Illustrations | ix
Acknowledgments | xi

Introduction: The Fragile and the Flimsy | 1

1 Watteau's *Délicatesse* | 13

2 Pastel and the Allure of Fragility | 33

3 Wax, Fire, and the Fashion for Permanence | 65

4 Clodion's Fragile Monuments | 85

Epilogue: This Is So Contemporary | 115

Notes | 123
Bibliography | 145
Index | 171

Illustrations

1. Fragonard shop entry at the Carrousel du Louvre mall, Paris, 2022 | 2
2. Jean-Honoré Fragonard, *The Warrior's Dream of Love*, ca. 1780–85 | 3
3. Fragonard, *The Warrior's Dream of Love* (before completion of the 1987 restoration), ca. 1780–85 | 4
4. Jean-François Benard after Jean Berain, *Grotesque*, second half of seventeenth century | 6
5. *Cravat End (France)*, ca. 1695 | 8
6. Antoine Watteau, *The Pilgrimage to the Isle of Cythera*, 1717 | 14
7. Watteau, *Actors at a Fair* (detail), ca. 1710 | 15
8. Watteau, *The Pleasures of the Ball*, ca. 1715–17 | 17
9. Roger de Piles, *Les premiers élémens de la peinture pratique*, 1684 | 19
10. Watteau, *The Pilgrimage to the Isle of Cythera* (detail), 1717 | 21
11. Watteau, *The Pilgrimage to the Isle of Cythera* (detail), 1717 | 21
12. Watteau, *The Pilgrimage to the Isle of Cythera* (detail), 1717 | 21
13. Watteau, *The Village Bride*, 1710–12 | 22
14. Watteau, *The Village Bride* (detail), 1710–12 | 23
15. Watteau, *Gersaint's Shop Sign*, 1720 | 27
16. Nicolas Loir, *Allegory of the Foundation of the Royal Academy of Painting and Sculpture*, 1666 | 28
17. Watteau, *Gersaint's Shop Sign* (detail), 1720 | 29
18. Maurice-Quentin de La Tour, *Louis Duval de L'Épinoy*, 1745 | 35
19. Louis XIII, *Portrait of René Potier, duc de Tresme*, ca. 1632–35 | 37
20. Robert Nanteuil, *Portrait of Monseigneur Louis Doni d'Attichy, Bishop of Riez*, 1663 | 38
21. Joseph Vivien, *The Sculptor François Girardon*, 1701 | 39
22. Rosalba Carriera, *John Law*, ca. 1720 | 40
23. Small devotional image of the Three Magi | 42
24. Small devotional image of the Three Magi | 42
25. Maurice-Quentin de La Tour, *Self-Portrait with Index Finger*, 1737 | 44
26. La Tour, *Preparation for the Portrait of Voltaire*, ca. 1735 | 45
27. La Tour, *Preparation for the Portrait of Voltaire*, ca. 1735 | 46
28. La Tour, *Portrait of Voltaire*, 1735 | 47
29. La Tour, *Gabriel Bernard de Rieux*, 1739–41 | 49
30. La Tour, *Buste d'un nègre*, ca. 1741 | 50
31. La Tour, *Gabriel Bernard de Rieux* (detail under raking light), 1739–41 | 51
32. La Tour, *Gabriel Bernard de Rieux* (detail), 1739–41 | 52
33. La Tour, *Jean-Jacques Rousseau*, ca. 1759–63 | 55
34. La Tour, *Jean Le Rond d'Alembert*, ca. 1752 | 56
35. La Tour, *Madame de Pompadour*, 1755 | 57
36. La Tour, *Princesse de Rohan*, ca. 1741 | 58

37. La Tour, *Jean Restout*, ca. 1738 | 59
38. La Tour, *Self-Portrait*, ca. 1742 | 60
39. La Tour, *Mme Le Riche de La Pouplinière, née Françoise-Catherine-Thérèse Boutinon des Hayes* (detail), ca. 1745 | 62
40. Joseph-Marie Vien, *Minerva*, 1754 | 66
41. Vien, *Daedalus Attaching the Wings of Icarus*, 1754 | 70
42. Vien, *Priestess Embroidering Temple Decorations*, 1755 | 73
43. François Boucher, *Jeanne-Antoinette Poisson, Marquise de Pompadour*, 1750 (with later additions) | 75
44. Jean-Charles François and Gilles Demarteau after Joseph-Marie Vien, *The Virgin*, second half of eighteenth century | 76
45. Pierre-François Cozette after Carle Van Loo, *The Vestal Tuccia*, 1763 | 77
46. Arnaud Vincent de Montpetit, *Louis XV*, 1774 | 82
47. Montpetit, *Alexis Piron*, 1777 | 83
48. Clodion (Claude Michel), *Mausoleum of Fifi*, ca. 1772 | 86
49. Clodion, *Mausoleum of Fifi* (detail), ca. 1772 | 87
50. Johan Tobias Sergel, *Amor and Psyche* (detail), ca. 1770–72 | 90
51. Clodion, *Vase with Putti*, 1760s | 92
52. Boucher, *Drawing of a Vase* | 93
53. Clodion, *Erigone*, ca. 1783 | 94
54. Clodion, *Erigone*, ca. 1783 | 94
55. Clodion, details of *Erigone*, ca. 1783 | 95
56. Clodion, *Bacchante and Satyr with Young Satyr*, ca. 1775–80 | 98
57. Nicolas Poussin, *A Bacchanalian Revel Before a Term*, 1632–33 | 99
58. Clodion, *Votaries of Bacchus*, early 1780s | 100
59. Clodion, *Votaries of Bacchus* (detail), early 1780s | 100
60. Clodion, *The Intoxication of Wine*, ca. 1780–90 | 102
61. Clodion, *Model for a Proposed Monument to Commemorate the Invention of the Balloon*, ca. 1784 | 104
62. Claude-Louis Desrais (print after), *Vue et perspective du jardin de Mr. Réveillon fabriquant de papiers . . .* , ca. 1783 | 106
63. Anonymous, *Ascension of Charles and Robert at the Tuileries*, 1783 | 106
64. Gabriel de Saint-Aubin, *Clodion's Montesquieu at the Salon of 1779*, 1779 | 107
65. Clodion, *Charles-Louis de Secondat, baron de La Brède et de Montesquieu*, 1783 | 108
66. Clodion (photograph after), *À la gloire des frères mongolfier* [sic], 1885–86 | 109
67. Clodion, *Model for a Proposed Monument to Commemorate the Invention of the Balloon* (detail), ca. 1784 | 110
68. Clodion, *Model for a Proposed Monument to Commemorate the Invention of the Balloon* (detail), ca. 1784 | 111
69. J. Chéreau, *Embrâsement Déplorable de la Machine Aërostatique des S.rs Miolan et Janinet, le Dimanche 11 Juillet 1784*, 1784 | 113
70. Anonymous, *La coquette phisicienne*, 1784 | 114

Acknowledgments

I began working on this book shortly after meeting two people whose friendship sustained me throughout the process. Aaron Wile's candor and empathy made him my most trusted reader from start to finish. Greg Mellen, during countless conversations, sharpened my thinking about culture, history, and the subtleties of social experience (in addition to answering my occasional queries about Italian, ancient Greek, and Latin). I am lucky to know them both.

Ewa Lajer-Burcharth and Henri Zerner provided the encouragement and advice that I needed to get the project launched. For feedback on drafts and formative conversations, I also want to thank Layla Bermeo, Nina Dubin, Marc Gotlieb, Michael Ann Holly, Melissa Hyde, Lindsay Kaplan, Robin Kelsey, Ethan Lasser, Mark Ledbury, Kevin Lotery, Erika Naginski, Jennifer Roberts, and Kristel Smentek. Thank you to Jennifer Chuong, Thea Goldring, Sarah Grandin, Ashley Hannebrink, Sarah Lund, Camran Mani, David Pullins, and Isaac Schamberg for help and camaraderie over the years. On pastel-related matters, I benefited from the expertise of Emily Beeny, Thea Burns, Neil Jeffares, and Xavier Salomon. Thank you to Tony Sigel for the patient and thorough counsel about terracotta. Comments from the anonymous readers at the *Art Bulletin* inspired me to hone my claims in chapter 1, a version of which appeared in the June 2018 issue published by the College Art Association. I am also grateful to the colleagues who gave me opportunities to present pieces of this project at various stages: Esther Bell, Pamela Berger, Francesca Borgo, Michelle Foa, Jennifer Van Horn, Matthew Hunter, Iris Moon, Avigail Moss, and Julia Vázquez.

Thank you to the many archivists, curators, and librarians who made the research process a pleasure. Delphine Valmalle and Marie Lionnet-de Loitière were exceptionally accommodating at the Centre de recherche et de restauration des musées de France. Jérémy Le Bellégo and Stéphanie Prenant offered much-needed assistance at the Musée des Beaux-Arts Antoine Lécuyer. Alexandre Leducq at the École nationale supérieure des beaux-arts and Virginie Frelin-Cartigny at the Musée des beaux-arts et d'archéologie de Besançon both helped me track down materials at important junctures.

The research and the early writing phases of this book depended on fellowships from the Center for Advanced Study in the Visual Arts, the American Council of Learned Societies, and the Sterling and Francine Clark Art Institute. My time as a guest scholar in the Lise Meitner Group on Decay, Loss, and Conservation in Art History at the Bibliotheca Hertziana energized me as I brought the project to a conclusion. Thank you to Francesca Borgo, Ornella Rodengo, and John Rattray for creating such a convivial environment in Rome. Boston College provided critical support, and I am supremely grateful to have such generous colleagues in the Department of Art, Art History, and Film.

I feel fortunate to publish this book with Penn State University Press. Ellie Goodman has my gratitude for her forthright guidance and sensitivity to my intentions as a writer. Maddie Caso fielded my many questions and managed all practicalities with aplomb. Thank you to Brian Beer, Jennifer Norton, and Laura Reed-Morrisson for overseeing the production process, and to Colleen O'Reilly for the scrupulous copyediting. The astute comments of the peer reviewers helped me refine my arguments.

Finally, my deepest thanks to my family. My parents, Mary Morgan and David Wunsch, have always modeled curiosity and an openness to complexity. Thank you to my wife, Rose Levine, and our son, Felix, for inspiring wonder and reminding me what matters. And thank you to my brother, Aaron Wunsch, who has been a lifelong thinking partner, and who taught me to care for fragile things. This book is dedicated to him.

Introduction

The Fragile and the Flimsy

What is the relationship between the exquisite delicacy of art and the debased flimsiness of disposable commodities? Few people today would deny that a distinction exists between these two forms of perishability. The Louvre may sit atop an enormous mall, but no one would confuse the art in the galleries with the fashionable goods in the basement shops. A world of difference separates, for example, the delicate brushstrokes of Jean-Honoré Fragonard's paintings from the latest season of trinkets and fragrances on display downstairs in the Fragonard perfumery (fig. 1). A painting by Fragonard such as *The Warrior's Dream of Love* (fig. 2) may, like perfume, conjure evanescent pleasure, but the museum ensures that we regard the fragility of the painting itself as much more than an expression of commercial ephemerality. When the museum's informational brochure cautions us that "works of art are unique and fragile" and that "touching, even lightly" can cause irreparable harm, the warning makes no reference to market worth. The significance of art's fragile materiality goes unspecified, but we are told that whatever unnamed essence it contains "must be preserved for future generations."[1] If the perishability of a commercial product reflects the fleetingness of fashion, then the fragility of art here stands for the opposite, representing something whose value transcends time.

This book is devoted to disputing such a neat division between the delicacy of art and the ephemerality of consumer goods. More specifically, it is a book about the fragile and decaying objects from eighteenth-century France that first prompted people to wish this slippery distinction into existence. The period witnessed an unprecedented proliferation of materially unstable art. Some artists made objects that were fragile by design, creating enormous pastel portraits that were vulnerable to the slightest touch, or constructing spectacularly breakable sculptures from attenuated pieces of clay. For

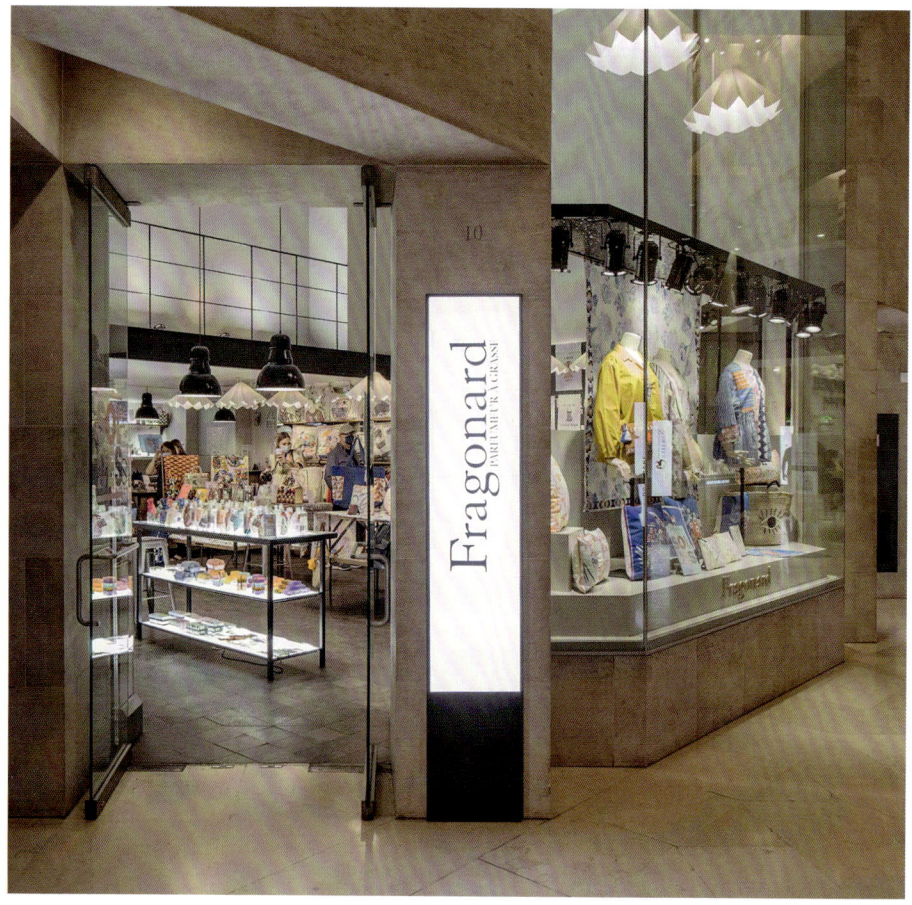

FIG. 1 Fragonard shop entry at the Carrousel du Louvre mall, Paris, 2022. Photo © Carrousel du Louvre.

other artists, impermanence was an unintended by-product of a search for novel and spontaneous effects. *The Warrior's Dream of Love* provides a telling example from this second category. Until the painting's restoration in 1987, it was considered unworthy of exhibition because it was in such poor condition.[2] The painting's decay stemmed from the process of its production: Fragonard employed an unusual quantity of a drying agent when painting it, which soon caused broad cracks to form across its surface (fig. 3).[3] The use of these siccative oils was a notorious problem among painters at the time, so much so that the French Royal Academy of Painting and Sculpture had issued warnings about it in the decades before Fragonard produced the picture.[4] These ingredients allowed artists to work more quickly and to produce atmospheric effects, but they resulted in damage within a matter of years, rendering paintings nearly unrecognizable.

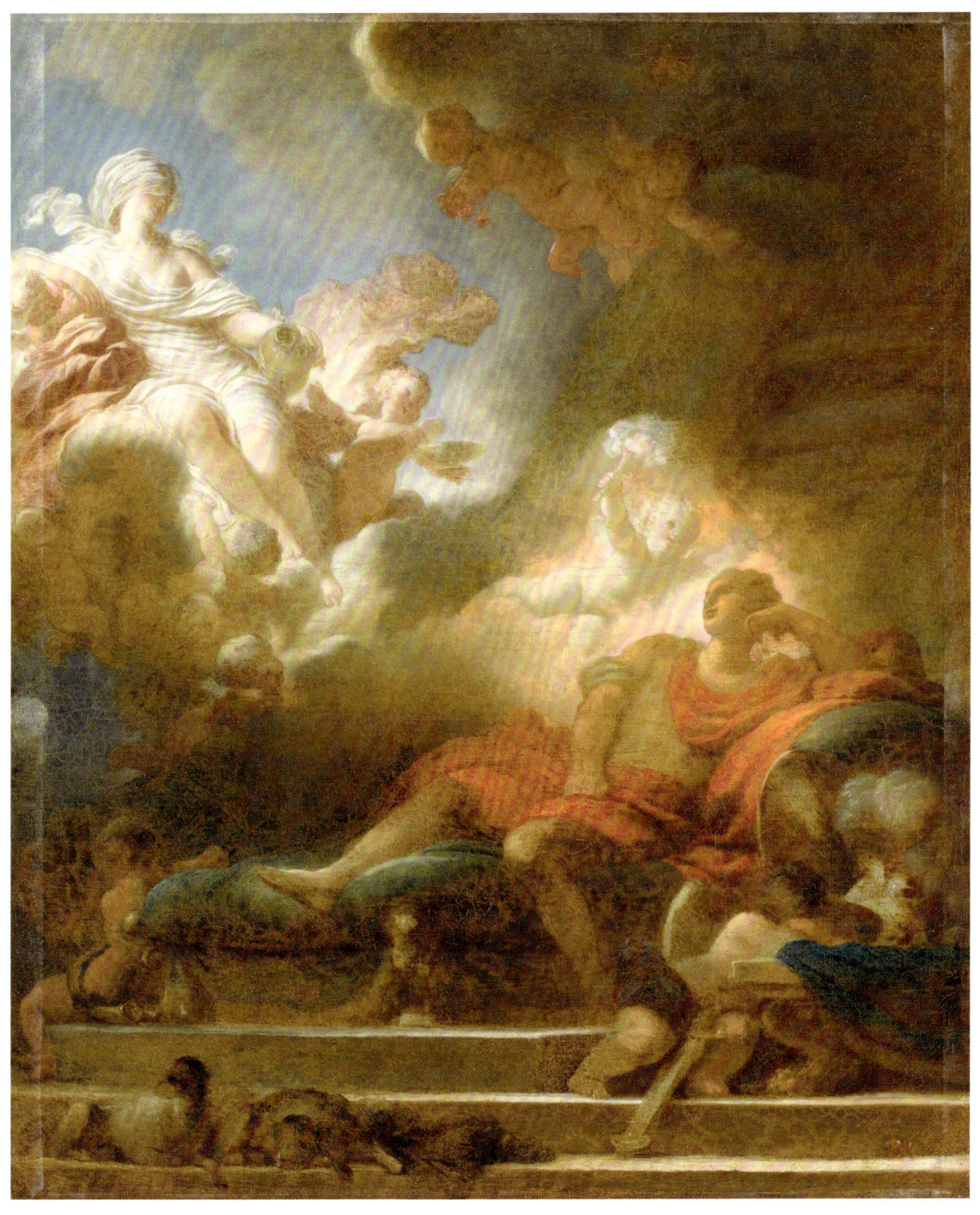

FIG. 2 Jean-Honoré Fragonard, *The Warrior's Dream of Love*, ca. 1780–85. Oil on canvas, 61.5 × 55 cm. Musée du Louvre, Paris. RF 2149. Photo © RMN-Grand Palais / Art Resource, NY (Stéphane Maréchalle).

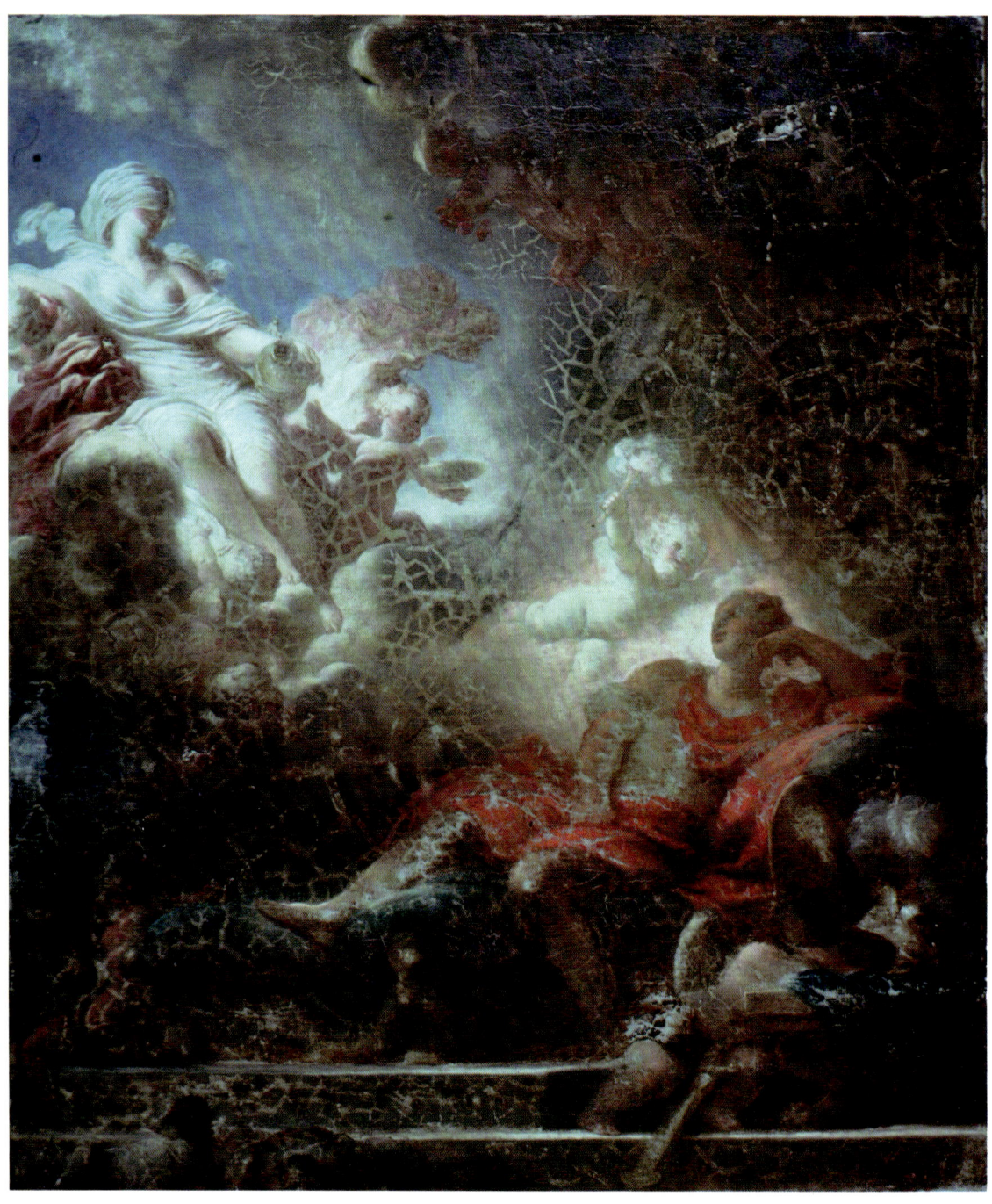

FIG. 3 Jean-Honoré Fragonard, *The Warrior's Dream of Love*, ca. 1780–85, before completion of the 1987 restoration. Oil on canvas, 61.5 × 55 cm. Musée du Louvre, Paris. RF 2149. Photo © Centre de recherche et de restauration des musées de France.

Such techniques developed in tandem with broader changes in the artistic economy. The eighteenth century was a pivotal moment in the history of the art market: private collections grew in both number and size, art increasingly changed hands at auction, and art dealers acquired a new professional status.[5] These commercial developments subjected art to competing temporal pressures. On the one hand, the commodification of art led to a new concern for issues of conservation.[6] Collectors prized art's materiality as the bearer of an artist's autographic touch and as a source of sensory pleasure, which meant that art's value became intertwined with its physical condition.[7] On the other hand, the market created short-term incentives that were at odds with the expectation of durability. Artists had to work quickly to make a living and to keep up with trends in taste, which could lead them to take technical shortcuts. In addition, the demand for sensuous surfaces and novel techniques among collectors pushed artists to become more experimental, sometimes causing them to sacrifice permanence in the process. The painter Jean-Baptiste Oudry warned about this tendency in a 1752 lecture to the Academy, explaining that artists had been led astray in their search for beguiling surface effects: "The seduction that it achieves passes like a dream, and all this beautiful work turns yellow in no time at all."[8]

To an extent, the eighteenth-century art market simply intensified a tension that had existed within artistic technique for centuries. Artists throughout history have balanced their desire for posterity's recognition against their impulse to take technical risks. Leonardo da Vinci, to cite one notable precedent, continually tested unusual combinations of materials that compromised the integrity of his work.[9] But the art market that emerged in the eighteenth century did more than amplify the degree of such experimentation. What makes the technical transformations of the period distinctive is their connection to a deeper shift in temporal expectations, an altered outlook rooted in the instability of fashion. As Francis Haskell has shown, the collecting culture of the eighteenth century led to a new awareness of taste's capriciousness as dealers and connoisseurs observed how talented artists often fell out of favor and slipped into oblivion.[10] This change in consciousness helps explain why artists at the time began to reconsider the goal of trying to please posterity at all. The sculptor Étienne-Maurice Falconet famously proclaimed that he worked only for viewers in his own time, an assertion that drew him into a protracted debate with Denis Diderot.[11] François Boucher made comparable statements on multiple occasions, according to one of his associates: "We often heard him say that he only worked for his century and that he was convinced that his works, so praised, so sought after by his contemporaries, would not receive the approval of posterity."[12] Such declarations did not always translate into technical practices—neither Boucher nor Falconet was particularly negligent in his workmanship. Their statements nonetheless point to a significant shift in the horizon of expectation from which artists regarded their future reception. The vicissitudes of commerce

INTRODUCTION (5)

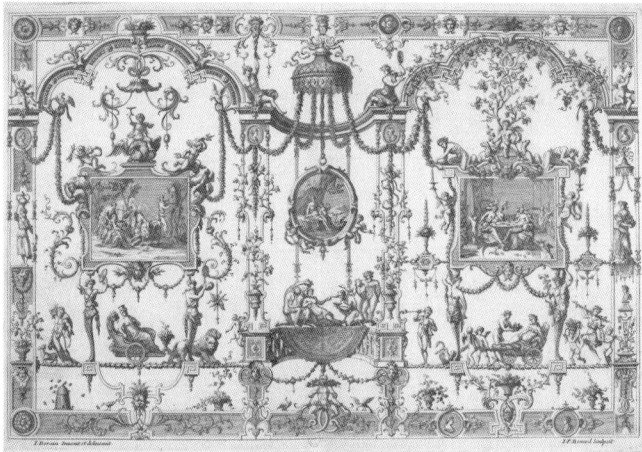

FIG. 4
Jean-François Benard after Jean Berain, *Grotesque*, second half of seventeenth century. Etching, 29.5 × 45.6 cm. Bibliothèque nationale de France, département des Estampes et de la photographie, Paris. HD-58-PET FOL. Photo: gallica.bnf.fr / BnF.

revealed the provisional nature of any cultural canon, highlighting the perils of aspiring to join its immortal ranks. And in a commercial sphere that could offer lucrative rewards in the present, the necessity of making physically permanent works could no longer be assumed.

The relationship between the market and material impermanence in eighteenth-century France has largely escaped the attention of art historians, perhaps because of a disciplinary tendency to see art's perishability as nothing more than an impediment to research. Because art historians generally study the relation between art and the period in which it was produced, we usually assume that the original appearance of an object is the only one that should matter to us. As a result, we leave questions of material instability to conservators and scientists, trusting them to halt the effects of time as best they can. When we do encounter signs of damage and temporal change in our objects of study, we typically regard these alterations as a distraction, not as a subject that demands interpretation.

This is not to say that art historians have been entirely indifferent to issues of temporality, delicacy, or instability. In fact, much of the scholarship on eighteenth-century French art addresses exactly these concerns but treats them as a question of form, not materiality. Anyone who has a passing familiarity with eighteenth-century French art knows that delicacy plays an important role in the style of the period. What we now call "Rococo"—and what was then simply known as the *goût moderne*—revolves around sinuous lines and asymmetrical shapes that appear to teeter on the brink of collapse. Foundational studies of the style trace its origins to the realm of court spectacle under Louis XIV, tracking its evolution from the playful palace decor of seventeenth-century artisans such as Jean Berain (fig. 4) to its apotheosis in the work of eighteenth-century painters such as Watteau, Boucher, and Fragonard.[13] Thanks to the groundbreaking scholarship of Katie Scott, we now have a much clearer sense of the social and political meanings that accrued to this style in the course of its evolution, as affluent Parisians turned airy and intricate forms into a complex language of power and prestige.[14] Subsequent scholarship has further underscored the seriousness of the Rococo's seemingly lighthearted aesthetic, connecting its formal and iconographic evocations of fleetingness to theories of pleasure, risk, and the mutability of subjective identity in Enlightenment France.[15]

What requires further attention is the connection between the stylistic manifestations of transience and its physical presence in art's very substance. Grasping this link is crucial not only to appreciating the technical features of eighteenth-century French art but also to understanding how the period fundamentally altered the relationship between art, time, and value. At the heart of this transformation, I argue, is the concept of delicacy itself. The salience of delicacy lies in its dual associations with personal refinement and material instability, a double meaning that came into relief in the commercial sphere at the turn of the eighteenth century. Before this time, the French term *délicatesse* principally applied to people, referring to a person's sensitivity to subtle pleasures—a meaning rooted in the Latin *delicatus*.[16] This idea of *délicatesse* occupied an important position within seventeenth-century French court society, where it signified an ineffable sophistication in behavior and conversation (throughout this book, I will use the French word *délicatesse* and its variants when referring to this courtly norm, reserving the English equivalent, *delicacy*, for moments when material fragility is also at issue). The Jesuit critic Dominique Bouhours remarked on the word's social significance in his 1671 study of language and wit, *Les entretiens d'Ariste et d'Eugène*, where he provided examples of the word's usage: "Un esprit *délicat*, une raillerie *délicate*, une pensée *délicate*; c'est une affaire *délicate*; tenir une conduite *délicate* avec quelqu'un. Il a beaucoup de *délicatesse* dans l'esprit; il sait toutes les *délicatesses* de la langue" (A *delicate* mind, a *delicate* mockery, a *delicate* thought, it is a *delicate* affair; to maintain *delicate* conduct with someone. He has great *delicacy* of spirit; he knows all the *delicacies* of language).[17] Such phrases placed *délicatesse* within a broader lexicon of terms that courtiers invoked as signs of gentility, such as *honnêteté*, *galanterie*, and *urbanité*.[18] Unlike these other terms, however, *délicatesse* developed a material connotation in the marketplace that overlapped with—and significantly disrupted—its social function.

Signs of the shift appeared in the 1690s, when French dictionaries began to emphasize that delicacy could designate a physical property of manufactured goods, citing the word "fragile" as a synonym: "DELICATE refers also to that which is weak or fragile, which is unable to resist attacks, impacts from foreign bodies. . . . Glass, talc, porcelain are fragile and delicate materials."[19] The reference to materials such as glass and porcelain reflects the types of commodities that were becoming increasingly prevalent in

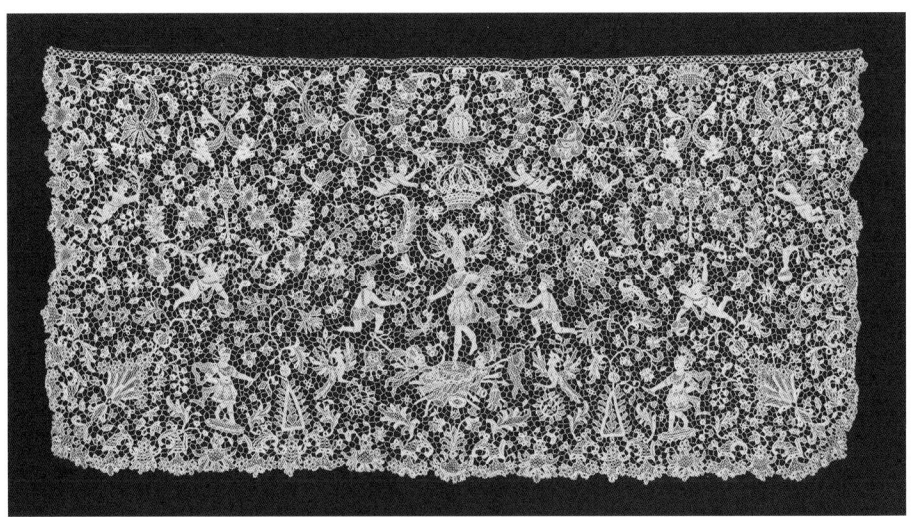

FIG. 5 *Cravat End (France)*, ca. 1695. Linen, 26.7 × 48.9 cm. Cooper Hewitt, New York. 1962-50-18-a. Bequest of Richard Cranch Greenleaf in memory of his mother, Adeline Emma Greenleaf.

the opulent decor of the Parisian elite.[20] Fueled by fortunes derived from colonial speculation and the expansion of credit markets, luxury consumption dramatically increased during this period.[21] Many of the most prized goods in this economy were characterized by their fragility.[22] Breakable ceramics displaced metal vessels on dining tables as porcelain encroached on silver's previously prominent position in the homes of the affluent.[23] Lace, which had been a key component of sartorial distinction across Europe since the early sixteenth century, reached new levels of diaphanous insubstantiality with the "point de France" lacemaking techniques that emerged in the late seventeenth century (fig. 5).[24]

Such objects offered a means of expressing the social norm of *délicatesse* in physical form, but they also highlighted a troubling problem in the process: by translating *délicatesse* into a saleable product, they provided an opportunity for class dissimulation. In a period when merchants and financiers began to compete with the old nobility for power and prestige, the commodification of courtly behavior was no small source of discomfort.[25] As luxury products became available to a wider range of consumers, the distinction between those who appreciated the refinement of these goods and those who simply flaunted their extravagance through hedonistic spending became the subject of intense debate.[26] Writers immediately derided the "false *délicatesse*" of provincials and pretenders to nobility who sought to purchase their way into polite society through ephemeral consumption.[27] The novelist and critic Charles Sorel, for example, ridiculed men who were so laden with lace that they resembled the "shop displays of merchants" and might even be mistaken for a "wandering boutique."[28] The polemicist Eustache

Le Noble, in his satire of contemporary manners, *L'école du monde*, similarly derided those who believed themselves to be "polite men" simply because they appreciated the "delicacy of lace."[29] Such comments are familiar to anyone who has studied the clashes between cultural and economic capital that resulted from the transition from feudalism to capitalism.[30] What the discourse of delicacy reveals, however, is the critical role that materiality came to play in these conflicts—a role that would ultimately reshape the conception of art itself.

Paintings and sculptures were far from the only fragile products implicated in the commodification of delicacy, and it was for this exact reason that their material instability called into question art's cohesion as a category. Perishability, because it linked art to the broader world of disposable commodities that proliferated in the eighteenth century's burgeoning consumer culture, had the potential to negate the very concept of art as a privileged domain of cultural experience. Art critics were quick to highlight the issue. Étienne La Font de Saint-Yenne was among the first to lay out the problem, condemning the "little durability" of contemporary paintings while aligning their ephemerality with glass, plaster, and other decorative materials that adorned fashionable Parisian interiors.[31] From this perspective, the distinction between art and mere manual labor, which artists had fought to establish during the preceding centuries on the premise that painting and sculpture constituted intellectual pursuits, quite literally appeared to crumble as the short-term interests of the market manifested themselves within art's materiality.[32] How could art maintain its exalted status when it was increasingly governed by the same physical and temporal forces that shaped the production and reception of other commodities? This was the dilemma that the physical instability of art made visible to eighteenth-century artists, critics, and collectors. It was also, as we will see, a problem that artists addressed through their materials and techniques. One way to respond was to reject fragility altogether, to promote materials and techniques with claims of indestructability. But the other strategy, the one that would ultimately have a more lasting impact, was to present art's delicacy as something distinct from that of other commercial products. Doing so meant investing material delicacy with new meaning, attaching it not to the fleetingness of fashion or the ephemeral patter of courtly conversation but to the indefinable essence of creative inspiration. It meant reclaiming the elusive aura that had surrounded courtly *délicatesse* for a different domain, ascribing its transcendent and ethereal powers to the specific class of delicate objects that we call art.

This book ultimately shows how the materiality of eighteenth-century French painting and sculpture transformed delicacy from a commodified extension of courtly sociability to a defining feature of art's irreducible essence. While France was not unique in witnessing the rise of fashion and consumer culture during this period, the French preoccupation with delicacy was distinctive. Period definitions of *délicatesse* make clear that the term's social meaning was central to France's self-conception. For Bouhours, *délicatesse* distinguished contemporary France from all other nations and eras: "In a word, I know of nothing more common in the kingdom than this *délicat* good sense that previously was so rare."[33] By the early eighteenth century, French writers commonly cited *délicatesse* as a key quality separating themselves from neighboring people.[34] Even the British acknowledged the specifically French character of *délicatesse*, albeit with a note of derision. John Dryden, for example, explained that for the French, *délicatesse* was the mark of greatest distinction: "*Délicate, & bien tourné*, are the highest commendations, which they bestow, on somewhat which they think a masterpiece."[35] This association of Frenchness with *délicatesse* is significant because it explains why the material delicacy of the commodity proved to be such a confounding problem within the country. Superfluous consumption, precisely because it was not a specifically French phenomenon, threatened to degrade and erase the defining feature of the nation. If courtly *délicatesse* morphed into nothing more than the physical delicacy of the ephemeral commodity, then France would lose its essential character, becoming, like England, a country organized entirely around the crass interests of the marketplace. As it became increasingly clear that social *délicatesse* would inevitably succumb to the commercial sphere, the purified delicacy of art offered an alternative form of distinction, one that endures today in the global perception of France as a sanctuary for high culture.

I track this transformation across a series of case studies that move chronologically through the eighteenth century, each focusing on a different material or technique. My examples are not meant to provide a comprehensive survey of eighteenth-century art. Instead, in order to highlight the evolving relationship between commercial forces and artistic practices, I focus on cases where the ties between these two domains are particularly evident. What unites the varied objects that I examine throughout this book is that they make visible, in their very materiality, the problem of defining art's temporal status under the conditions of its commodification. Chapter 1 establishes the connection between commerce and material instability in the early eighteenth-century art market. I explore these conditions through the example of Antoine Watteau, an artist whose oil paintings were delicate in two senses of the word: their ravishing surface effects were *délicat* in their indescribable allure, but they were also physically delicate because of the unusual techniques that Watteau used to create them. Watteau's working methods responded to the commercial pressures that artists faced at the time. In a period of declining royal and religious patronage, an emerging private art market placed new emphasis on speed and novelty over durability. In this context, delicacy's charm became increasingly difficult to disentangle from its pitfalls.

Chapter 2 examines how, for the generation after Watteau, material delicacy emerged as a full-fledged aesthetic sensibility—something that art buyers did not merely tolerate but actively sought in their pursuit of novel fashions. I concentrate on the demand for pastel, a highly fragile medium that came to dominate the eighteenth-century portraiture market. Pastellists such as Maurice-Quentin de La Tour aestheticized the instability of their works by aligning the fugitive materiality of pastel with the evanescent personalities of portrait sitters. The socially mobile buyers of these works similarly connected material delicacy with social *délicatesse*, which they invoked to advance their position in the realm of polite manners.

By midcentury, however, such materials and techniques faced a growing backlash. Critics and collectors expressed new concern about the potential ephemerality of contemporary art, and artists sought to allay their fears. Chapter 3 turns to these efforts, focusing on the painter Joseph-Marie Vien's ill-fated experiments with a supposedly imperishable method of painting in molten wax known as encaustic. Vien's efforts belonged to a larger group of "innovations" in the chemistry of painting from the time that promised to yield the appearance of delicacy while remaining durable. Most of these inventions are now long forgotten, and their present obscurity is understandable; the majority of them were, in fact, less durable than conventional methods of oil painting, and they proved to be products of the mercurial marketplace that they claimed to transcend. But these techniques were more than oddities of history—they underscored the power of the commercial sphere to absorb every attempt to curb its influence, converting any object into an ephemeral commodity.

If nothing existed beyond the market's turbulent forces, then how could art be salvaged from vanity, corruption, and fashion? Chapter 4 examines how this question loomed over the booming market for fragile terracotta sculptures in the 1770s and 1780s. These objects played into existing critiques of ephemeral consumption, but skillful practitioners in the medium presented its fragility in nobler terms, appealing to the emerging discourse of artistic spontaneity and the temporal instability of inspiration. Claude Michel, better known as Clodion, was the most notable among these artists, producing fanciful terracotta sculptures with a tantalizing sense of weightlessness and fragility. While Clodion's work has often been interpreted as a swan song of Rococo frivolity before the onset of the Revolution, closer scrutiny suggests that he represented the beginning of a new paradigm. By integrating the debased volatility of the marketplace with the ostensibly purified temporality of aesthetic expression and experience, Clodion embodied the union of artistry and commercial spectacle that would endure long after the fall of the old regime.

In the book's epilogue, I address these aftereffects, examining the relationship between art, ephemerality, and capitalism in the twenty-first century. While scholars have often detected echoes of the Rococo within a subset of contemporary art that evokes the stylistic ostentation and libidinal themes of the eighteenth century, I take a different approach. My concern is not so much with formal and iconographic similarities across these eras but with structural continuities in the economy of culture that continue to bind the temporality of artistic production with the dynamics of consumer capitalism. The performance art of Tino Sehgal, which bears no obvious resemblance to Rococo painting and sculpture, serves as a case study for highlighting these underlying economic forces. Sehgal's work consists of temporary "situations" in which performers engage gallery visitors in conversation or repeat choreographed movements. Sehgal refuses to allow any documentation of his work, insisting that it survives only in the form of memory and oral tradition. Yet this very rejection of objecthood has served as a source of publicity, attracting audiences worldwide to his exhibitions and prompting museums to purchase the right to stage his work for enormous sums of money. By pushing to an extreme the commodification of transience, Sehgal's art lays bare a fact that had first become visible in the delicate paintings and sculptures of the eighteenth century: in a competitive marketplace for public attention, what the artist monetizes is not a durable repository of value but a rarified form of subjective experience whose perishability only heightens its aura of exclusivity.

The history of delicacy in art, then, is much more than a story of changing technical priorities. Throughout the eighteenth century, delicacy structured debates over morality, status, and power. It determined who belonged within a group and who was excluded from it. Physical instability provided a way to think through the social instability brought about by the rise of capitalism and the erosion of aristocratic distinction. For artists, these developments entailed both danger and opportunity. The risk was that art would come to be seen simply as one more manifestation of a degraded and superficial delicacy that pervaded a world of false appearances and upended hierarchies. Yet the growing suspicion that surrounded fragile consumer goods also created an opening that artists could exploit: it generated demand for a subset of commodities whose ties to ephemeral consumption could be plausibly disavowed, a type of object that existed in the marketplace while appearing to transcend it. Art came to fulfill this need. It did so only after artists and their audiences reimagined what the fragility of paintings and sculptures represented, turning a material weakness into a metaphysical strength. Delicacy, once reconceived, emerged as the very property through which art secured its privileged position within the conditions of commercial modernity. While this transformation was specific to the social and economic context of the eighteenth century, its effects remain palpable today. If we want to understand why some forms of perishability carry prestige while others elicit scorn, then we need to study the history of delicacy as both a material property and an idea.

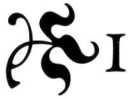

Watteau's *Délicatesse*

Few artists better captured the pleasures of *délicatesse* than the painter Antoine Watteau. The term comes up again and again in remembrances of him after his untimely death in 1721 at the age of thirty-seven. His friend Antoine La Roque praised "the most *délicates* and piquant perfections of his art," writing that "his figures have all the *délicatesse* . . . that one could desire."[1] His dealer, Edme-François Gersaint, insisted that *délicatesse* distinguished Watteau's work from that of his closest imitators, who lacked his "*délicatesse* of design."[2] A century later, the writer and painter Charles-Louis-François Le Carpentier cited Watteau as the ultimate exemplar of this quality, asking, "where, indeed, can be found as much *délicatesse* as in the touch of Watteau?"[3]

Scholars, too, have appreciated the seductions of Watteau's *délicatesse*. Norman Bryson's methodologically pathbreaking study traces Watteau's ineffable charm to the "semantic void" in his work—a refusal of signification that sends the viewer into flights of reverie.[4] Other art historians have put the phenomenon in period-specific terms, connecting Watteau's imaginary scenes of leisure and love with the norms of *honnêteté* and *délicatesse* that structured aristocratic sociability.[5] Celebrated paintings such as *The Pilgrimage to the Isle of Cythera* (fig. 6) not only depict these elite modes of social exchange but enact them upon the viewer, ravishing the eye through their subtle and indescribable effects.[6]

What requires greater examination, however, is the connection between this pleasurable side of Watteau's *délicatesse* and a more vexing one. Watteau's paintings were, quite literally, delicate objects, physically unstable and prone to decay. Twenty-five years after his death, the damage was already overwhelming. "This painter enjoyed a great reputation during his life," wrote one commentator in 1746, "but his reputation today has greatly declined; the majority of his works could not sustain themselves, which we attribute to the negligence with which he painted."[7] Art historians have tended to focus on Watteau's best-preserved works, but lesser-studied examples, such as *Actors at*

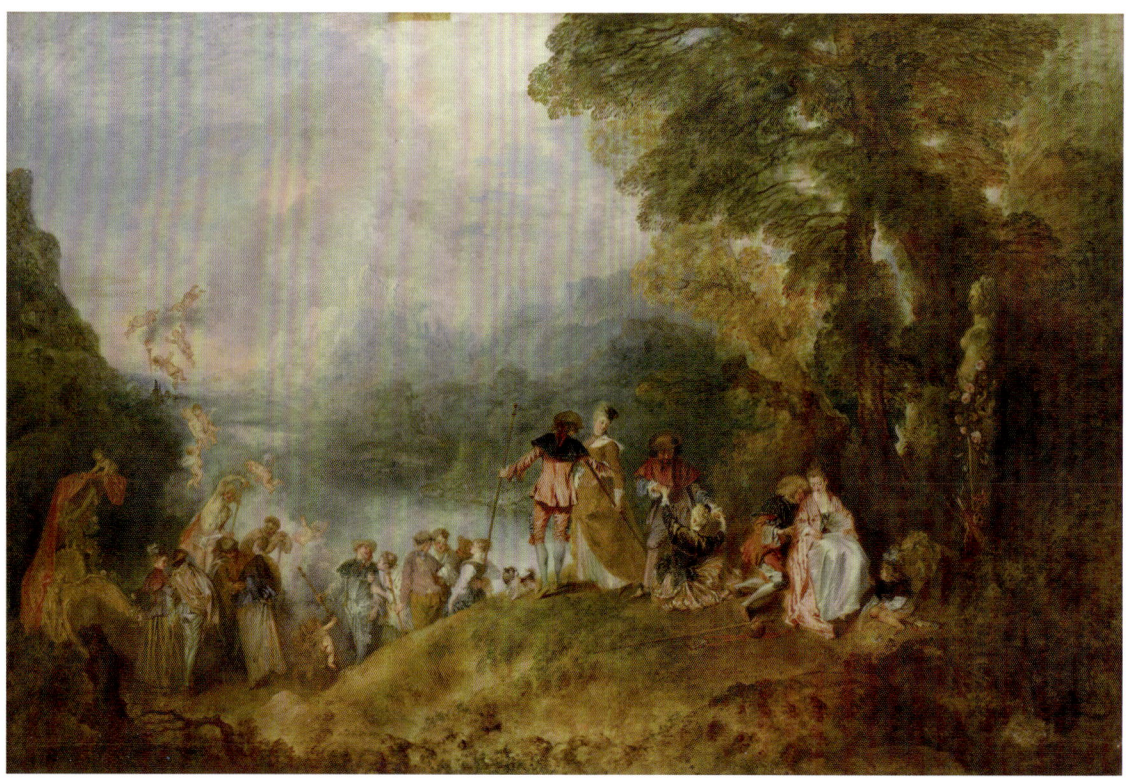

FIG. 6 Antoine Watteau, *The Pilgrimage to the Isle of Cythera*, 1717. Oil on canvas, 129 × 195 cm. Musée du Louvre, Paris. INV 8525. Photo © RMN-Grand Palais / Art Resource, NY (Stéphane Maréchalle).

a Fair (fig. 7), make clear what eighteenth-century viewers deplored: darkened colors and deep cracks pervade the painting's surface. Nearly all of Watteau's contemporaries bemoaned the results of his short-sighted indifference to the survival of his work and his reckless abandonment of sound technique. "His paintings suffered a little from the impatience and fickleness that formed his character," Gersaint wrote.[8] The print merchant and connoisseur Pierre-Jean Mariette claimed that Watteau simply "did not care to paint properly."[9] The comte de Caylus, an amateur and antiquarian, similarly attributed the decay of Watteau's paintings to his "laziness and indolence."[10]

The physical instability of Watteau's decaying paintings might appear unrelated to the *délicat* pleasures of his virtuosic brushwork, or perhaps even at odds with it. Murky colors and gaping crevices certainly make it difficult to appreciate the subtlety of touch that audiences so admired. But the two issues are more intertwined than they first appear. The inimitable qualities of Watteau's paintings, after all, were not easily separated from his rejection of traditional technique. And the sense of facility and

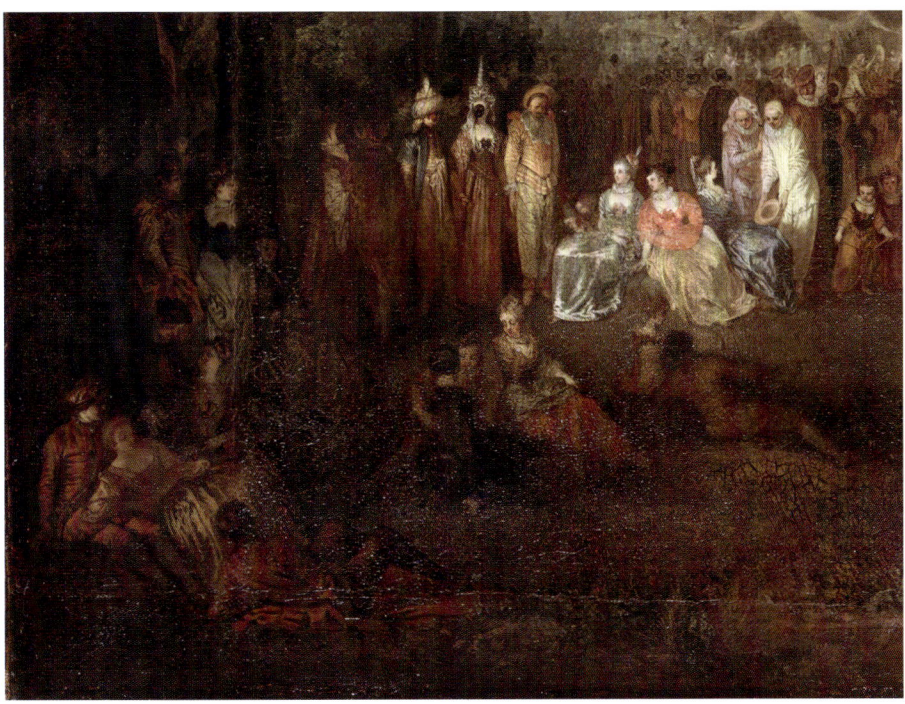

FIG. 7 Antoine Watteau, *Actors at a Fair* (detail), ca. 1710. Oil on canvas, 64.7 × 91.3 cm. Schlösser und Gärten, Charlottenburg Palace, Berlin. GK I 5602. Photo: Stiftung Preußische Schlösser und Gärten Berlin-Brandenburg (SPSG) / Jörg P. Anders.

spontaneity that viewers praised in his rapid brushwork was intimately linked to the "impatience" that guided his hand.

Watteau, then, provides an opportunity to examine how delicacy's multiple meanings began to converge in the French art world of the early eighteenth century. His paintings were, to be sure, an extreme demonstration of delicacy's aesthetic charm as well as its material hazards.[11] Outliers, though, have a way of making obvious the latent forces that operate within a culture at large. Watteau's working habits, reckless and mercurial as they seem, can be understood as an outsized response to the changing market conditions that surrounded French artists more generally at the time. In the chapter that follows, I situate Watteau's techniques within the commercial pressures that pushed artists and their viewers to sacrifice material permanence in favor of transient delights. Watteau emerges as a crucial figure in this history, both participating in and reflecting on a burgeoning culture of ephemeral consumption in which the pursuit of durability ceased to be a universal aspiration. In his unique disposition and distinctive methods, he reveals a broader economy in which delicacy's charm and its perils became increasingly difficult for artists, critics, and collectors to separate.

A Brief History of Permanence

For centuries before Watteau's time, French painters had little doubt about their obligation to produce work that would physically endure. When artists formed the first guild to regulate painting and sculpture in Paris in 1391, they established clear guidelines ensuring the durability of their productions. Fourteen of the nineteen original statutes of the guild pertained to the necessity of using high-quality materials and preparing the painting surface properly.[12] Rotten and worm-eaten wood was forbidden as a support, as was any wood still saturated with fresh sap. Only colors and primers of an established standard were acceptable, and materials were subject to inspection and guild approval. These measures served as a guarantee to patrons of the arts, the church and the nobility chief among them. When Henry III confirmed the guild's statutes in the sixteenth century, the decree came with a preamble that explained how the regulations prevented shoddily manufactured objects from sullying "sacred sites dedicated in honor of God, and of us, princes of our blood and our nobles."[13]

By the middle of the seventeenth century, however, the guild's technical guidelines were no longer universal prescriptions. When a group of artists received permission from the king to break from the guild and establish the French Royal Academy of Painting and Sculpture, they did so on the grounds that art was an intellectual pursuit, not simply a mechanical one.[14] The Academy shied away from detailed discussion of materials and techniques in order to emphasize the status of painting as a liberal art. This development was a crucial step in the loosening of craft standards, but it was not enough to free artists from the expectation of making works that would last. Much to the contrary, the Academy's right to exist came from the king, and the productions of all its members were meant to stand as lasting testimony to his glories. To justify their work, academicians needed to immerse themselves in a rhetoric of royal eternalization. André Félibien, chronicler of the arts under Louis XIV and secretary to the Academy, made this logic clear when he told the king, "Painting . . . only needs to find a material durable enough to conserve what it marks, to render immortal the name of your majesty."[15] Félibien reminded painters that their livelihoods depended on their ability to produce permanent representations of great men, the royal patron above all others.[16] Artists thus entered into an implicit pact with their sponsor: he would provide them with the financial and institutional protection to sustain their profession, while they gave him immortal material form in their work.

By the time Watteau entered the Academy in 1712, however, this agreement was increasingly open to question. In the final years of Louis XIV's reign, with the country in financial disarray after disastrous military campaigns, royal sponsorship for the arts was in decline.[17] State-sponsored projects did not disappear entirely, and the shift should be understood as a diminishment of opportunity rather than a complete cessation.[18]

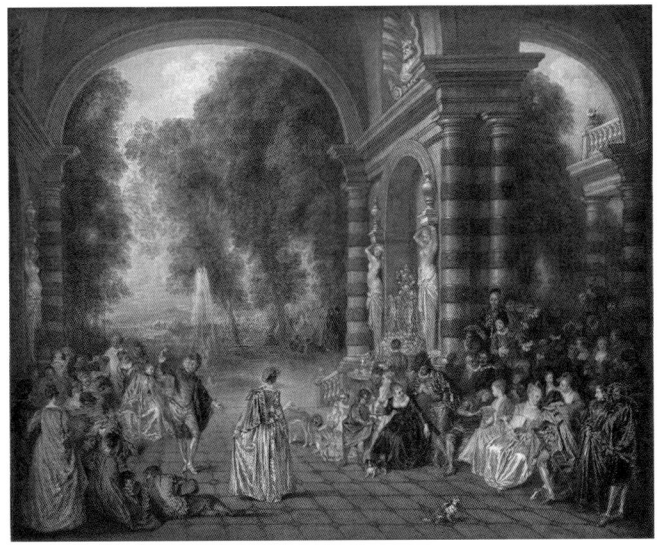

FIG. 8
Antoine Watteau, *The Pleasures of the Ball*, ca. 1715–17. Oil on canvas, 52.5 × 65.2 cm. Dulwich Picture Gallery, London. DPG156.

The change was nonetheless significant given the simultaneous reduction in religious patronage, which sharply decreased as Jansenist opposition to lavish decoration permeated many Parisian parishes, and upheaval surrounding the 1713 papal bull *Unigenitus* hindered large-scale artistic campaigns for several decades.[19] Artists, faced with these economic pressures, increasingly turned to an emerging private art market to support themselves.

The buyers in this marketplace acquired works of art with more varied expectations than the institutional patrons who had preceded them.[20] Some continued to see the objects that they purchased as tools of self-glorification, a means of establishing a reputation that would resound for posterity. For others, however, the capacity of a painting to communicate with the future was often less important than the pleasures that it provided in the present moment. They treated their collections not as inviolable memorials but as spaces in flux, selling works as readily as they bought them.[21]

Various attempts have been made to quantify rates of commercial circulation during the eighteenth century.[22] Scholars have mined trade almanacs and shop inventories for statistics, often coming to different conclusions about precisely when and where a "consumer revolution" occurred in Europe.[23] But if we restrict our perspective to the collecting culture through which Watteau's works circulated, we quickly see the degree to which his pictures were subject to regular trade. Provenance records indicate that most of his paintings passed through multiple collections over the course of the eighteenth century.[24] *The Pleasures of the Ball*, for instance, changed hands no fewer than ten times (fig. 8).[25] Watteau's most devoted collector, the amateur Jean de Jullienne, offers a particularly clear demonstration of the phenomenon. Jullienne purchased a

WATTEAU'S *DÉLICATESSE* (17)

vast number of Watteau's paintings, supported by a formidable fortune from his family's textile dyeing business and their early investments in France's colonial empire.[26] Yet his ownership of Watteau's paintings was temporary; by 1756 he had bought and subsequently sold at least 36 of the artist's canvases.[27] Jettisoning works appears to have been a common practice for Jullienne, who deaccessioned 119 paintings from his collection during his lifetime—more than a third of what he owned at the time of his death.[28] This kind of collection, in other words, functioned according to a different sense of time from the old repositories of art that it was coming to displace. A private collection was not necessarily an enduring monument destined for the future but a space in which pictures came and went.

The rhythm of this commerce did not, on its own, dictate any change in the durability of art. A thriving art market had arisen in the Dutch Republic a century earlier with no appreciable decline in the permanence of paintings.[29] Dutch painters continued to operate under strict guild regulation, which ensured that commercial forces had little effect on the soundness of craftsmanship.[30] In France, where artists enjoyed the possibility of working outside the guild and its craft traditions, circumstances were different.[31] Artists' materials and techniques were less easily sequestered from the temporal pressures of commerce.

Collectors, of course, still had reason to be wary of shoddily crafted paintings—decay affected the resale value of objects, and buyers stood to lose money on works by artists who used unreliable techniques. Auction records from the second half of the eighteenth century suggest that signs of decay in Watteau's paintings diminished their sale prices.[32] Resale value, however, does not necessarily weigh on the artist, who derives income only from the original sale and whose career may have ended by the time the market has responded to the effects of decay. Moreover, collectors in the eighteenth-century art market were not always dissuaded from acquiring works that had the potential to deteriorate—demand for Watteau's work overall remained strong through the 1770s, long after the hazards of his techniques were common knowledge.[33] Not all purchases, after all, are investments, and not all investments are made rationally. On the contrary, one of the hallmarks of consumer behavior is the tendency to prioritize short-term desires over long-term interests, whether out of deliberate hedonism, irrational decision-making, or some combination of the two.[34] Critical reflection on the issue dates to the eighteenth century, when moral philosophers struggled to understand the role of sentiment in the marketplace.[35]

Many of the collectors who dominated the French art market had, in fact, generated their fortunes in an emotionally inflected world of speculative finance that revolved around well-timed intuitions about when to buy and sell.[36] The explosion of investment in French colonial enterprises during the late 1710s, which had been engineered through the complex financial instruments devised by the Scottish banker John Law, made obvious the subjective dynamics of capital allocation as fabulous expectations and cataclysmic fears produced wild fluctuations in wealth.[37] For collectors who had profited from this economy, the purchase of a potentially unstable painting would have constituted no more of a risk than the financial bets that had rewarded them in the past. And for a painter addressing this audience, success demanded a brush that was swift and responsive to demand, not necessarily one that produced durable effects.

Permanence in Doubt

Let us turn to where the problem began: with Watteau at work on a painting. Watteau followed few of the commonly accepted practices of the period for ensuring the longevity of his paintings. He worked with oil paints, a medium that was widely recognized to require special precautions.[38] By the beginning of the eighteenth century, artists had painted in oil for more than two hundred years, a sufficiently long period for them to notice that pictures in the medium could degrade over time. Technical guides emphasized, however, that any such deterioration was largely avoidable through the use of proper techniques.[39] Fastidious work habits were understood to be especially important. A painter's palette, for instance, needed to be clean and well-ordered to avoid the contamination of colors (fig. 9). Artist manuals described elaborate daily palette-cleaning rituals, which ensured the purity and integrity of one's materials.[40] Paint needed to be removed from the palette at the end of the workday and properly stored if it was to be reused.[41] Depending on when the artist planned to work again, some colors could be transferred to a fresh palette for later use, whereas others needed to be submerged in water for safekeeping. With the colors removed from the palette, the artist then needed to scrub it clean and coat it with oil. Only then was it fit for another day's work.

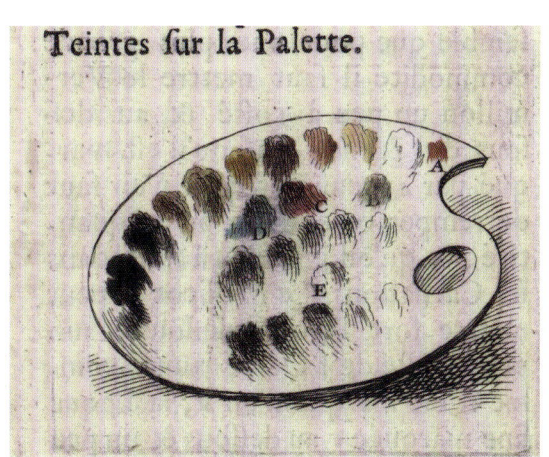

FIG. 9
Roger de Piles, *Les premiers élémens de la peinture pratique*, 1684, page 47. Ghent University. BIB.1490047.

Watteau, we are told, followed these steps infrequently, if at all. He replaced the colors on his palette only on rare occasions, and he cleaned it even less often.[42] Grime soon accumulated not just on his palette but also in the cup of oil where he wiped his brushes, which became a mix of "filth, dust, and colors."[43] Unkempt working conditions were not the only problem that Watteau's contemporaries lamented. Particularly troublesome, they all remarked, was his excessive use of *huile grasse* ("fatty oil"), a medium that accelerated the drying process and could produce thinly painted atmospheric effects.[44] Watteau was hardly the first artist to have used this medium—recipes for it abound in artist manuals going back to the early seventeenth century.[45] The trouble arose from the reckless abandon with which he availed himself of it. Caylus described how Watteau, in an effort to work more quickly, "rubbed *huile grasse* indiscriminately all over his canvases and repainted on top."[46] Gersaint provided similar testimony and detailed the disastrous results: Watteau's "paintings perish from this day by day; they have totally changed color or they become cracked [*très-alès*] beyond repair."[47]

The destructive effects of *huile grasse* set in quickly. When Oudry warned of its dangers in his 1752 lecture to the Academy, he remarked that paintings made with excessive *huile grasse* "conserve their freshness for very little time and become unrecognizable by the end of a couple of years and sometimes even sooner."[48] Such dramatic deterioration stems from the unequal drying speed of the different levels of paint. As the *huile grasse* dries and contracts, it pulls the surface of the picture apart. In contrast to the fine craquelure that naturally develops on the surface of paintings over a long period of time, these fast-forming cracks open wide and run deep.[49] Just how many of Watteau's paintings fell victim to the damage of *huile grasse* remains unclear. Mariette wrote that "nearly all have suffered," and Gersaint admitted that paintings by Watteau immune from these effects "are rare, in truth."[50]

Watteau's best-known paintings tend to be among this well-preserved minority, providing glimpses of instability only on close inspection. Step near *The Pilgrimage to the Isle of Cythera*, for example, and you will find a network of deep cracks circling around the arced body of the shirtless oarsman (fig. 10).[51] Like ripples on the surface of a pond, these ruptures in the painted surface fan outward and dissipate. As they move away from the oarsman, they draw our eyes to disturbances on other parts of the canvas. Concentric rings of fractured paint radiate from a section of open sky (fig. 11). Lower and to the right, crevices cut across the faces of the cavorting lovers (fig. 12).[52]

In other works, such as *The Village Bride*, the effects of *huile grasse* become much clearer, with gaping fissures running across much of the picture's surface (fig. 13). Art historians, looking past the cracks, have sometimes seen in the subject matter of this painting a meditation on "time's passage," whether in the "inevitable sense of movement" that characterizes the winding wedding procession or in the diaphanous trees and ethereal clouds that hover above them.[53] But if time is a depicted subject of the painting,

FIG. 10
Antoine Watteau, *The Pilgrimage to the Isle of Cythera* (detail), 1717. Oil on canvas, 129 × 195 cm. Musée du Louvre, Paris. INV 8525. Photo: author.

FIG. 11
Antoine Watteau, *The Pilgrimage to the Isle of Cythera* (detail), 1717. Oil on canvas, 129 × 195 cm. Musée du Louvre, Paris. INV 8525. Photo: author.

FIG. 12
Antoine Watteau, *The Pilgrimage to the Isle of Cythera* (detail), 1717. Oil on canvas, 129 × 195 cm. Musée du Louvre, Paris. INV 8525. Photo © RMN-Grand Palais / Art Resource, NY (Stéphane Maréchalle).

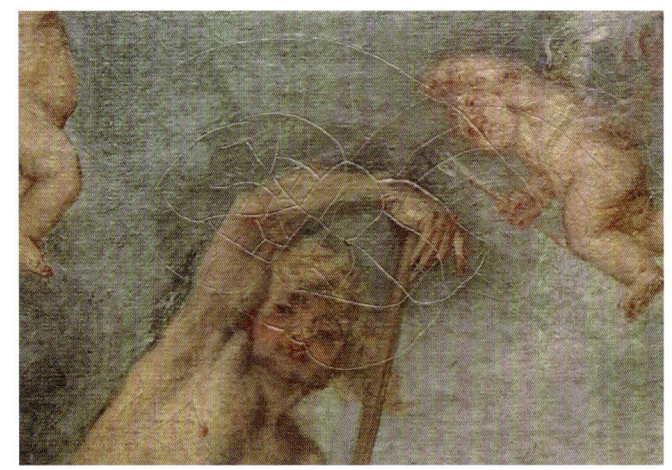

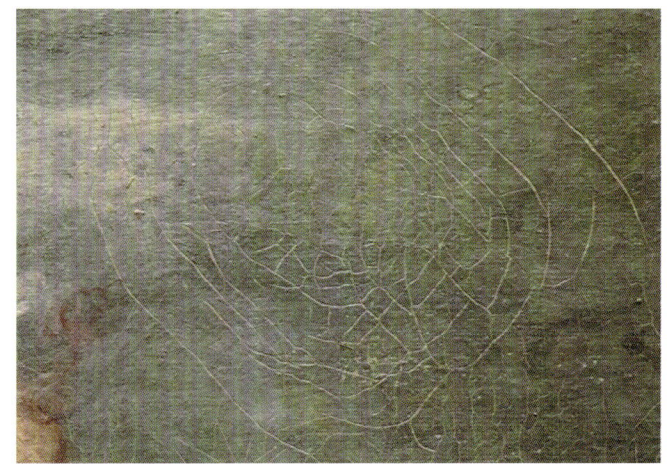

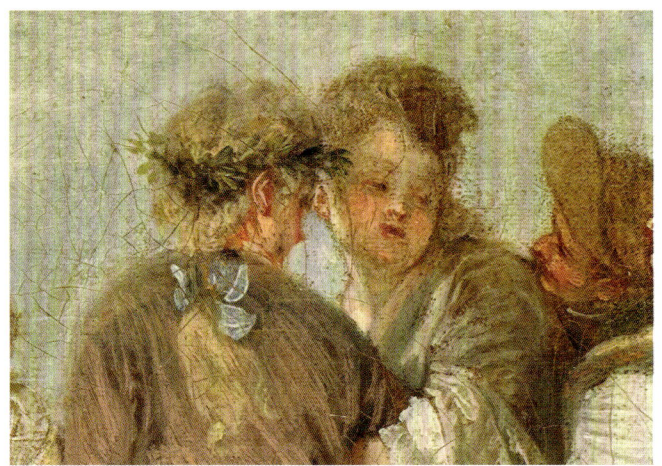

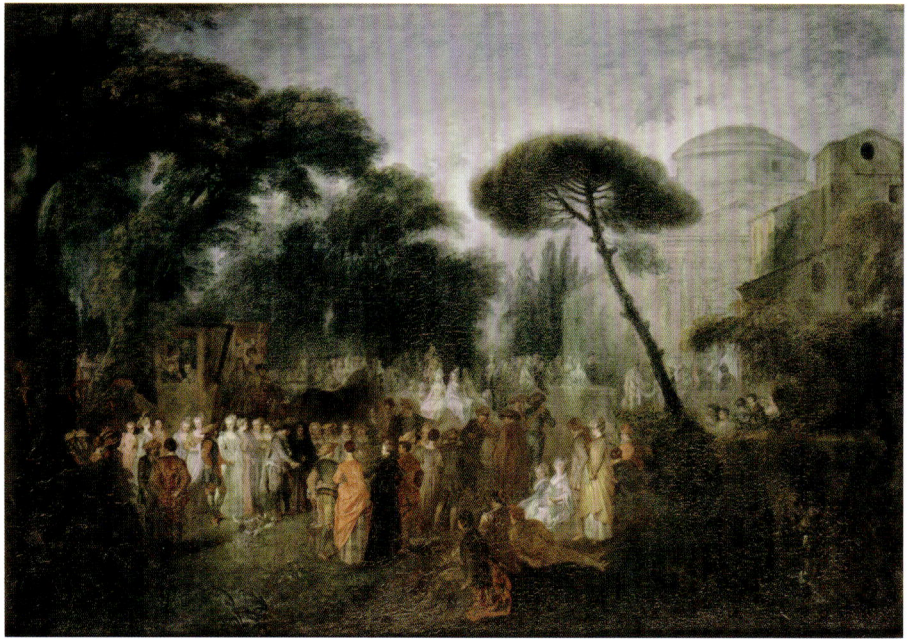

FIG. 13 Antoine Watteau, *The Village Bride*, 1710–12. Oil on canvas, 65 × 92 cm. Schlösser und Gärten, Charlottenburg Palace, Berlin. GK I 5603. Photo: Stiftung Preußische Schlösser und Gärten Berlin-Brandenburg (SPSG) / Jörg P. Anders.

FIG. 14 (*opposite*) Antoine Watteau, *The Village Bride* (detail), 1710–12. Oil on canvas, 65 × 92 cm. Schlösser und Gärten, Charlottenburg Palace, Berlin. GK I 5603. Photo: Stiftung Preußische Schlösser und Gärten Berlin-Brandenburg (SPSG) / Jörg P. Anders.

then it has long been overwritten by time's material effects. Wedding attendants break into a fragmented mass of oil and pigment, becoming an almost illegible mosaic of paint chips (fig. 14). Edmond de Goncourt described the painting as a "sad ruin" in the late nineteenth century, but its problems had become clear well over a century before that.[54] After having passed through the homes of several French collectors in the first half of the eighteenth century, the painting entered the collection of Frederick the Great in Prussia by 1750, when it was described as "torn through the faces, hands, and clothes."[55] Attempts to restore the painting go back at least to that date, perhaps even earlier.[56]

Watteau's friends and acquaintances saw cracks like these as the unfortunate product of his desire to finish paintings quickly. The fact that he is thought to have produced more than two hundred paintings during the period of roughly a decade when he was active gives some indication of his speed, but it was his studio habits that particularly called attention to his haste.[57] His entire working process was designed to create paintings with a minimal investment of time. We know of almost no compositional sketches that he executed in preparation for paintings.[58] He preferred instead to draw from life

(22) A DELICATE MATTER

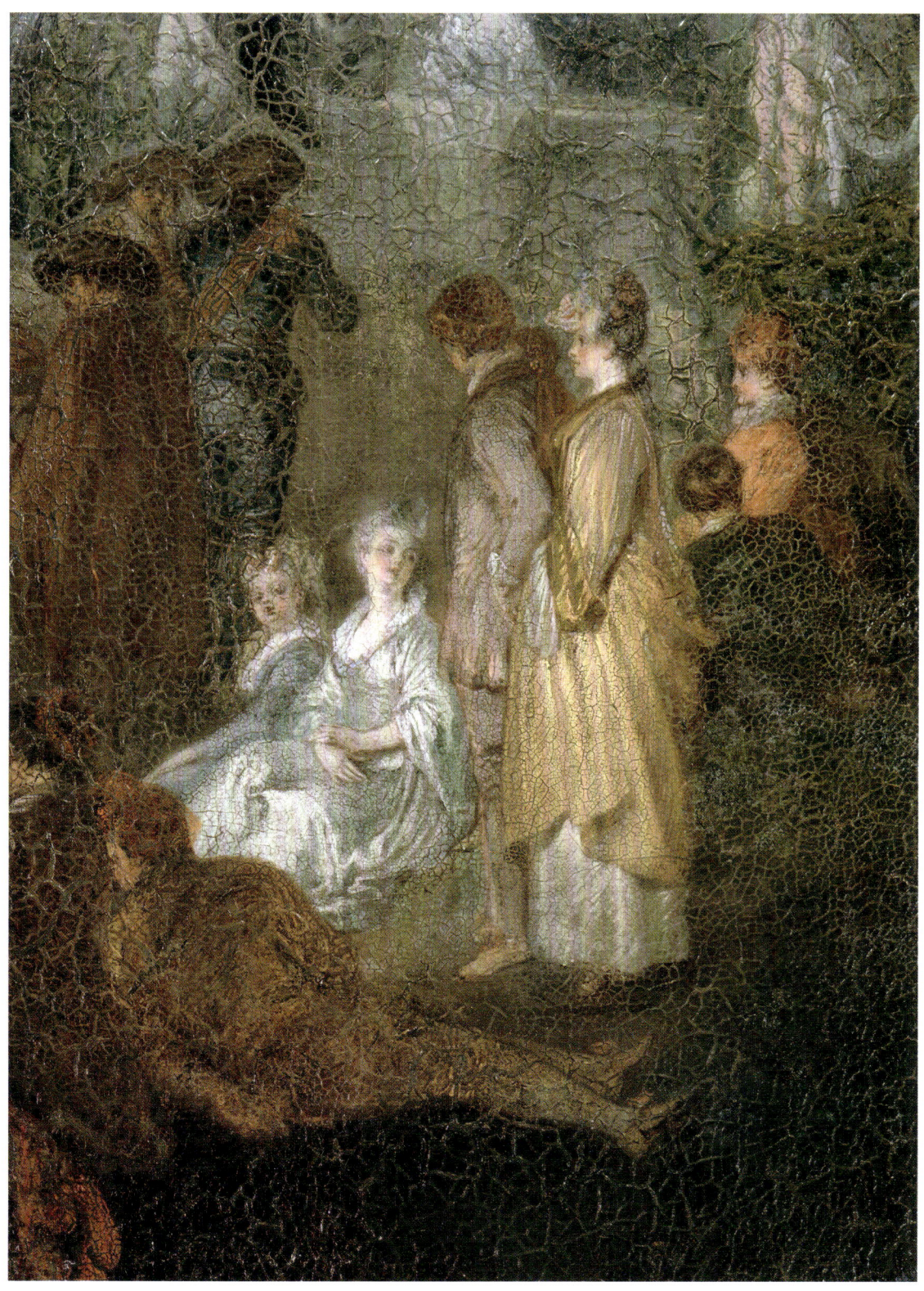

without a particular painting in mind, filling his sketchbooks with figure studies that he could reuse across multiple works.[59] To make a painting, he would apparently flip through his drawing albums to find a few stock figures that he could insert into the work, composing the scene as he painted.[60]

It is tempting to take these hasty work habits as nothing more than confirmation of Watteau's impatient and indifferent personality, a corroboration of the psychological characterizations offered by his contemporaries. Yet the rapidity with which he worked can also be understood as a response to the demands of the market surrounding him. It was not simply the fact that working quickly was necessary to generate more income, or that buyers expected artists to keep up with the latest fashion. Speed of production also spoke to the aesthetic priorities of collectors who saw in the swift movements of an artist's brush a pleasing sense of ease and facility. The veneration of these qualities stemmed from the aristocratic ideal of nonchalance or *sprezzatura*, which established an association between painterly immediacy and the improvisational witticisms that had long structured elite sociability.[61] Writing in 1708, the art theorist Roger de Piles explicitly connected fluidity of brushwork with these forms of social distinction, unifying them under the term "elegance": "Elegance in general is a manner of saying or doing things . . . with *politesse* in giving a turn to things such as will strike people of a *délicat* mind."[62] He remarks that one finds this quality in paintings that are "little polished, even careless [*négligés*]," explaining that the apparent effortlessness of such works overcomes their faults, charming the eye.[63]

Art historians have noted the conflicted status of terms such as *facilité* and *négligence* among eighteenth-century art theorists, who spent countless pages trying to distinguish between an agreeable swiftness of the brush and a hurried sloppiness.[64] What needs to be examined more carefully, however, is how the efforts to draw this distinction emerged from an attempt to separate the temporality of social intercourse from the supposedly degraded rhythms of commerce. In truth, the difference between the noble elegance of an unrestrained brush and the base self-interest of painting quickly to satisfy market demand was not always clear. The difficulty of distinguishing between these modes of painting did not stop the leadership of the Academy from trying. Antoine Coypel, soon to become director of the Academy, delivered a lecture on brushwork in 1713 that spoke directly to the dangers of a financially motivated speed in technique. After noting the importance of a "facile, agreeable, and light hand," he warned that these skills were like "riches that are only worthy of consideration in the hands of sagacious people who employ them with a sense for the apropos."[65] Coypel then shifted from using money as a metaphor for artistic technique to treating it as an actual cause for excessively rapid brushwork: "One often wishes to paint quickly because of the miserable principle of interest . . . [avarice] is what makes one run after gain sooner than glory and that makes us abandon the care to do things well for the desire to do a lot."[66] Coypel reminded the artists of the Academy that true glory awaited them in the future, which meant that they should paint with care. He quoted the words of the ancient Greek painter Zeuxis: "I work so much on what I paint because I paint for posterity."[67] The fact that none of Zeuxis's paintings had actually survived apparently did not bother Coypel. What mattered to him was Zeuxis's *devotion* to the future, a commitment that contemporary artists, in their putatively vulgar attachment to money, no longer seemed to be honoring.

A conflict between long-term posterity and immediate economic interest emerged as a key theme in the doctrine of the Academy under Coypel's direction in the following years.[68] The old obligation of artists to make durable monuments to their royal patron, Coypel felt, needed to be reestablished in a period of challenging financial circumstances. In 1714, a year before the death of Louis XIV, Coypel called on artists to make objects that would deliver an image of their illustrious ruler to future generations: "May painting and sculpture . . . transmit to the most distant posterity the crowning achievements and virtues of a king whose precious days give us the pleasure of ours."[69] In a reprisal of the foundational rhetoric of the Academy, he spoke of the "glory of assuring immortality to those who should never die."[70] Such declarations were clearly meant to echo the sort of statements that Félibien had made throughout the second half of the seventeenth century, reiterating the duty of artists to offer immortal testimony of the king's glories in exchange for his continued sponsorship. Unlike the pronouncements of the previous century, however, Coypel's words betrayed an anxiety about the terms of this agreement. In an implicit acknowledgment of declining state funding for the arts after a period of ruinous military expenditures, Coypel spoke hopefully of a "happy peace" that would renew investment in cultural affairs.[71] Such hopes, however, would go largely unfulfilled. In the years after the death of Louis XIV, there was no great return to the massive program of state-sponsored artistic production that had defined the height of his reign. During the regency period that followed, and into the early years of Louis XV's rule, patronage had never been more in question. Artists had to pursue alternative sources of income, and a growing commercial sphere offered them new opportunities. In this sense, we can understand the opposition that Coypel saw developing between posterity and avarice— or perhaps simple economic necessity. An object made for the king needed to stand as durable evidence of his glory for future generations, but what expectations existed for an object made for an unspecified buyer, hanging on a gallery wall?

Market Time

By probing the connection between Watteau's working habits and the market in which he operated, I do not wish to insinuate that he was some kind of mercenary huckster. We have little reason to doubt Gersaint, Watteau's dealer, when he claims that the artist became uncomfortable with the enormous revenues that his paintings generated and sometimes insisted on lowering their prices.[72] What I am suggesting instead is that the emerging art market produced an understanding of cultural temporality that differed markedly from the posterity-minded ethos that had predominated under earlier systems of patronage. An economy in which paintings are continually bought and sold, in contrast to a system in which artworks reside indefinitely in an institution that treats them as evidence of its everlasting splendor, presupposes a radically different understanding of art's place in history. This is not to say that royal and religious patrons maintained unwavering tastes or that they never redecorated; it is simply to recognize that such changes were subsumed within a broader rhetoric of institutional endurance and artistic eternalization. For example, the Superintendent of Royal Buildings under Louis XIV, Jean-Baptiste Colbert, officially barred the practice of selling or deaccessioning works from the royal collections, creating the impression of the crown as an everlasting protector of its holdings.[73] No such rules obtained among private collectors, and artists could hardly envision the fate of their work after it entered the open market. In this context, it was not the personal acquisitiveness of the artist but the broader structure of the artistic economy that challenged traditional assumptions about the futurity of art. To grasp the full extent of art's temporal reorganization in the commercial sphere and the nature of Watteau's relationship to it, we need to consider his material practices alongside his subject matter.

No single work speaks to the temporal implications of art's entry into the market more than the shop sign that Watteau painted for Gersaint's storefront in 1720 (fig. 15). The picture presents a moment of bustling activity within Paris's emerging consumer culture. On the right side, potential buyers admire paintings alongside mirrors and other luxury objects. On the left, objects are literally in circulation: a shop worker carries a large mirror while another handles a portrait of Louis XIV, loading it into a crate for shipment or perhaps unpacking it for display.[74]

Scholars have devoted much energy to deciphering the significance of these objects and gestures. The portrait of Louis XIV has often served as the focal point for analysis, its position in the wooden crate sometimes being interpreted as a symbolic entombment of the recently deceased king.[75] Subsequent interpretations have resisted such macabre intimations, seeing the movement of the king's portrait as a celebration of commercial circulation, an advertisement for the kinds of pictures that a gallery like this one would have continually bought and sold.[76]

The symbolic reading of the king's entombment and the more literal interpretation of the portrait's sale are hardly incompatible. The end of the king's reign and art's commercialization, after all, were connected. Louis XIV's portrait had long stood as an emblem for the system of royal patronage that had structured the artistic economy when state support sheltered art from the demands of the marketplace. When royal portraits

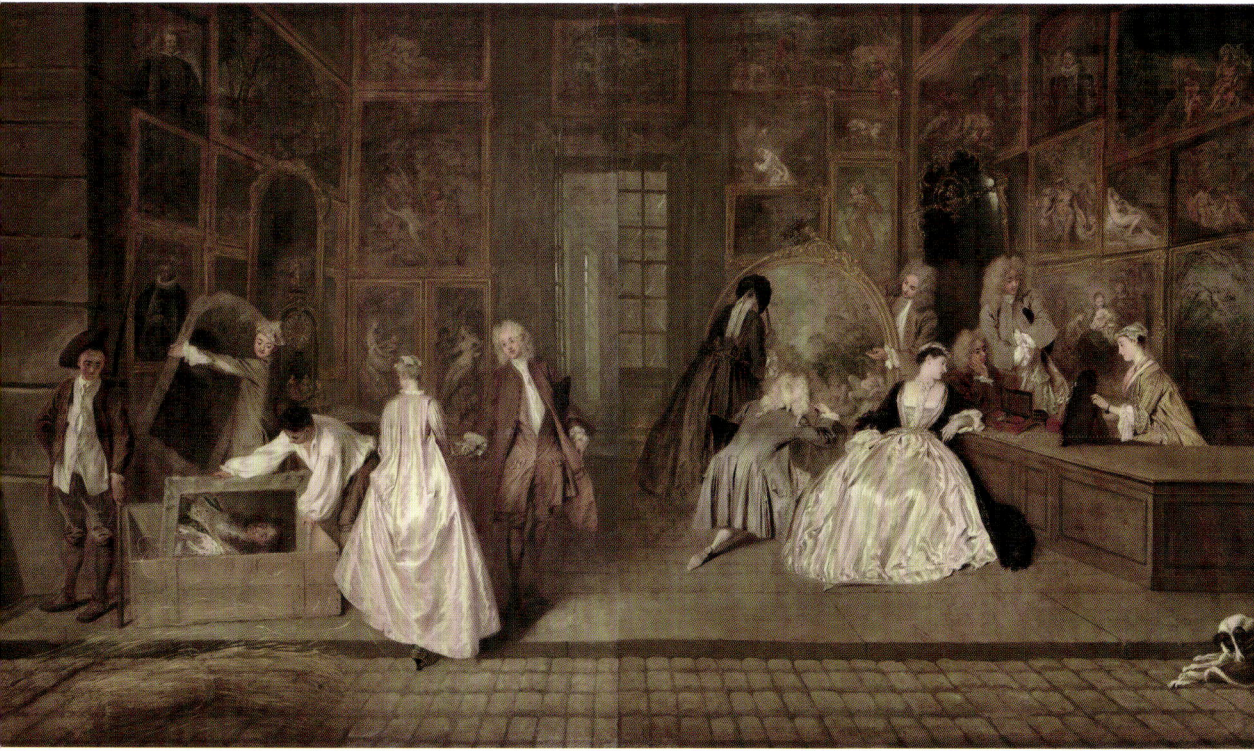

FIG. 15 Antoine Watteau, *Gersaint's Shop Sign*, 1720. Oil on canvas, 163 × 308 cm. Schlösser und Gärten, Charlottenburg Palace, Berlin. GK I 1200–1201. Photo: Stiftung Preußische Schlösser und Gärten Berlin-Brandenburg (SPSG) / Roland Handrick.

like these appeared embedded within seventeenth-century paintings by members of the Academy, they underscored art's stable and enduring status under its institutional sponsor. Typical in this regard is Nicolas Loir's *Allegory of the Foundation of the Royal Academy of Painting and Sculpture* from 1666 (fig. 16), in which Minerva and Fame hold the king's portrait in the sky while Time unveils the arts of painting and sculpture. The king's portrait is here both a source of inspiration to the arts and an example of the supposedly everlasting imagery that was produced with his support. Loir's painting makes clear that because of the mutually beneficial relationship between the arts and their royal benefactor, time was no threat. This particular painting still hung in the halls of the Academy during Watteau's life, but the idea of time that it allegorized had lost its supremacy.[77] If the sale of the king's portrait in Watteau's painting can be said to symbolize any broader historical transformation, it is the weakening of that temporal order, the decline of that institutional stability.

Watteau wrests the royal portrait from the absolutist realm of immortal images, incorporating it into the mobile and fluctuating forces of the commercial sphere. In

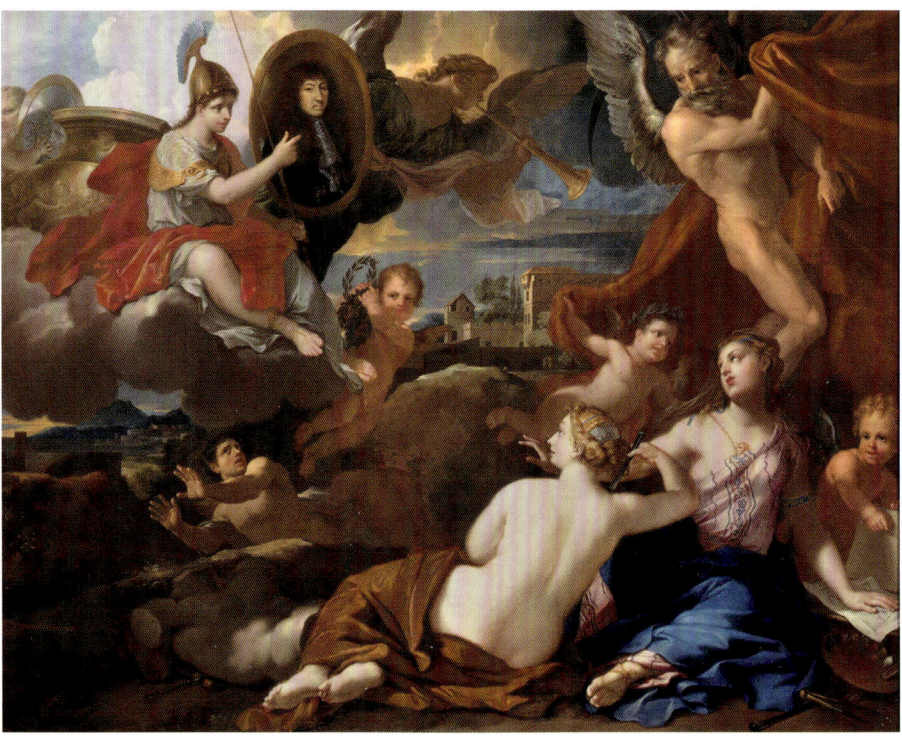

FIG. 16 Nicolas Loir, *Allegory of the Foundation of the Royal Academy of Painting and Sculpture*, 1666. Oil on canvas, 141 × 185.5 cm. Châteaux de Versailles et de Trianon, Versailles. MV 8650. Photo © RMN-Grand Palais / Art Resource, NY (Gérard Blot).

the emerging marketplace, the notion that art is the domain of immortality is reduced to a joke. Watteau shows painting for what it had become: a material object subject to the physical realities of the world, easily packaged and sold. In this sense, the king's portrait in the crate offers both an iconographic symbol and a very tangible depiction of the practical realities surrounding the life of art in the world of commercial exchange. We might see it equally as an allegory of royal patronage's dethronement and as a matter-of-fact illustration of the physical travails that paintings were expected to undergo as a result. Painting, Watteau shows us, no longer had a permanent home.

In the world of commerce, an artist's work entered an amorphous network where it became difficult to track, often never to be seen again. Gersaint himself spoke of the vanishing status of objects in the emerging art market, describing how paintings in private collections "gradually disperse themselves without one perceiving in what hands they pass."[78] Estate sales of famous collectors, he noted, sometimes provided the last opportunity to see paintings before they disappeared: "One could hardly name today the collections where a tenth of these paintings find themselves placed."[79] Under

(28) A DELICATE MATTER

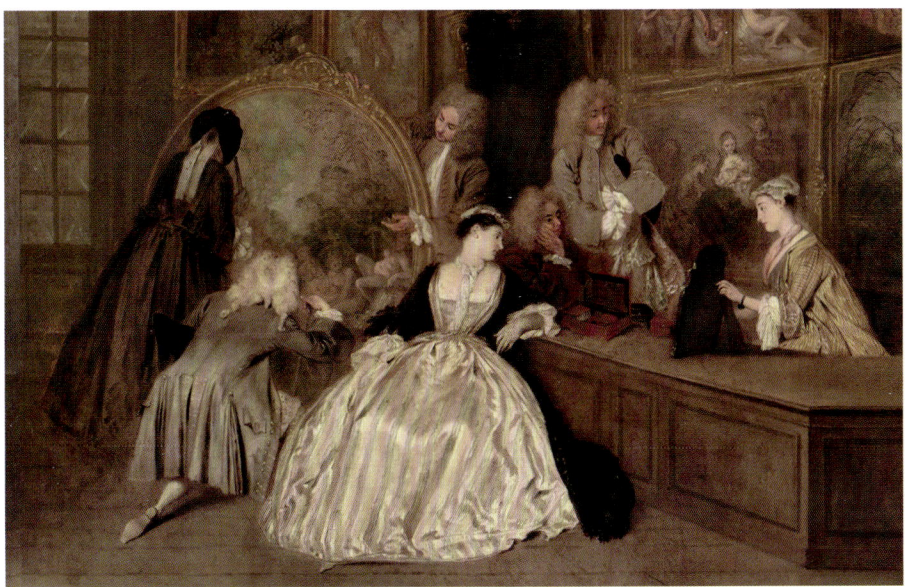

FIG. 17 Antoine Watteau, *Gersaint's Shop Sign* (detail), 1720. Oil on canvas, 163 × 308 cm. Schlösser und Gärten, Charlottenburg Palace, Berlin. GK I 1200–1201. Photo: Stiftung Preußische Schlösser und Gärten Berlin-Brandenburg (SPSG) / Roland Handrick.

these conditions, the old obligation of the painter to make materially durable works could no longer be taken for granted. Even the most carefully crafted object could be packed up, shipped off, and rendered untraceable for posterity. A painting, no matter how it was made, faced an uncertain fate. Material stability had become just one factor in art's contingent relationship to the future.

In the commercial sphere, painting's survival depended as much on its ability to attract an audience as it did on its material durability. As the right half of Watteau's shop sign makes clear (fig. 17), a picture needed to entice a consumer in the present moment before it had any hope of enduring into the future. For an emerging audience of buyers who gravitated toward paintings like Watteau's, their initial point of interest was less the durability of a painting's surface than the subjective flights of imagination prompted by the sensuous application of paint.[80] Watteau's work spoke to a new type of viewer, an amateur, whose attachment to art was based on pleasure and affective experience rather than dispassionate analysis.[81] Unlike the connoisseur, whose identity depended on "knowledge" and "discernment," the amateur was defined principally by "love."[82] Though amateurs often made their own forays into artistic practice, frequently trying their hand in the forgiving media of drawing and etching, such efforts hardly constituted a thoroughgoing technical initiation in the material underpinnings of art—nor was such a background required.[83] The affection these viewers had for particular paintings demanded no more erudition or justification than the attraction that they might have felt for another person. Both forms of desire were understood to be unlearned, and the amateur freely conflated artistic preferences with libidinal impulses.[84] The viewer who stoops before the landscape painting in Watteau's shop sign, it is often observed, may take equal pleasure in the fluid brushstrokes before his eyes and in the nude figures that they depict.[85] In either case, durability is far from the central preoccupation in this indulgence of desire.

Desire, of course, can be fleeting. Part of what defined the new generation of art buyers was the mercurial nature of their whims, which could be as ephemeral as the paintings that they acquired. Gersaint compared some aspiring collectors to adolescents who are drawn to "beauties that soon fade away."[86] Later in the century, Denis Diderot would offer in his *Salon de 1765* what is perhaps the bluntest description of the impetuous urges that came to be seen in matters of art and love: "One leaves the loveliest woman for no other reason than the duration of her affection; one becomes bored with the sweetest of pleasures without quite knowing why. Why would painting have any advantage in the matter?"[87]

The market of fluctuating desires through which Watteau's paintings circulated was, in this sense, not so different from the world of fleeting flirtations that his *fêtes galantes* are so often said to depict. It is sometimes claimed that Watteau's enchanted landscapes show love not as an enduring bond between people but as a process subject to perpetual change, temporalized and inherently unstable.[88] This temporal understanding of desire links the world within the *fêtes galantes* to the commercial reality outside them. Watteau's shop sign makes this connection clear enough. The figures within the gallery space could just as easily belong to one of his pastoral scenes. Here in a commercial showroom, they take part in another kind of courtship ritual, one conducted not simply among people but also between buyers and objects. The large oval landscape painting around which some of them gather performs the role of the principal seducer. Its beguiling effects may be short-lived, but so may love itself. Change and exchange, in Watteau's world, is the logic of love and commerce alike.

Some of the most probing commentary on this phenomenon came from those who opposed it. By the 1740s, as the condition of Watteau's paintings worsened, critics pointed to his work as an emblem of commerce's corrupting effects on the material integrity of art. In expressing these complaints, no voice was stronger than that of the art critic Étienne La Font de Saint-Yenne. In his first major piece of art criticism, published in 1747, he positioned Watteau's paintings at the center of a systemic analysis of the relationship between the marketplace and ephemerality:

> Might it be permitted that I make several reproaches on behalf of the public to nearly all of our painters at present on the little durability of their coloring

that ten years at most removes and effaces to the point of bringing to nothing paintings that were bought at high prices and that used to enchant us. Such are those of the charming Watteau, who would be the most seductive and piquant of all the moderns if he were not lacking in this one area. What are most of his paintings today? An unformed assemblage of discordant colors that leaves neither life nor resemblance in the figures.[89]

The mention of "high prices" and fleeting enchantment were key to La Font's argument. Permanence, he claimed, had no place in the market's system of value. Beyond Watteau, he cited as evidence the enormously successful decorative painter Pierre-Charles Trémolières, whose flesh tones had apparently changed greatly in the seven years that had elapsed since his death: "To what distasteful degree have the pinks of Sr. Tremoillere [sic] faded today, which he made so fashionable?"[90] La Font pointed, also, to the "little knowledge of our French painters in the choice of colors," observing that the majority of artists now bought their pigments pre-prepared. He also suggested that "economy" had prompted artists to shun expensive and durable colors, such as lapis lazuli, in favor of fugitive alternatives.[91]

What makes La Font's criticisms especially revealing is the connection that they establish between material instability and other forms of flux brought on by fashion and consumption. He linked art's physical fragility to the modish taste for pinkish hues, describing the colors as a symbol for fleetingness across the arts: "Everything is the color of roses and conserves the same durability."[92] Subject matter and genre, too, shaped how La Font understood the temporality of the art market, as the tradition of history painting gave way to portraits and decorative schemes for home interiors that were constantly being remodeled. Admirable works of the past now found themselves under "the dust of attics and the filth of coach houses" or, worse still, turned into carriage decorations, "dragged in the streets, to be subjected there to the ravages of the mud, and to be exposed every day without any defense to the threat of being left in pieces by the knock of the dirtiest wagon, street carts, or the impetuous march of these carriages."[93] Even at Versailles, he noted, the great historical works of the past had been packed away, on the verge of "a coming and inevitable decay from lack of air and exhibition."[94]

Some of these claims were almost certainly exaggerations, and La Font was hardly a disinterested observer. As Thomas Crow and Katie Scott have shown, La Font belonged to a social circle of noble and non-noble elites who felt marginalized by the monarchy's growing allegiance to an ascendant financial class.[95] La Font's assertions about the deleterious effects of luxury markets and declining royal patronage can therefore be understood as a proxy war in a broader conflict over governmental policy and fiscal affairs. And yet, his analysis of the forces driving artistic production in an age of consumption remains instructive, even if we reject his more hyperbolic statements and hectoring tone. Technical art history has largely substantiated his assertion that painters during this period relied increasingly on pre-prepared materials from color merchants, outsourcing the labor and knowledge that had once been confined to the artist's workshop.[96] State sponsorship for the arts had indisputably declined since the height of Louis XIV's reign, and the physical disrepair of patrimony in royal collections had been commented upon since the 1720s.[97] Scholars have also corroborated La Font's view that artistic tastes began to change more rapidly during the eighteenth century, as fashion undermined previously stable artistic hierarchies.[98] La Font's insight, then, was to identify the common thread of temporal instability running through these seemingly disparate developments. The physical movement of paintings, the shifting proclivities of buyers, and the unstable materials used by artists all became, in La Font's view, interconnected pieces of a system in which commercial circulation undermined different forms of cultural stability.

Where La Font's ideological inclinations distorted his perspective was in the lessons that he took from the loss of this stability. His characterization of Watteau as both "charming" and "seductive" offers an instructive example. Both terms had historically been used to describe the flickering displays of wit and flirtation that defined court sociability.[99] La Font gave these words a double-edged meaning, ostensibly using them to commend Watteau while incorporating them into a cautionary tale of commercial debasement. The physical decay of Watteau's work, in this account, becomes an implicit metaphor of moral decay, a sign of noble charms perverted through the excesses of the marketplace and consumer demand. The problem with this interpretation is not the economic relation that it establishes between the *délicat* pleasures of Watteau's paintings and the delicate materiality of their cracked surfaces but in the implication that this relation is borne of corruption and depravity. Take away the high-minded appeals to virtue, and we are left with a remarkably incisive account of the financial forces that link the courtly allure of Watteau's paintings to their technical properties.

Watteau's work captured, in sum, the way the art market of the early eighteenth century formed a bridge between the fleeting pleasures of an older aristocratic order and the ephemeral "seductions" of an emerging commercial sphere. While Watteau's detractors described this connection in negative terms, they were not the only people to recognize or respond to it. Watteau, by showing how a burgeoning consumer culture could support a new degree of material experimentation, opened a path for other artists in the generation that followed to take greater technical risks. Much more, in fact, was left for them to explore. Watteau had made clear that *délicat* charm was enough to persuade buyers to overlook the physical impermanence of an object, but what remained to be seen was the degree to which material instability itself could become a source of attraction.

2

Pastel and the Allure of Fragility

One of the traditional functions of a portrait is to leave a lasting likeness of a person for future generations. "Through painting, the faces of the dead go on living for a very long time," declared Leon Battista Alberti in his treatise *On Painting* from 1435.[1] The idea was hardly new at the time, and it would become a truism in theoretical writings on art in the centuries that followed.[2] In eighteenth-century France, however, a development called this principle into question: hundreds of Parisian artists and amateurs began producing portraits in pastel, an exceptionally fragile medium that consisted of little more than powdered pigment clinging to paper.[3]

Pastels present a host of issues that vex conservators to this day.[4] Like all works on paper, they are sensitive to light and susceptible to mold, but the most significant threat to the medium relates to the tenuous adhesion of its particles to the underlying support.[5] Large shocks will knock a cloud of pigment into the air, and small vibrations during transport can incrementally loosen the powder from the paper. Even nearby street traffic poses a hazard—in the early twentieth century, Henri de Rothschild was so concerned that a bus route near his home in Paris endangered a pastel portrait in his collection that he arranged for the construction of a new house in a more tranquil neighborhood to protect the work.[6] Such precaution is warranted. Recent scientific research suggests that minor tremors gradually weaken the bond between pastel and its support, causing material fatigue that remains invisible until the cumulative effect passes a threshold, resulting in sudden and catastrophic damage.[7]

How did a medium beset by instability suddenly come to dominate a genre that had traditionally been charged with immortalization? Histories of pastel portraiture tend to treat its fragility as an unfortunate byproduct of its virtues.[8] The medium offered portraitists numerous advantages. Its subtle colors and powdery textures were well suited to capturing the nuances of skin, especially the powdered faces of eighteenth-century Europeans whose cosmetics shared a number of ingredients with pastel.[9] Unlike the glossy finish of oil on canvas, the matte surface of pastel allowed light to penetrate and scatter among its particles, producing a radiant glow.[10] Pastel also enabled artists to work quickly, with no need to wait for layers of paint to dry—a benefit that was particularly important in the context of portraiture, where artists needed to avoid exhausting their subjects with long modeling sessions. For these reasons, we might imagine, eighteenth-century portraitists and collectors may simply have decided that the merits of pastel outweighed the risks of its fragility.

What this explanation does not adequately convey, however, is the centrality of fragility to the medium's social meaning and aesthetic effect. In the world of elite sociability where pastel earned its adherents, the medium's physical delicacy took on symbolic significance, allowing artists to convey the social *délicatesse* of their sitters in material form. The most skillful practitioners of pastel, such as the renowned portraitist Maurice-Quentin de La Tour, particularly capitalized on this metaphorical potential. In La Tour's hands, the friable substance became a physical surrogate for the evanescent personalities of his sitters, a transubstantiated manifestation of the elusive soul behind the face. Critics registered this effect by equating La Tour's medium with the spiritual essence of his subjects, suggesting that the weightless presence of the sitter's inner life lay between his fingers: "He knows, with his subtle and magic touch how to seize and fix the volatile salt of wit [*esprit*], so quick to evaporate in the hands of anyone, even among those who possess it."[11]

As a materialized proxy for social *délicatesse*, pastel became one of the most important commodified expressions of courtly sociability among the newly affluent. While the market for pastels was not restricted to any single demographic, many of the largest and most ambitious pastels to attract interest at the Salon depicted recently ennobled financiers.[12] La Tour's meteoric rise, for example, depended on clients such as Louis Duval de l'Épinoy (fig. 18), who amassed his fortunes through speculation in John Law's "System" and investment in France's expanding colonial empire.[13] La Tour's pastels manifested the transitory signs of worldly comportment that such men needed to secure their position in the domain of *mœurs délicates*. The portrait of Duval typifies the effect, showing the sitter turning toward the viewer with a faint smirk while grasping a pinch of snuff—the powdered tobacco between his fingers echoing the materiality of the portrait itself. The combination of fugitive gestures, rendered in a medium that appears no less mutable, creates the impression of a fleeting social encounter. The French writer and salon hostess Madame de Graffigny admired the portrait for this atmosphere of momentary social exchange, observing that the sitter "makes you laugh with his laughing air."[14]

The strategic deployment of pastel's physical delicacy as a metonym for social *délicatesse* nonetheless came with risks. By commodifying a courtly mode of conduct and making its privileges available for purchase, pastellists opened themselves to accusations

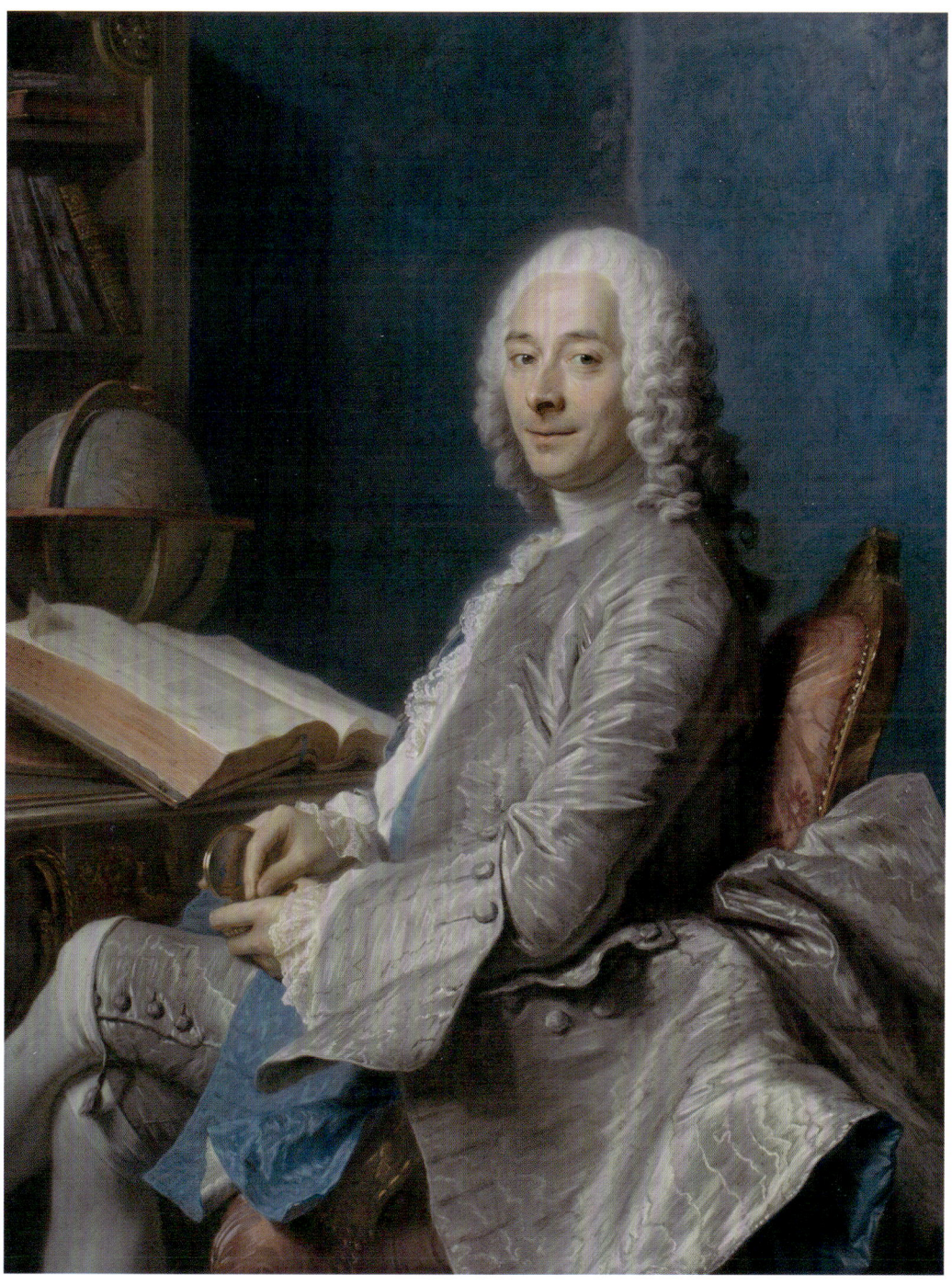

FIG. 18 Maurice-Quentin de La Tour, *Louis Duval de L'Épinoy*, 1745. Pastel on paper, 120 × 93 cm. Museu Calouste Gulbenkian, Lisbon. Inv. 2380. Photo: Calouste Gulbenkian Foundation (Catarina Gomes Ferreira).

of enabling social duplicity. Critics were quick to level the charge, using it to attach new meaning to pastel's fragility. "It is the same with everything that is in fashion," La Font wrote dismissively of pastel, describing the "fragile crayons" less as a signifier of ineffable subjectivity than as an emblem for the vulgar and short-sighted interests of the commercial sphere.[15]

The instability of pastel, then, was hardly an incidental side effect of its virtues. In a period of diminishing aristocratic authority and increasing financial mobility, fragility became integral to both the medium's value and its vulnerability as an instrument of social differentiation. As this chapter will show, the shifting meanings of pastel's fragility presented artists with significant challenges and possibilities. La Tour, who worked exclusively in pastel, made these promises and pitfalls especially evident. Having capitalized on the allure of pastel's delicate materiality at the outset of his career, he became increasingly consumed by the search for a reliable means of stabilizing his work, struggling to remake his image as a disinterested intellectual committed to posterity. At stake in these developments was not just the survival of pastel as a medium but the future of art's relationship with consumer capitalism. Pastel, in its rise and eventual fall, would demonstrate how the alignment of social *délicatesse* with the material delicacy of a saleable object was a perilous artistic enterprise—one that would ultimately force artists to disavow delicacy's association with commercial ephemerality if they wished to harness its power as an autonomous aesthetic value.

The Rise of a Social Medium

The ties between pastel and the socioeconomic transformations of the eighteenth century become evident when we consider why the medium achieved popularity when it did. Pastel itself had existed well before the eighteenth century. Conservators generally use the term "pastel" to describe any fabricated drawing stick consisting of three main ingredients: pigment to provide color, an extender such as gypsum or kaolin to add bulk, and an adhesive to bind the ingredients together.[16] Artists as early as the fifteenth century had fashioned such implements, which they soon described as "pastels," borrowing a term that apothecaries had used to designate the medicinal lozenges that they created from paste.[17] Painters such as Leonardo and Barocci experimented with some version of the medium in their preparatory sketches, using it to test color relationships and to add life to drawings.[18] Yet, for most of the early modern era, few artists would have considered using pastels for finished works. The story of how opinions about the medium changed has typically been told through the technical innovations of artists from Robert Nanteuil to Rosalba Carriera, who expanded pastel's coloristic range and textural effects.[19] There is much truth to this narrative, and the contributions of these

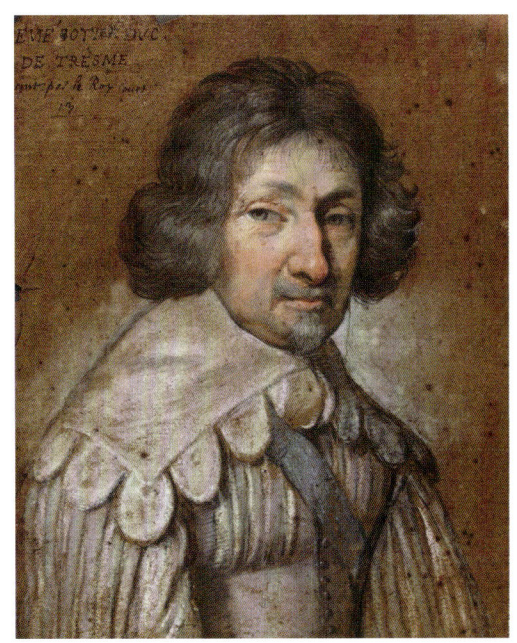

FIG. 19
Louis XIII, *Portrait of René Potier, duc de Tresme*, ca. 1632–35. Pastel on paper, 18.1 × 15.1 cm. Musée du Louvre, Paris. RF 54529. Photo © RMN-Grand Palais / Art Resource, NY (Martine Beck-Coppola).

artists deserve recognition. But their success also needs to be understood as a product of the social field in which they worked, particularly the worldly sphere of polite manners in which pastel's materiality could take on new meaning.

This transformation in attitudes toward pastel began not only in the work of professional artists but also in the realm of aristocratic amateurs who sought a medium for making portraits that would be cleaner and more convenient than oils. Louis XIII was among the first of these amateurs to experiment with pastel, using it to create portraits of his retinue (fig. 19).[20] According to André Félibien, the king asked the painter Simon Vouet to tutor him in pastel: "This sort of work being clean and fairly quick, his majesty wanted Vouet to teach him to draw and paint in this manner in order to be able to amuse himself by making portraits of his closest courtiers."[21] Members of the aristocracy soon followed suit. A painting guide from 1651 explained that pastel was the medium of choice for nobles who did not wish to sully their hands with oil paint: "The nobility is able to take good advantage of them in making naturally colored portraits and other things, without being obliged to involve themselves with oils."[22]

The cleanliness and convenience of pastel granted it a place among the various games, musical performances, and other types of entertainment that formed the basis of social interaction in salon and court society.[23] Pastel, like all of these pleasurable pursuits, could be seamlessly integrated into a culture of *délicat* conversation and exchange. It could also take this interpersonal engagement as its subject, capturing a moment of

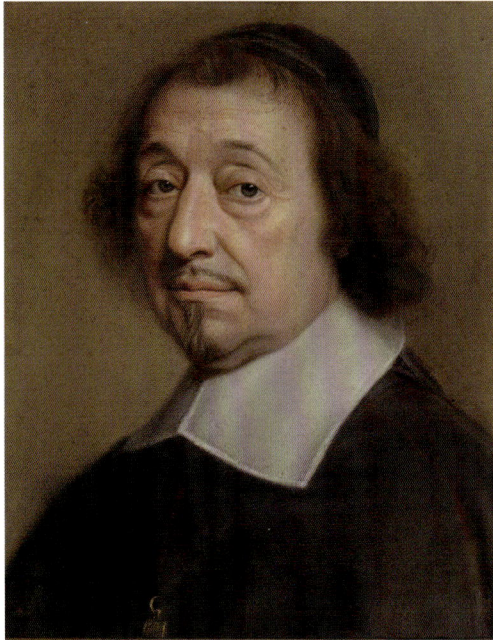

FIG. 20
Robert Nanteuil, *Portrait of Monseigneur Louis Doni d'Attichy, Bishop of Riez*, 1663. Pastel on paper, 34.3 × 27.9 cm. J. Paul Getty Museum, Los Angeles. 98.GG.13. Digital image courtesy of the Getty's Open Content Program.

encounter between artist and sitter. Nanteuil took ample advantage of these conditions in the second half of the seventeenth century, using pastels to sketch portraits while entertaining his models with comedic conversation.[24] His witty repartee helped animate the faces of his subjects, which he quickly recorded on paper. Many of Nanteuil's pastels were studies for his engravings, but he nonetheless developed them into highly refined pictures that verged on independent works of art (fig. 20).[25]

A significant market for such works, however, would not emerge until the rituals of court migrated into the commercial sphere of the eighteenth century. Only in this context did professional artists begin to consider pastel as a profitable alternative to oil painting, freeing it from its preparatory function and granting it an increasingly public role. The first artist to pursue this path seriously was the portraitist Joseph Vivien, who was received into the Academy as a "painter of portraits in pastel" in 1698.[26] According to one eighteenth-century biographer, Vivien's choice of medium was something of a promotional strategy in what was becoming a competitive portrait market: "Seeking to distinguish himself, he painted in pastel, a type of painting that is fresher, more brilliant, mellower than oil, but that is not so durable."[27] In the following years, Vivien exhibited dozens of his fragile portraits in the public Salon exhibitions that the Academy had sporadically begun to organize.[28] His pictures were larger and more highly finished than anything previously attempted in the medium (fig. 21), and they made an ambitious claim for pastel's capacity to compete with oil painting in the realm of

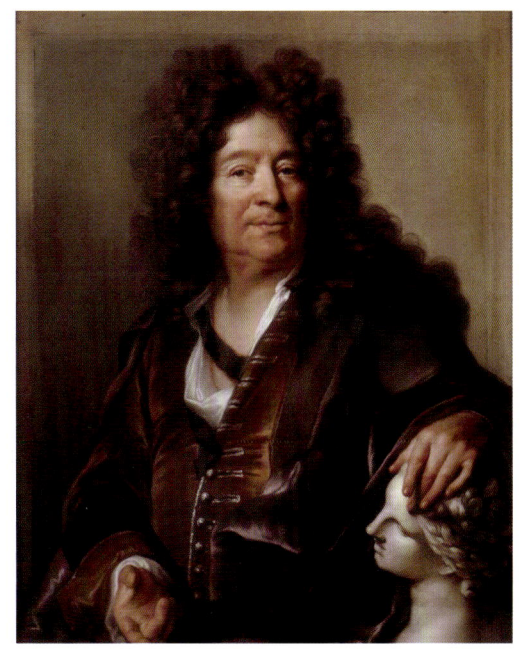

FIG. 21
Joseph Vivien, *The Sculptor François Girardon*, 1701. Pastel on paper, 70 × 80 cm. Musée du Louvre, Paris. INV 33291. Photo © RMN-Grand Palais / Art Resource, NY (Michèle Bellot).

portraiture. "He makes us discover," a critic at the time remarked, "the same force, the same simplicity and *délicatesse* that one finds in the oil works of our great masters."[29] Not all his patrons, however, were convinced. The Bavarian court apparently sought Vivien's services on the condition that he work in oil, advising him that pastel was too fragile to survive for posterity.[30]

The true turning point in attitudes toward pastel occurred in 1720, when the Venetian-born portraitist Rosalba Carriera came to visit Paris. Carriera had begun working in pastel at the turn of the eighteenth century, developing a steady stream of business from the many European travelers who passed through Venice. The speed with which pastels could be completed was important in this context, allowing Carriera to produce portraits in less than a week's time for visitors who stayed in her city only briefly.[31] A savvy businesswoman, Carriera eschewed the financial protection of any single patron or court, instead forcing her buyers to compete for her attention, driving up her prices in the process.[32] She earned the admiration of the court aristocracy, but she also benefited from the growing wealth of merchants, bankers, and speculators (she herself invested her earnings in a wide range of ventures, ultimately drawing a substantial portion of her income from the interest payments she received).[33] This broader context of Europe's transition toward capitalism proved crucial to her success in Paris, where she arrived at the height of speculative exuberance for John Law's System.[34] Carriera, in fact, became close with the Law family during her time in Paris and created

PASTEL AND THE ALLURE OF FRAGILITY (39)

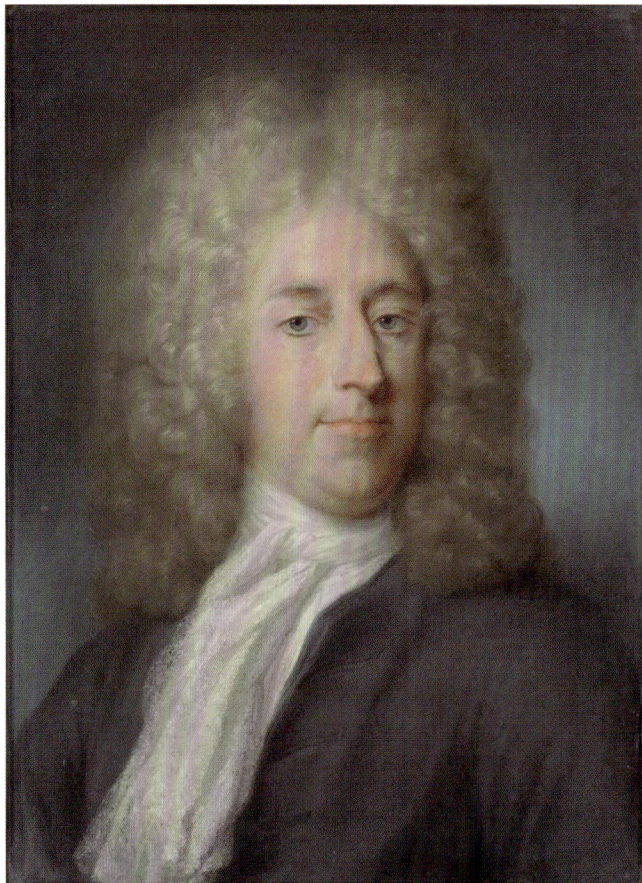

FIG. 22
Rosalba Carriera, *John Law*, ca. 1720. Pastel on paper, 60 × 45 cm. Private family collection.

multiple portraits for them, including one of John Law himself, a version of which has recently been rediscovered (fig. 22).[35] Carriera's ties to the world of French finance were further facilitated by the art collector Pierre Crozat, whom she had met when he traveled through southern Europe some years earlier. The son of a provincial banker and brother of a powerful financier, Crozat had a considerable fortune at his disposal. His brother, Antoine Crozat, was a director of France's leading slave trading business, the French Indies Company, from 1701 to 1718, greatly enriching the family through speculation in French colonial enterprises.[36] Pierre Crozat was therefore a prime example of the newly moneyed art collectors who increasingly set the cultural agenda in France.[37]

The social background of these men is important to understanding their interest in pastel in two respects. First, the broader context of speculative finance helps explain why such buyers were willing to wager money on works in a medium as unstable as pastel. As Neil De Marchi and Hans J. Van Miegroet have argued in the context of British art, the new forms of capitalist speculation that arose during the eighteenth century produced a mode of risk calculation that was as applicable to the acquisition of art as it was to the purchase of financial instruments.[38] For buyers such as Crozat and Law, the chances that they took on fragile pastels were trivial compared to the financial stakes of their overseas investments. Secondly, the fragile materiality of pastel offered these *arrivistes* an important form of social currency, linking their consumption to the realm of ephemeral courtly diversion. Carriera herself enabled this sociable understanding of her work by presenting it less as a commodity than as an extension of her courtesy. She avoided open discussion of prices in her correspondence, and her clients generally used the language of friendship to describe their interactions.[39] It is telling, for example, that when Mariette admired Carriera's pastels, he did so in terms borrowed from the realm of aristocratic manners, telling her that all of Paris "has, like me, recognized in your work the same pleasant character of *politesse* which makes the commerce of your friendship so precious."[40]

Carriera further encouraged this civilized and worldly interpretation of her work by blurring the boundary between professional activities and the polite arts of feminine leisure. The French collector and naturalist Antoine-Joseph Dezallier d'Argenville, for instance, noted that pastel was just one of Carriera's many talents, which also included "pleasing concerts" that she performed for guests on the harpsichord.[41] These social rituals were necessary, in part, because of Carriera's gender, which required her to be careful about revealing her professional ambitions.[42] But the fiction that money played an incidental role in the production of her portraits was also beneficial to her clients, particularly affluent buyers whose efforts to convert wealth into status were subject to suspicion. The rhetoric of friendship and amiable conversation surrounding her work came as much from her patrons as it did from Carriera herself, suggesting that both parties saw an advantage in obscuring the line between social and monetary commerce.[43]

In this context, the provisional materiality of pastel was as much an asset as it was a liability, helping to frame the work of art in terms of fleeting conviviality. This is not to say that Carriera and her clients were unconcerned about the vulnerability of pastel to damage. Crozat had noted the issue early on, writing to Carriera: "It is a shame that these beautiful works are subject to ruin."[44] "Could you not," he asked hopefully, "make use of pastels with a more solid color?"[45] Crozat encountered the fragility of pastels firsthand; a portrait that he purchased from Carriera arrived badly damaged when its glass covering shattered into "a hundred pieces" during shipment.[46] Carriera, too, apparently felt anxious about the fate of her works as they were transported across Europe. Behind her pictures, she would sometimes hide small devotional images of the Three Magi, which were thought to protect travelers during long journeys (figs. 23 and 24).[47] But this concern for the practical problems of pastel's fragility coexisted with an awareness of the sociable poetics that it enabled, the language of "lightness," "vivacity," and "*esprit*" that Carriera's French admirers ascribed to her work.[48]

FIGS. 23 & 24
Small devotional image of the Three Magi, folded behind the strainer of Rosalba Carriera's *Portrait of a Man in a Pilgrim's Costume*. The Frick Collection, New York.

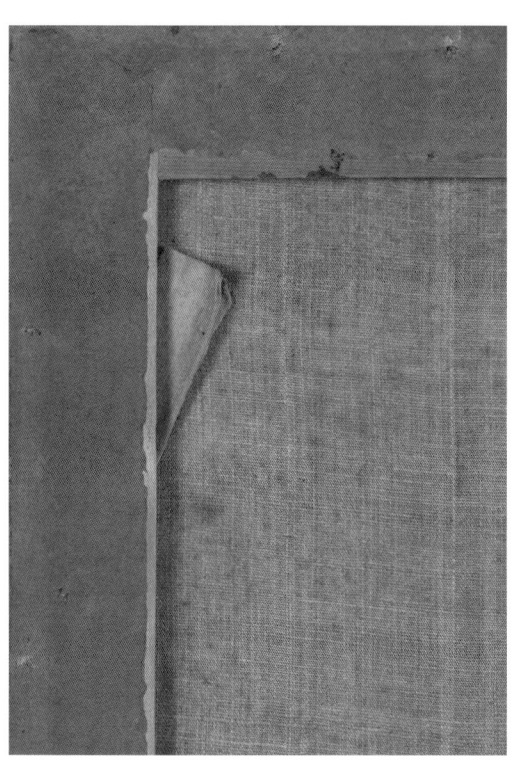

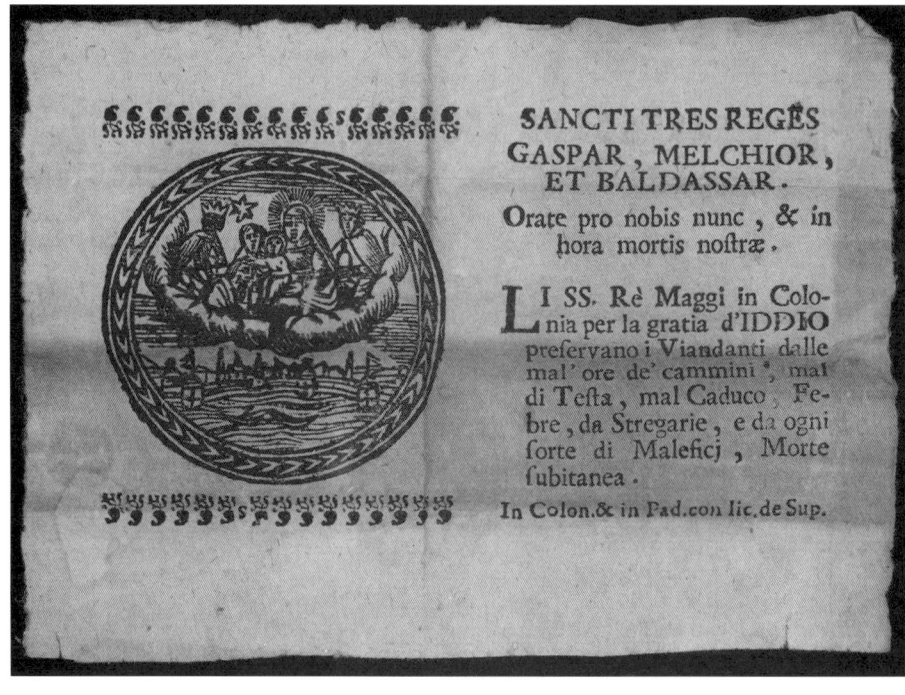

SANCTI TRES REGES GASPAR, MELCHIOR, ET BALDASSAR.

Orate pro nobis nunc, & in hora mortis nostræ.

LI SS. Rè Maggi in Colonia per la gratia d'IDDIO preservano i Viandanti dalle mal' ore de' cammini, mal di Testa, mal Caduco, Febre, da Stregarie, e da ogni sorte di Maleficj, Morte subitanea.

In Colon.& in Pad.con lic.de Sup.

Carriera would only begin to explore the potential symbiosis between pastel, sociability, and capitalism before returning to Venice. The dramatic collapse of Law's System in December 1720, which left Carriera seeking to recover money that the Law family owed to her, temporarily interrupted the economic opportunities that she had found in the French capital.[49] But her visit to Paris would prove pivotal for the future direction of the arts in France. In the decades that followed, other artists would pick up where she left off, taking the risks and commercial possibilities of pastel to a greater extreme.

Selling Fragility

Visitors to the 1737 Paris Salon exhibition encountered a jocular face (fig. 25). Hanging on the wall where the public first entered the gallery was a self-portrait by Maurice-Quentin de La Tour, a charismatic pastellist who had just joined the Academy as a provisional member.[50] La Tour understood the promotional potential of the exhibition, and he used his self-portrait to introduce himself to Parisian audiences. In the illusionistic composition, he smiles from inside a circular window, his elbow resting on the ledge while his hand points backward. We might understand the gesture as a gentle joke at the expense of La Tour's competitors, the cocksure artist directing a derisive finger at the other works that hung on the Salon wall.[51] But the pose serves an additional purpose. As La Tour's finger retreats back into the window frame, it brings our attention to the surface of the work itself, beckoning us to inspect the crumbly substance that separates his world from ours. It was a bold statement, one that announced not only La Tour's talent for self-promotion but also his plans to sell the public on his fragile medium.

La Tour had come to Paris from his home in northeastern France as a teenager in 1719, seeking to make a life as an artist.[52] No doubt taking inspiration from the fervor surrounding Carriera's visit to France the next year, he soon adopted pastel as his sole medium. By this time, pastel portraits appeared with growing frequency in elite spaces of Parisian hospitality, the salons and "appartements de société" that brought together a diverse cast of characters from aristocratic, bourgeois, and intellectual circles.[53] The speed and relative ease with which pastels could be executed made them ideally suited to the context, providing an efficient means for keeping appearances up to date. Charlotte Aïssé, a prominent figure in Parisian salons throughout the 1720s, wrote in 1727 that the fast-paced process of pastel portraiture combined pleasurable amusement with the serious work of monitoring one's image: "It is a three-hour affair . . . you lean on a table where the painter works; that allows you to amuse yourself seeing the drawing, and to make sure that you do not have a disagreeable appearance."[54] La Tour showed an early talent for navigating this social terrain. As one of his contemporaries put it, "he

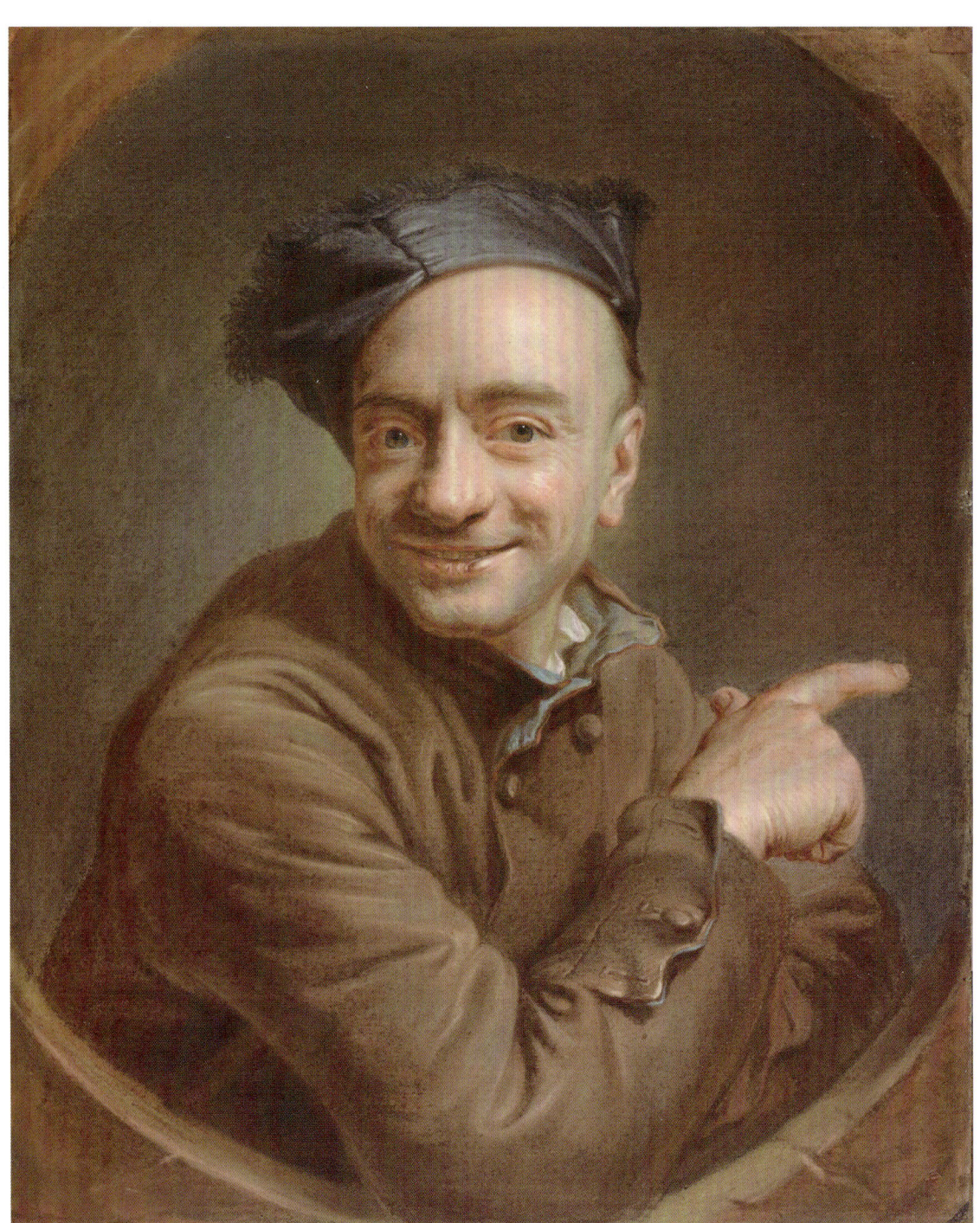

FIG. 25 (*opposite*) Maurice-Quentin de La Tour, *Self-Portrait with Index Finger*, 1737, pastel on paper, 59 × 49 cm. Musée du Louvre, Paris. RF 54298. Photo © RMN-Grand Palais / Art Resource, NY (Michel Urtado).

FIG. 26 Maurice-Quentin de La Tour, *Preparation for the Portrait of Voltaire*, ca. 1735. Pastel on paper, 26.5 × 18 cm. Nationalmuseum, Stockholm. NMB 1946. Photo: Erik Cornelius / Nationalmuseum.

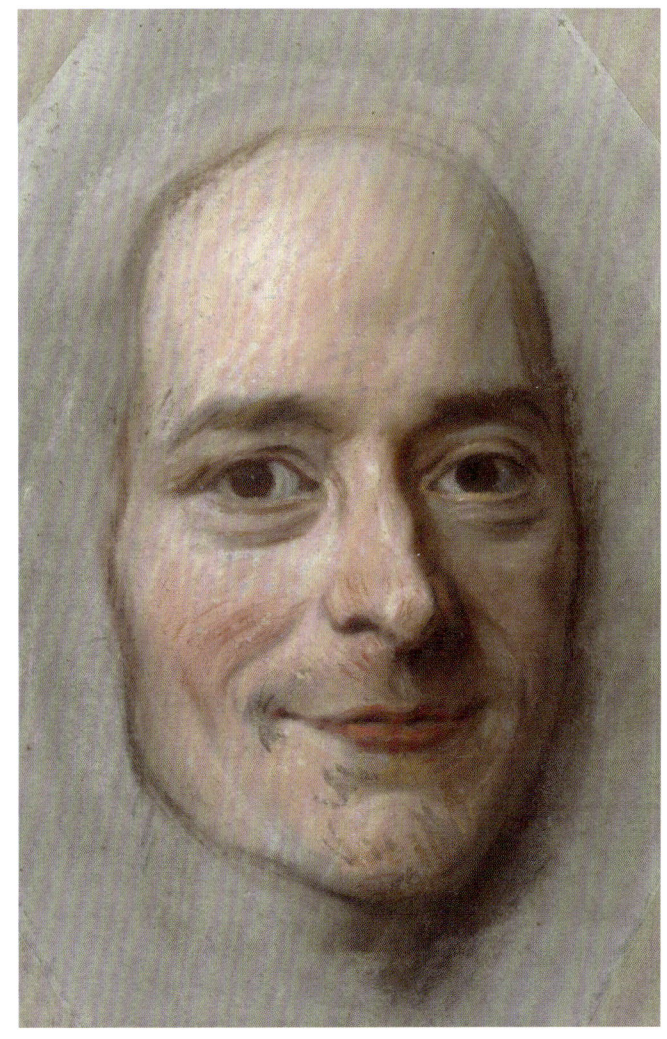

promoted himself as a painter of portraits; he did them in pastel, put little time into it, did not tire his models; they found them to be good likenesses; he wasn't expensive."[55]

We get a sense of La Tour's canny integration of sociability and commerce through an early commission that he received from Voltaire. La Tour attracted the philosopher to his studio in 1735, sketching a series of animated studies of Voltaire's smiling face (figs. 26 and 27).[56] These preparatory works became the basis for a more finished portrait, a version of which now hangs in Voltaire's château in Switzerland (fig. 28). Standing before a half-drawn curtain, he bears the trappings of both luxury and intellect. He appears dressed in a fashionable gray coat with elaborate gold trim, a ruffled lace cuff protruding from the sleeve, and an open book in his hand. With his other

PASTEL AND THE ALLURE OF FRAGILITY (45)

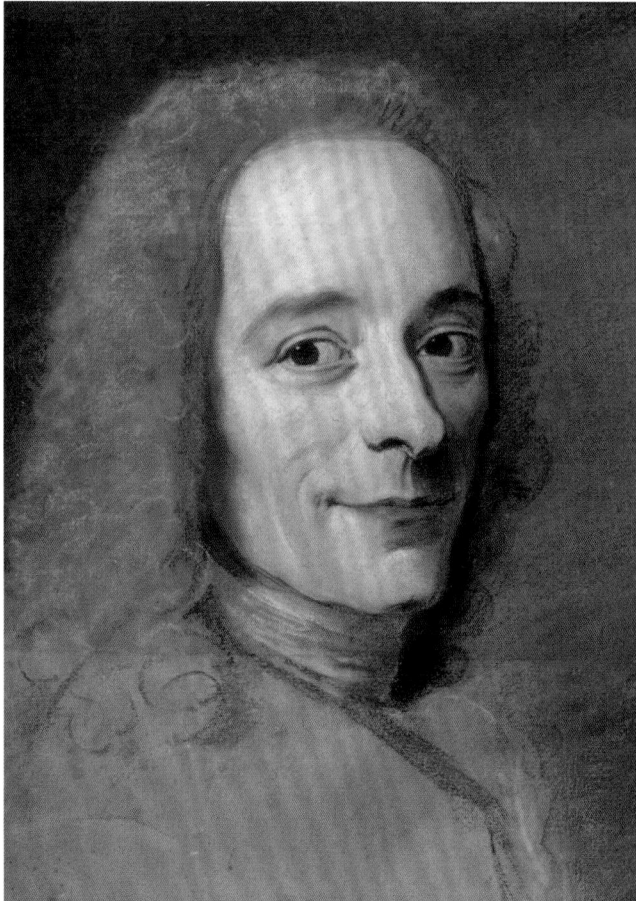

FIG. 27
Maurice-Quentin de La Tour, *Preparation for the Portrait of Voltaire*, ca. 1735. Pastel on paper, 36 × 28.5 cm. Musée Antoine Lécuyer, Saint-Quentin. 1995.6.1. Photo © Musée des Beaux-Arts Antoine Lécuyer, Saint-Quentin (Aisne).

FIG. 28 (*opposite*)
Maurice-Quentin de La Tour, *Portrait of Voltaire*, 1735. Pastel on paper, 60 × 50 cm. Château de Ferney, Ferney-Voltaire. FER1999000097. Photo © David Bordes / CMN Dist. / Art Resource, NY.

hand on his hip and his chest thrust forward, he smiles at the viewer with the relaxed affability of a man at home in the pleasures of his world.

The portrait nicely captures the ethos of pleasure, luxury, and immediacy that had become the hallmarks of "worldliness" in Parisian consumer society. Voltaire himself would distill these principles in his poem "Le Mondain" (The worldly man), which he wrote within a year of sitting for La Tour's portrait. Rejecting the Christian condemnation of worldly indulgence as moral vice, the poem defends commerce and transitory pleasure as guiding virtues. Its narrator revels in the glittering decor of an opulent Parisian home, arguing that his momentary joys are no less gratifying because of their transience: "The earthly paradise is where I am."[57] The poem's culminating image, a champagne cork that pops "like a bolt of lightning," stands as its unifying symbol: "It shoots, we laugh, it hits the ceiling."[58] Champagne, a newly popular French invention, encapsulated the mixture of consumption and conviviality that defined Voltaire's

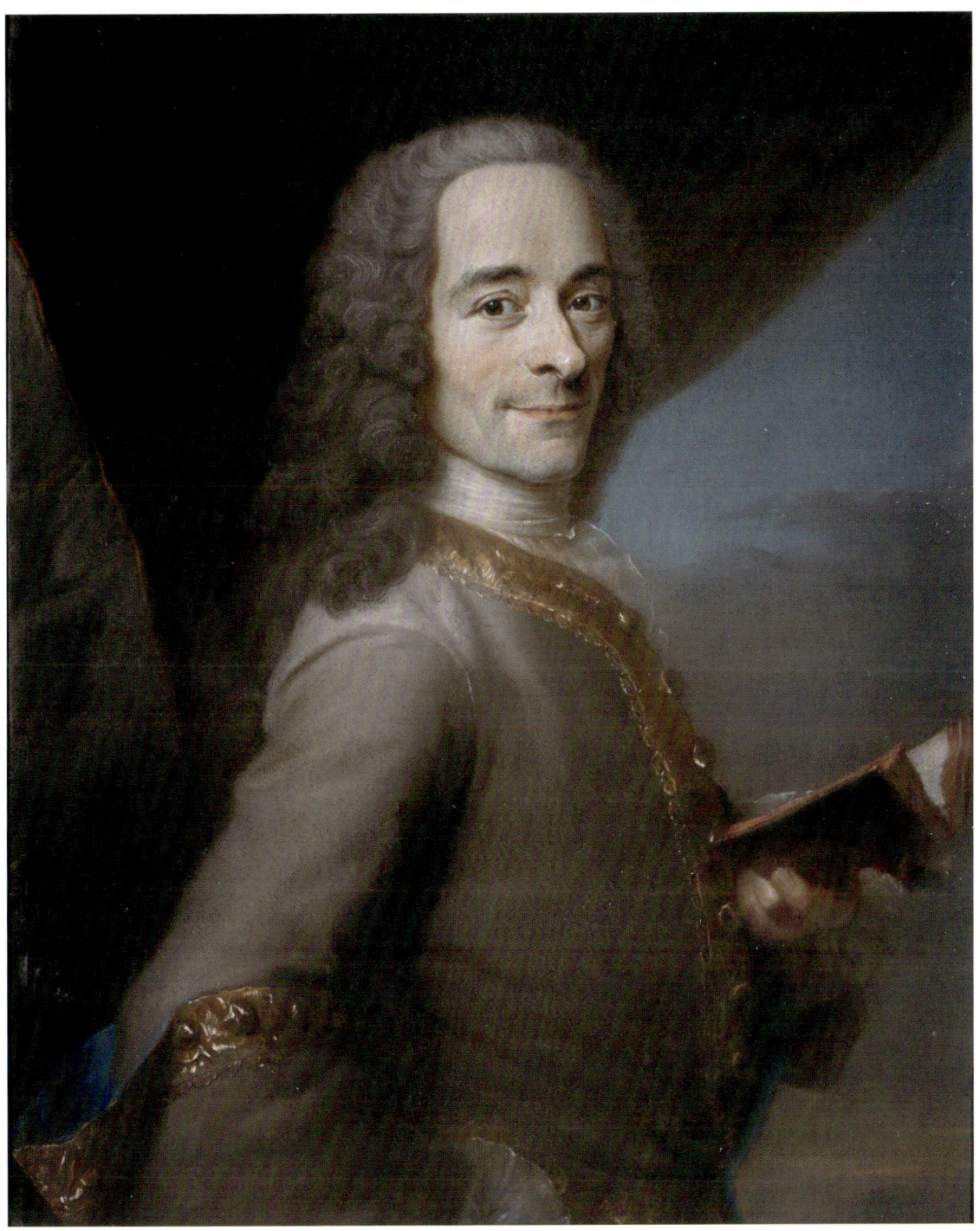

conception of "worldliness."[59] He characterizes the champagne's "bubbling foam" as "the sparkling image of the French," an emblem not only of perishable pleasure but also of patriotism and civility, a product worthy of the "honnête homme."[60] By tying unbridled consumerism to the refined norms of aristocratic behavior, Voltaire legitimized the fleeting pleasures of commerce through an appeal to courtly sociability.[61]

Voltaire does not mention pastel in this defense of worldly existence, but it was precisely this link between social performance and ephemeral consumption that the medium materialized. La Tour's portrait of Voltaire shows the medium's capacity to integrate the two. The picture's delicate materiality, with all the airy lightness of champagne, perfectly instantiates the sensuous and momentary pleasures that Voltaire lauded. La Tour fuses the captivating precarity of the medium with the social effervescence of the sitter, suspending Voltaire's transitory expression in a field of fine particulate. Each feature of the face is synchronized to heighten the impression of an intimate encounter: the subtle pinch of the eyelid and the wrinkle of flesh at the corner of the mouth, the fold of the cheek and the slight contour of the lip, all of which coalesce into a faint smile. Voltaire exchanges a knowing glance with the artist, and by extension, the viewer, inviting us to imagine ourselves as members of a privileged social circle. If Voltaire believed that commercial opulence could be redeemed through association with elite sociability, then the portrait enacts that process of purification before our eyes.

La Tour recognized as much, and he would enhance this connection between commerce and worldly behavior in the years that followed. An unusual opportunity came through one of his next clients: the legendary gadabout and financier Gabriel Bernard de Rieux (fig. 29). Rieux was the epitome of Voltaire's worldly man. Officially, he served as president of the Paris Court of Accounts, which was responsible for auditing the activities of other financiers. In practice, this function had become largely symbolic by the beginning of the eighteenth century, when the court was led by venal officeholders like Rieux who lacked the interest or investigative authority to regulate a financial system that they themselves manipulated for personal gain.[62] Instead, Rieux devoted the majority of his time to spending the enormous fortune that his father had accumulated through his investment in the slave trade and loans to the French state.[63] His excesses were apparently known throughout Paris, as Madame de Graffigny wrote in a letter to a friend in 1745: "Are you really the only person in the world who has not heard talk of Mr. de Rieux, the son, the inheritor of Samuel Bernard, who nearly found the means to wipe out his riches?"[64]

In La Tour's portrait, we find a less salacious image of Rieux but one that equally revolves around wealth and lavish consumption. The signs of luxury are everywhere: a gilded inkstand and ebony snuffbox lie on the table, while porcelain vases, *chinoiserie* figures, and an ornately carved clock line the edges of the room. Light shines on an enormous globe mounted on a floor stand, its face turned to show the west coast of

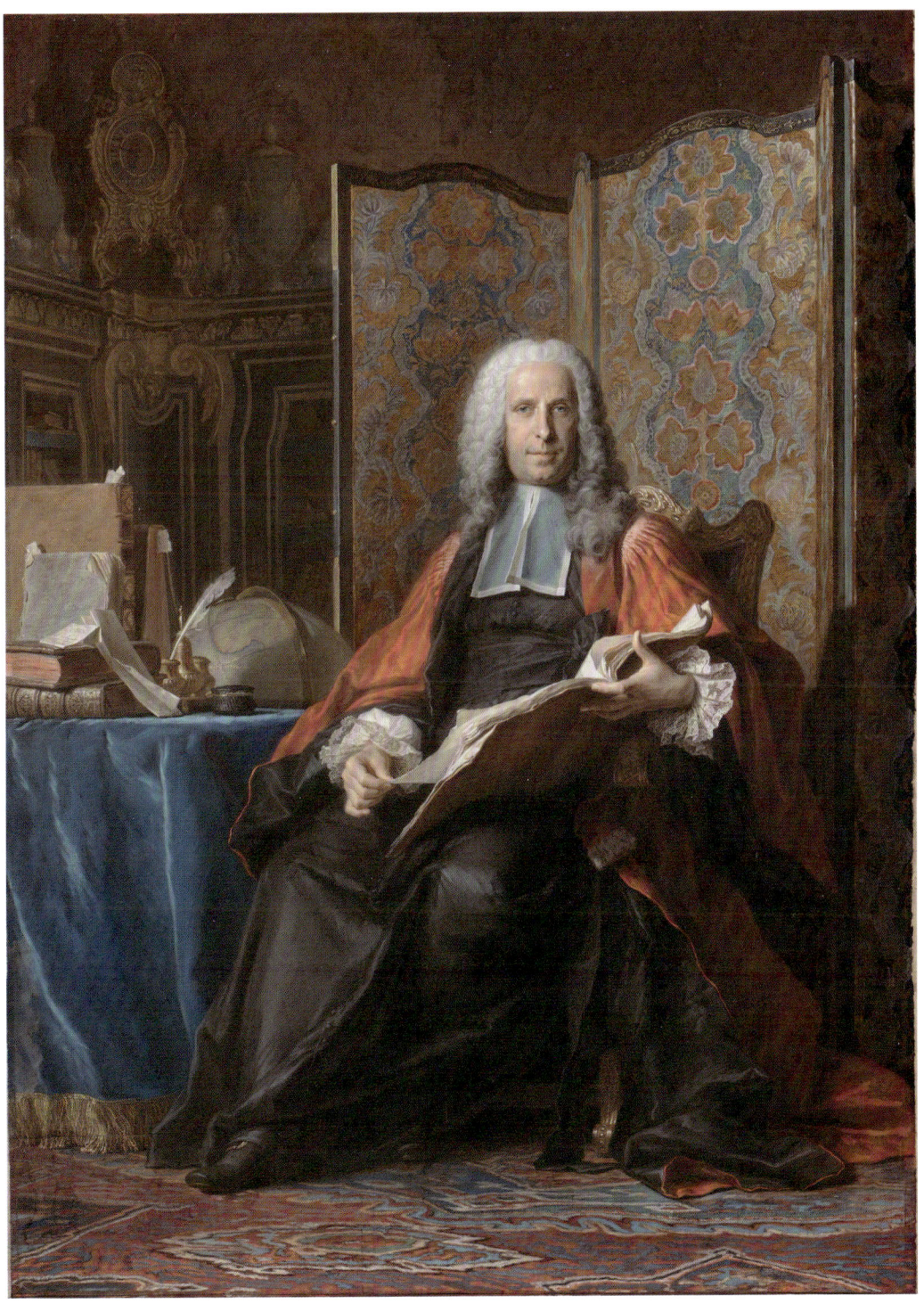

FIG. 29 Maurice-Quentin de La Tour, *Gabriel Bernard de Rieux*, 1739–41. Pastel and gouache on blue paper, mounted on canvas, 200.7 × 149.9 cm. J. Paul Getty Museum, Los Angeles. 94.PC.39. Digital image courtesy of the Getty's Open Content Program.

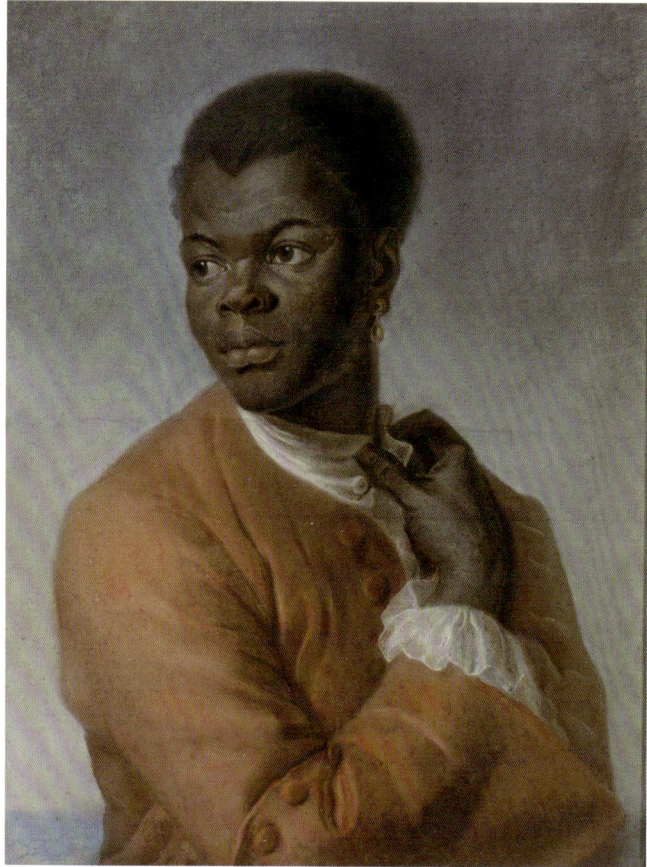

FIG. 30
Maurice-Quentin de La Tour, *Buste d'un nègre*, ca. 1741. Pastel on paper, 65 × 53.5 cm. Musée d'Art et d'Histoire, Geneva. Bequest of Edouard Sarasin, 1917. Inv. 1917-0028. Photo © Musée d'art et d'histoire, Ville de Genève (Yves Siza).

Africa. The geographic reference, juxtaposed as it was at the 1741 Salon with La Tour's depiction of an unidentified Black man in a livery jacket (fig. 30), offers an oblique reminder that Rieux's fortunes depended on enslavement and colonization.[65] Rieux's portrait, however, conveys nothing of that system's violent realities. It spectacularizes, instead, the sumptuous consumer products that those brutalities made possible, sublimating grotesque exploitation into tasteful finery.[66]

The most extravagant display of this material refinement is, of course, the portrait of Rieux as a physical object in and of itself. It is difficult to overstate the amount of work that went into constructing it. A critic at the time noted that the elaborate frame and enormous glass covering would have been extraordinarily expensive on their own.[67] To create a portrait on this scale, La Tour needed to assemble it from ten different pieces of paper.[68] He cut the paper in irregular shapes that roughly corresponded to the forms within the picture, concealing the seams between each sheet along the edges of objects. Seen up close, under raking light, these seams become visible (fig. 31).

FIG. 31
Maurice-Quentin de La Tour, *Gabriel Bernard de Rieux* (detail under raking light), 1739–41. Pastel and gouache on blue paper, mounted on canvas, 200.7 × 149.9 cm. J. Paul Getty Museum, Los Angeles. 94.PC.39.

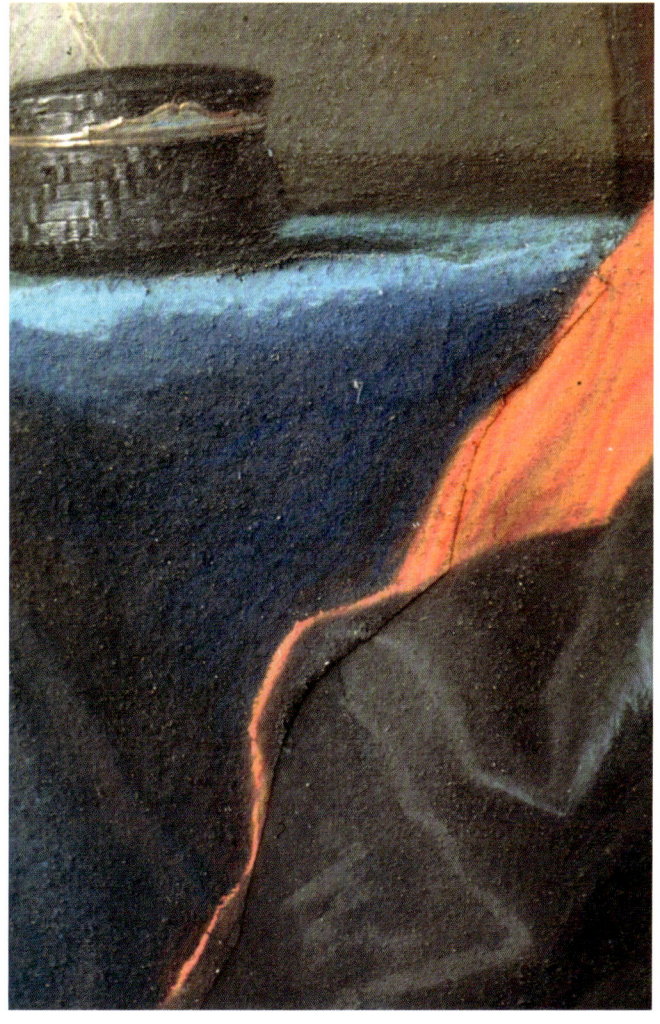

Paper is, in fact, crucial to the visual economy of the picture, serving to unite its form and subject matter. Consider the enormous paper object that lies in the middle of the composition, page after page unfurling across Rieux's lap (fig. 32). Its soft-cover binding indicates that it may be an account ledger of the sort that Rieux would have used to record his expenses.[69] Alternatively, it could represent one of the manuscripts that Rieux acquired for his formidable library, cultivating his image as a man who appreciated arts and letters.[70] In either case, the object invites the viewer to consider the delicate construction of the picture itself, to examine paper as a physical thing. La Tour delineates the edge of every page in all its rippling specificity. He carefully renders the individual curls at the corners, and he draws attention to the thinness of each sheet

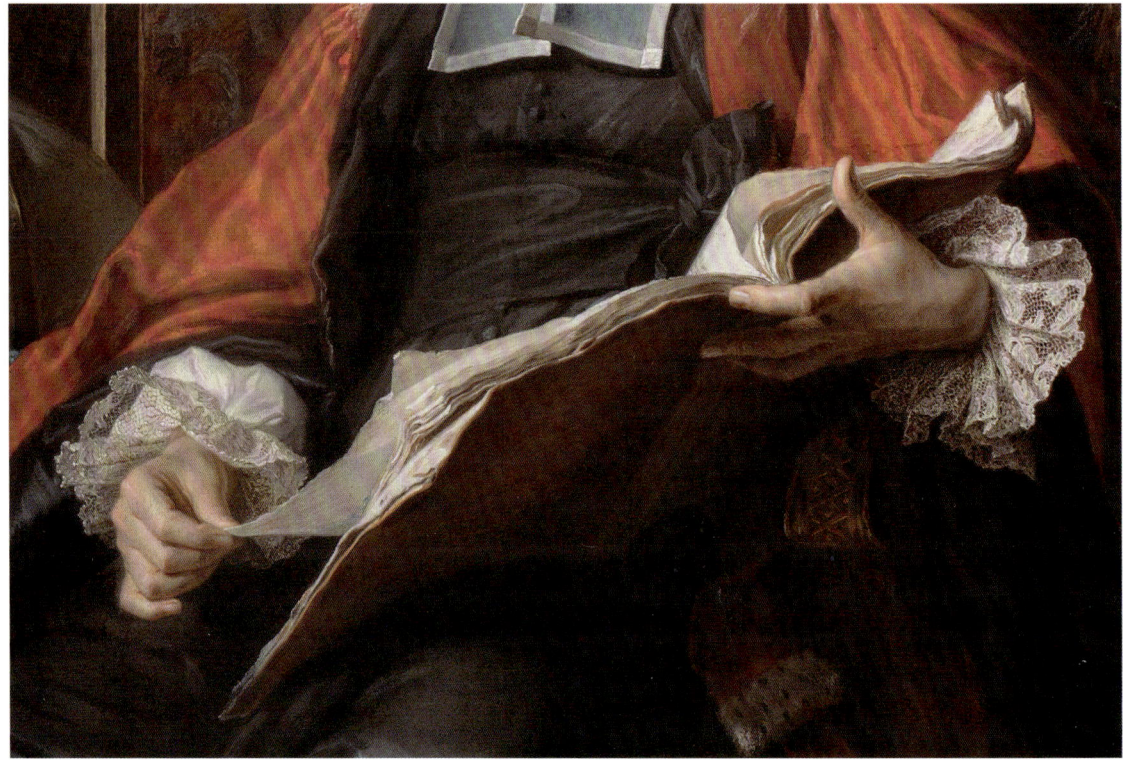

FIG. 32 Maurice-Quentin de La Tour, *Gabriel Bernard de Rieux* (detail), 1739–41. Pastel and gouache on blue paper, mounted on canvas, 200.7 × 149.9 cm. J. Paul Getty Museum, Los Angeles. 94.PC.39. Digital image courtesy of the Getty's Open Content Program.

by depicting the gaps of air between them. Rieux's diaphanous lace cuffs brush against the paper, a contiguity that highlights the insubstantiality of each material. With his right hand, Rieux grasps the corner of a single sheet, as if showing us the material lying underneath him.

The effect stunned viewers at the Salon, who marveled over the refinement of Rieux's appearance. "The most sumptuous people are jealous of the cuffs," one critic testified; "they sense the lightness of the wig, the fine weft and finish of the fabric, the delicacy and the immense detail of the lace."[71] Rieux, as a financier who needed to demonstrate his social *délicatesse* through the material delicacy of his possessions, was surely pleased by the response. La Tour, too, benefited from the portrait's thematization of delicacy. The *Mercure de France* addressed an ode to him in verse when the portrait went on display, praising "your candor and *politesse*, your *esprit*, your frankness, and your *délicatesse*."[72] These qualities described a mode of interpersonal behavior, but they also applied to what La Tour managed to materialize on the page. La Tour's talent resided in his capacity to work across these categories, to express a mode of *délicat* sociability through an exploration of material delicacy on the grandest of scales.

Saving Face

The alignment of art with the norms of courtly sociability was, from the outset, based on a tenuous set of preconditions. In order for the commercial aspects of art to be presented as an extension of civilized behavior, the marketplace needed to be seen as supporting and not superseding longstanding social hierarchies. This pretext, however, was vulnerable to attack. Any person who trafficked in art forms associated with polite society could easily be accused of placing commerce above courtesy. By the middle of the eighteenth century, such allegations had begun to spread. Ironically, many of the same authors who had promoted and engaged in the artistic appropriation of courtly norms were among the first to level charges, avoiding culpability by laying blame on others.[73] The phenomenon played out across the arts, but its effects were not equally felt. To label a writer's work excessively *délicat* was often just another way of saying that it lacked gravity and depth, that it was inconsequential and would soon be forgotten. But for visual artists, delicacy was a tangible attribute of physical things. The figurative implications of fragility blurred into the literal ones. For this reason, the critical turn against the commercialization of *délicatesse* proved especially difficult for pastellists to navigate.

While the effects of these critiques were different in literature, it was among writers that the terms of the broader debate were first articulated. By the 1730s, authors directed growing skepticism toward the expressions of wit and politeness that filled the worldly lexicon. The Jesuit minister and political writer Charles-Irénée Castel, abbé de Saint-Pierre, gave voice to these suspicions in a letter to Voltaire from 1739: "Devote no more of your life to entertaining witty women and other such children; dream of instructing men, of instructing those who instruct us and governing those who govern us, give us finally models of history. It is true that this requires great ambition and great patience, and I do not know yet if you have enough of them, but go and try. Quit your vain works in order to march toward sublime glory."[74] This invocation of history and public interest as the true guarantors of artistic glory would become central to the Enlightenment cult of posterity that arose in the decades that followed.[75] The lighthearted conversational norms of the salon were increasingly dismissed as the fashionable artifice of feminine amusement, while history became the ostensible purview of independent, masculine thinkers.[76]

Writers soon found ways to adapt to these norms without entirely giving up on the forms of expression that they had taken from court society. The qualities that connected their work to ephemeral sociability—wit, insubstantiality, artifice—were a matter of subjective interpretation. The relative lightness or gravity of a written phrase was difficult to weigh in one's hand. As a result, a writer like Voltaire could present himself as an autonomous *philosophe* devoted to the cause of posterity even as he remained enmeshed within networks of worldly sociability. Because the distinction between a sociable wit and an independent intellectual was clearer in theory than in practice, it was possible for a writer to have it both ways. But visual artists had to contend with criticisms of a more practical nature, ones that could be tested more objectively.

For pastellists, the issue was especially palpable, and no artist bore the burden more than La Tour. A pivotal moment arrived with the publication of La Font's review of the 1746 Salon, in which he singled out pastels for special criticism. "I come to the pastels," he wrote, "an excessively fashionable type of painting, and to which Sir de la Tour has given a vogue and credit that seem impossible to augment."[77] La Font contrasted the convenience of pastel with the difficulties of oil, expressing his fear that the former would soon overtake the latter: "One ought to fear that the ease and speed of their fragile crayons do not bring about the neglect of oil, much slower in truth, but infinitely more learned, and incomparable for durability."[78]

The complaints that La Font lodged against pastellists were, in part, similar to those that he had made against Watteau. He argued that commercial pressures, in a period of declining patronage, drove artists to transient materials and techniques: "The volatile beauties of crayons . . . are as fragile as the glass that protects them, and will disappear upon the first drop of the picture, or upon the penetration of the least humidity in the location where they are placed."[79] But pastel portraits, he suggested, also spoke to a more offensive sensibility, one that he connected to grave social maladies. As portraits, they evinced what he saw as a growing vanity in society, a superficial attachment to appearances. He observed that portraitists no longer depicted heroes of historical importance but provided flattering images of anyone who could afford them.[80] Such pictures, La Font argued, would be of little interest to future generations even if they survived. He went so far as to claim that most contemporary portraits, because they were shaped by fashion and the fleeting concerns of the present, would not even interest the immediate descendants of their subjects, "who will abandon their features to the dust of the attic and to the teeth of mice."[81]

In the aftermath of La Font's diatribe, pastels became a frequent target of denunciation in an emerging critique of a commercialized worldly sphere. In certain contexts, the word pastel itself became a metaphor for shallowness and inconsequentiality. When the abbé de Voisenon sought to distinguish Voltaire from frivolous contemporaries in 1749, he drew upon these metaphorical associations, describing Voltaire as "a painter whose coloring never fades; all the others are, in truth, only poor pastels."[82]

Voltaire, by this time, had distanced himself from the ephemeral excesses that he described in *Le Mondain*, embracing an identity as a philosopher devoted to the

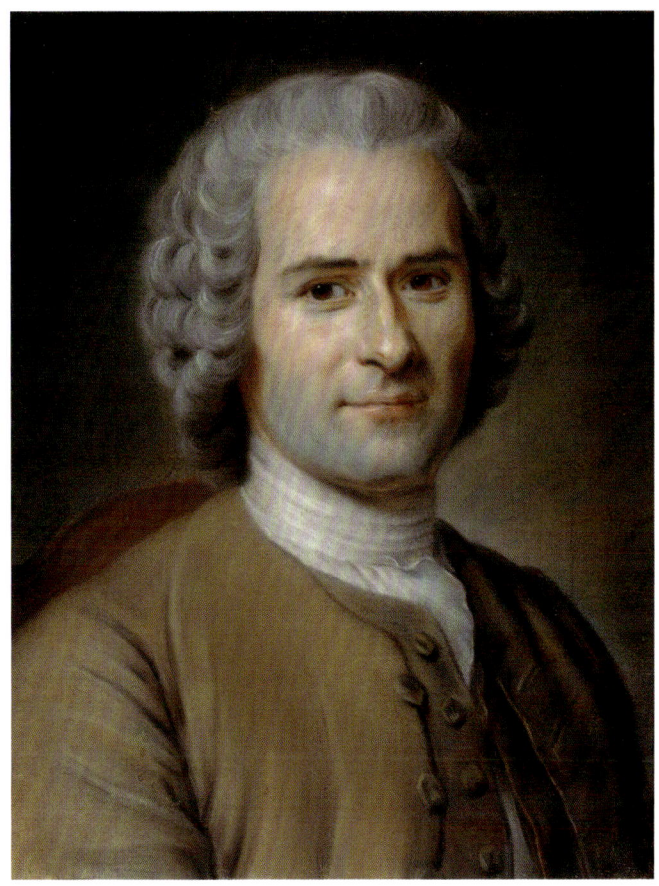

FIG. 33
Maurice-Quentin de La Tour, *Jean-Jacques Rousseau*, ca. 1759–63 (autograph replica of 1753 Salon submission). Pastel on paper, 46.5 × 38 cm. Musée d'art et d'histoire, Geneva. Bequest of Jean-Charles Coindet, 1876. Inv. 1876-0009. Photo © Musée d'art et d'histoire, Ville de Genève (Jean-Marc Yersin).

cause of history.[83] La Tour attempted a similar transformation, with varying degrees of success. One way to demonstrate his commitment to history was through his clientele. He increasingly pursued the patronage of Enlightenment intellectuals, telling figures such as Montesquieu that he wished to have the privilege of "transmitting to posterity" their likenesses.[84] Montesquieu did not accept the invitation, but many other *philosophes* obliged. La Tour's submissions to the 1753 Salon exhibition, which included portraits of Jean-Jacques Rousseau and Jean Le Rond d'Alembert, were exemplary in this regard (figs. 33 and 34). Set against simplified backdrops without signs of luxury, these bust-length depictions of "great men" shifted attention away from La Tour's connections with wealthy financiers, and they satisfied critics who condemned what they regarded as the co-optation of portraiture by moneyed interests.[85] Surveying the 1753 Salon, the comte de Caylus commended La Tour for supposedly shunning such affluent buyers, writing that "[La Tour] prefers the consolation of making portraits of illustrious men to the advantage of making those of opulent people."[86] La Font, in his

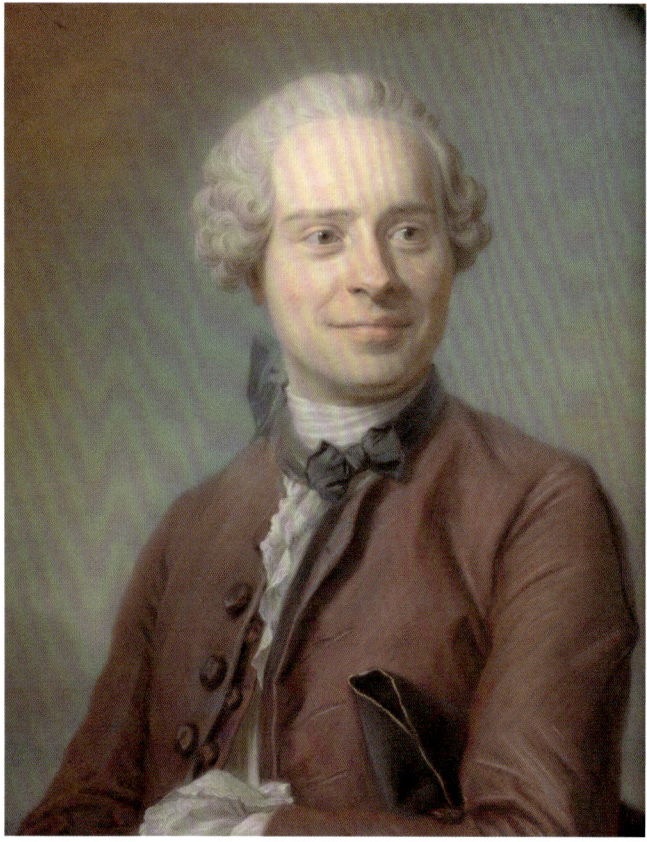

FIG. 34
Maurice-Quentin de La Tour, *Jean Le Rond d'Alembert*, ca. 1752. Pastel on paper, 56.3 × 46 cm. Musée du Louvre, Paris. RF 3893. Photo © RMN-Grand Palais / Art Resource, NY (R. G. Berizzi).

review of the Salon that year, repeated his broader assertion that portraitists catered to a "crowd of obscure men, without name, without talent, without reputation," but he singled out La Tour's depiction of "illustrious authors" as an exception, declaring that these portraits "will transmit to posterity the spirit of their physiognomies."[87] For a moment, La Font was prepared to forget his misgivings about the fragility of the medium in which La Tour had recorded these faces.

Gender, too, played an important role in the reimagining of La Tour's relationship with history. Six out of the eighteen portraits that he exhibited in 1753 depicted women, but they received little mention among the critics who celebrated La Tour's newfound commitment to the needs of posterity.[88] For La Font, the Salon was all too crowded with "the great many portraits of people of the fair sex," and he asserted that women used art as a kind of mirror "to adore themselves without end."[89] La Tour and his female patrons needed to be cautious about playing into this emerging stereotype of the woman who transforms portraiture into an ephemeral instrument of fashion and vanity. La Tour's portrait of Madame de Pompadour, exhibited at the 1755 Salon,

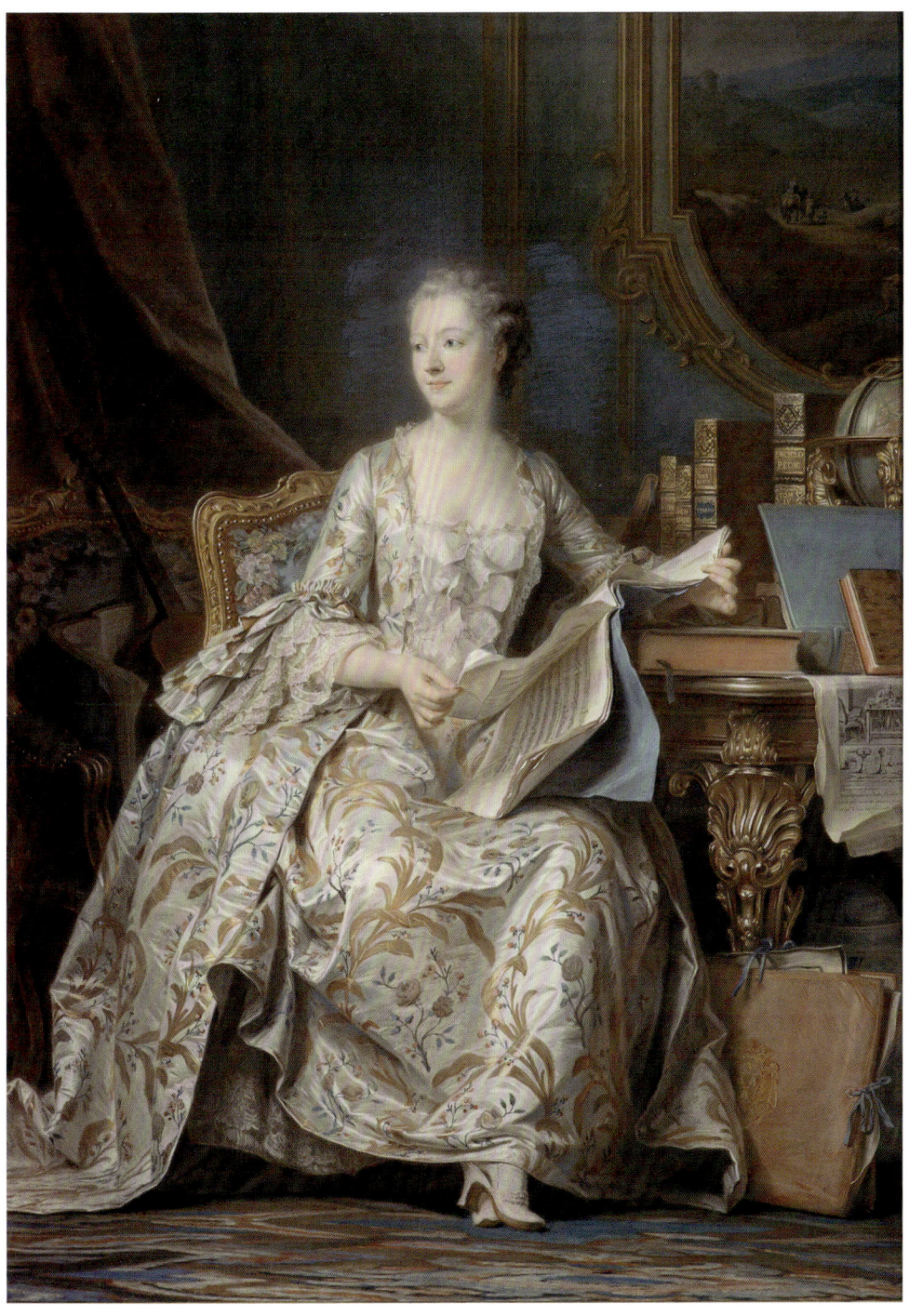

FIG. 35 Maurice-Quentin de La Tour, *Madame de Pompadour*, 1755. Pastel on paper, 177.5 × 131 cm. Musée du Louvre, Paris. INV 27614. Photo © Musée du Louvre, Dist. RMN-Grand Palais / Laurent Castel / Art Resource, NY.

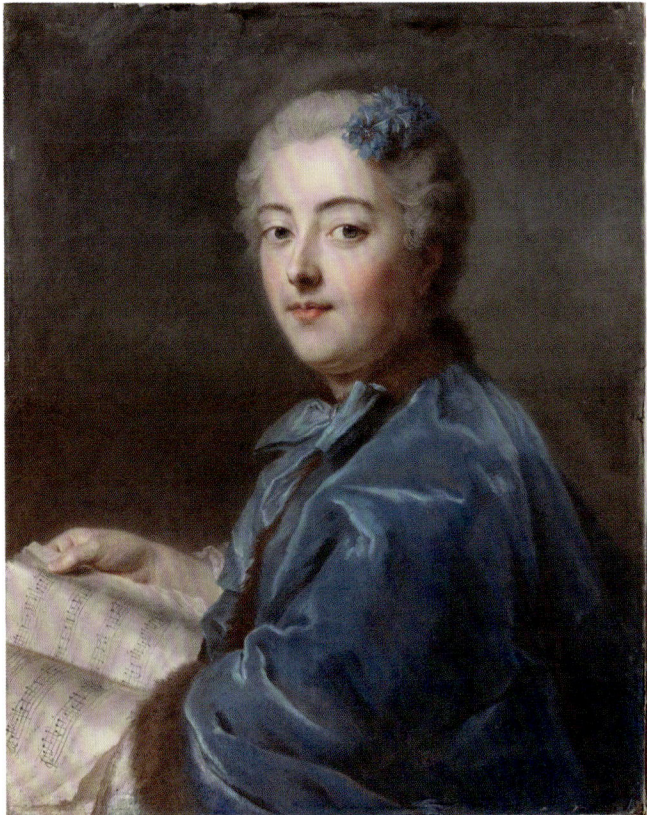

FIG. 36
Maurice-Quentin de La Tour, *Princesse de Rohan*, ca. 1741. Pastel on paper, 58 × 48 cm. Nationalmuseum, Stockholm. NMB 2650. Photo: Linn Ahlgren / Nationalmuseum.

provides particularly vivid evidence of their efforts to counter such assertions (fig. 35). Pompadour's presentation in a silk robe within a sumptuously decorated interior can hardly be described as austere, yet these elements, as many scholars have noted, are integrated into a larger message about the sitter's status as a learned supporter of art, philosophy, and history.[90] The portfolio of prints at Pompadour's feet and the engraving visible on the table offer a reminder of her patronage of the arts. The tomes at her side form a weighty reading list that includes Voltaire's *Henriade* along with volumes from the *Encyclopédie* and Montesquieu's *Esprit des loix*. While the unfurled pages of music in Pompadour's lap recall the flowing paper in La Tour's depiction of Rieux, any intimation of the portrait's own unstable materiality is here counterbalanced by the surrounding iconographic evocations of cultural and intellectual solidity.

La Tour's efforts to reframe the temporality of his work through style and subject matter, however, remained difficult to reconcile with the material properties of his medium. Even his defenders sometimes struggled to justify his decision to work in

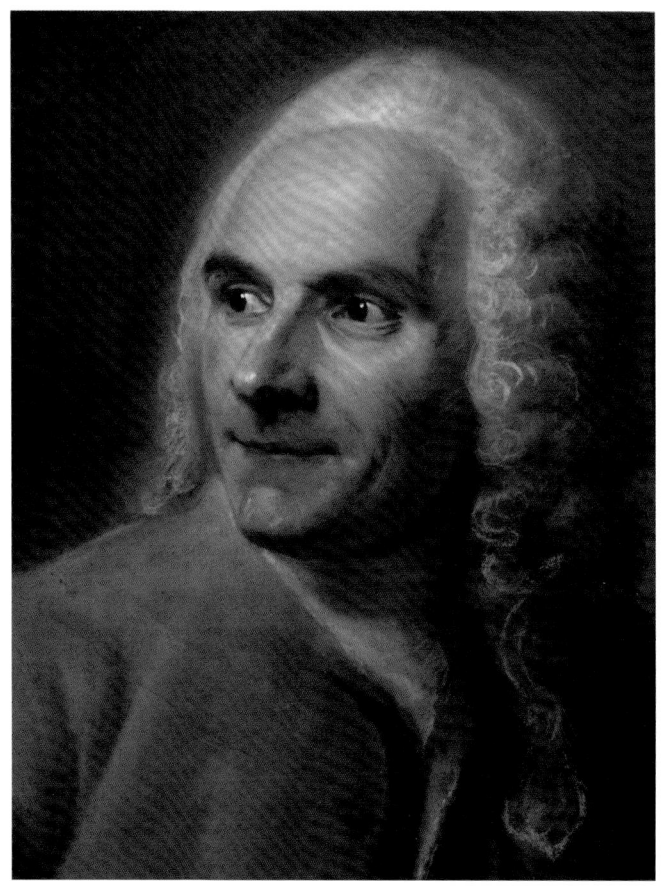

FIG. 37
Maurice-Quentin de La Tour, *Jean Restout*, ca. 1738. 41 × 31 cm. Musée Antoine Lécuyer, Saint-Quentin. LT 8. Photo © Musée des Beaux-Arts Antoine Lécuyer, Saint-Quentin (Aisne).

pastel. One critic, writing in 1748, praised La Tour's portraits before acknowledging their regrettable material composition: "In truth, we will have to lament that he did not become attached to oil.... The idea that the portraits of La Tour will not have the duration that they merit having is distressing for those with an interest in the glory of famous artists."[91]

La Tour, for his part, had already begun searching for a means of stabilizing his work. Recent technical analysis has revealed traces of sturgeon glue in La Tour's portrait of the princesse de Rohan from 1741 (fig. 36), though it is unclear whether the artist applied the fixative when he created the work or if it was added at a later date.[92] Tidelines, which stem from the application of a wet solution to the pastel, appear on several early preparatory studies (fig. 37), providing further clues about La Tour's experimentation. By 1745, the *Mercure de France* alerted readers that La Tour "had the good fortune of finding a varnish that, without altering in the slightest the freshness and flower of

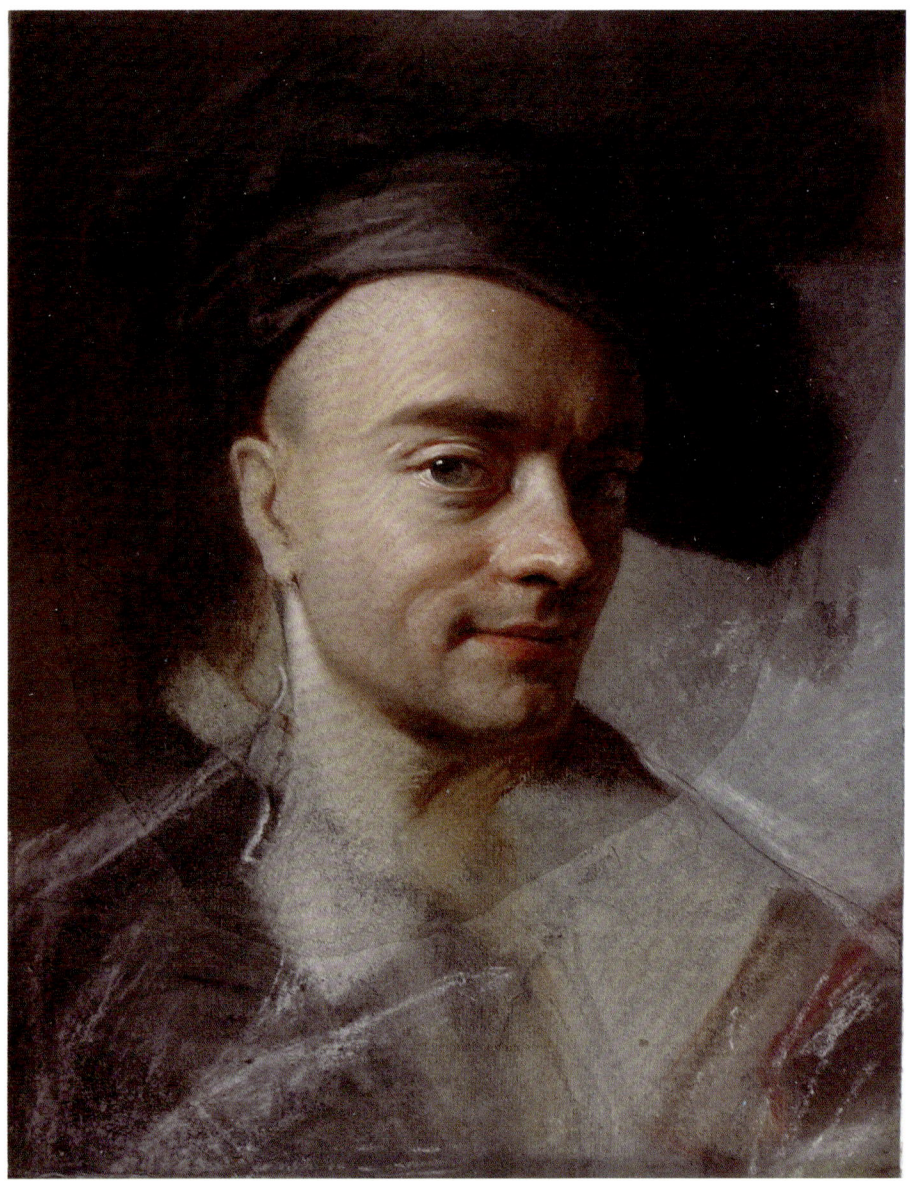

FIG. 38 Maurice-Quentin de La Tour, *Self-Portrait*, ca. 1742. Pastel on paper with fixative, 39 × 31 cm. Musée Antoine Lécuyer, Saint-Quentin. LT 3. Photo © Musée des Beaux-Arts Antoine Lécuyer, Saint-Quentin (Aisne).

his pastel, fixes it such that the most violent shock cannot disturb it."[93] The declaration proved overly optimistic. The darkened veil over several of La Tour's abandoned sketches (fig. 38) makes clear that his glues could have a noticeable impact on the appearance of his work. More troublingly, as his contemporaries would soon observe, his efforts to fix his pastels often had the opposite of the desired effect, ruining entire portraits. One critic, writing in 1750, stated that La Tour "became fixated on a varnish that he believes he invented and that very often spoils everything that he has done."[94]

Signs of these frustrations grew throughout the 1750s, when claims abounded about secret inventions that could preserve pastels. Entrepreneurs came forward to market new recipes for fixatives, often guarding the details in order to profit from them. Most notable among these enterprising inventors was the engineer and architect Antoine-Joseph Loriot, whose techniques came to fascinate La Tour.[95] In 1753, Loriot presented evidence to the Academy that he could fix pastels without altering their appearance. A report in the Academy's archives describes the problems that Loriot sought to remedy and makes clear the doubts surrounding pastels at the time: "Dryness causes pastel to come loose in the long run; humidity brings about mold in some of its colors; in placing it behind well sealed glass, the pastel usually gets pressed upon it, which removes the delicate texture and alters the picture; movement in transport knocks part of it to the bottom of the frame, which happens even when remaining at rest in apartments simply from the rattling caused by passing coaches; finally the colors appear gradually to lose their brilliance such that no painter can hope to see his pictures pass to posterity."[96] After inspecting work that Loriot had treated, leaders of the Academy concluded that his method greatly surpassed any alternative solution to these problems. He was awarded a generous pension in exchange for a description of his process, which was to remain sealed until the time of his death.[97] In the meantime, Loriot was free to profit from his technique, offering his services to artists and collectors for a fee.[98] His discovery generated significant publicity, and the fact that its details remained secret only heightened the fervor surrounding it.[99]

When La Tour asked Loriot about the process, he was apparently rebuffed. Mariette described how La Tour tortured himself over the secret: "Misfortune had it that he decided to see if he could succeed in fixing pastel in the manner of Loriot, who claimed to have found the secret and who refused to communicate it to him."[100] La Tour had been working on Mariette's portrait at the time, and he attempted to fix it in what he thought was a version of Loriot's technique. Mariette never saw the work again: "They inform me that the picture had suffered so greatly that he threw it in the fire out of frustration." Apparently, the incident was not an isolated one. "This was not the only time," Mariette explained, "that he acted this way with his own works."[101]

La Tour's failure to recreate Loriot's secret method may have stemmed from the fact that the secret itself proved far cruder and less reliable than the fanfare surrounding it had suggested. When the details of the process were revealed in 1780, the shortcomings were evident.[102] Loriot instructed artists to begin by soaking a short-bristled brush in a mixture of wine spirits and fish glue.[103] He then recommended finding a small metal rod—or, if necessary, the arm from a sculptor's compass—and dragging it across the

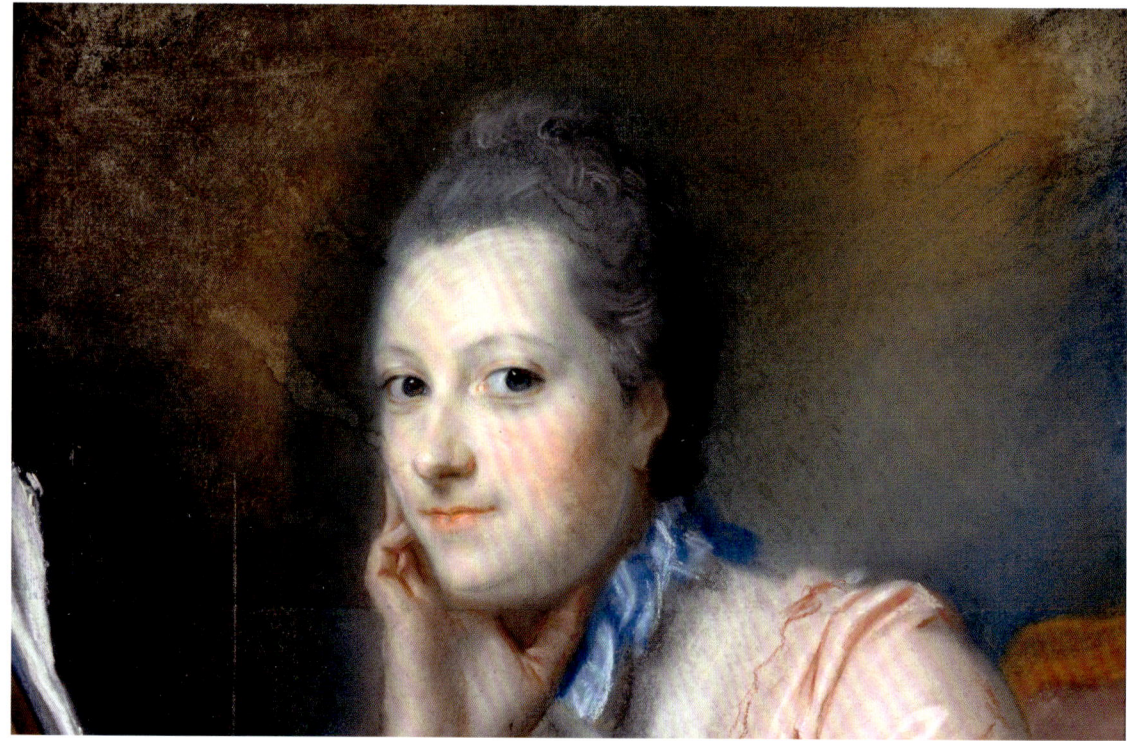

FIG. 39 Maurice-Quentin de La Tour, *Mme Le Riche de La Pouplinière, née Françoise-Catherine-Thérèse Boutinon des Hayes* (detail), ca. 1745. Pastel on paper, 68 × 53 cm. Musée Antoine Lécuyer, Saint-Quentin. LT 21. Photo © Musée des Beaux-Arts Antoine Lécuyer, Saint-Quentin (Aisne).

bristles of the brush. This motion, Loriot explained, would send a shower of adhesive through the air, which would then settle on the picture's surface, fixing it in place. In an era before spray bottles and atomizers, the method was one of the only ways to apply fluid to pastel without directly touching its fragile surface. But such spattering was also highly imprecise, making it difficult to disperse the fluid evenly. Irregular stains on some of La Tour's pictures suggest that he may have practiced a version of this technique and suffered the consequences (fig. 39).

These failed experiments have long been treated as technical footnotes in the literature on La Tour, but their significance goes beyond their mechanical particularities.[104] They point to the central conflict of La Tour's career: the struggle to reconcile an art based on lighthearted immediacy with the need to preserve that immediacy for the future. The sense of contingency and fleetingness that had opened the path for La Tour's success here confronted its limits, in the place where pigment mingled with coagulated fish glue on the page. What was at stake in La Tour's search for a reliable fixative was not simply the future of his work but also the aesthetic principles on which it was based. The technical problem of finding a fixative became a proxy for a broader cultural conflict, a divide between the spirit of worldly ephemerality that catalyzed artistic innovation and a historical concern over what the legacy of those innovations would be.

La Tour attempted to transcend that divide, to show that art could rise from the commercialized domain of fleeting entertainment and enter the more illustrious realm of history. In pursuing this goal, he sought to follow the example of his colleagues in literature and philosophy, who honed their ideas in salon conversation before incorporating them into immortal tomes destined for posterity. But in the absence of a reliable way of preserving pastels, La Tour's work remained stubbornly earthbound, far below the heavenly pantheon that Enlightenment philosophers had begun to imagine for themselves.

La Tour had mastered only one half of the equation that came to govern the intellectual culture of the Enlightenment: he embraced the new forms of extemporaneous expression generated by polite society and the marketplace, but he failed to find a way to assure their permanence. His inability to reconcile these two ambitions would haunt the reception of his work for the remainder of his career. By the 1760s, the praise that critics once showered on La Tour's pastels was increasingly qualified. "Nothing could be added to the truth of nature and to the character of resemblance of these portraits; they seem to breathe," wrote one anonymous critic in 1769, before adding: "It is a shame that there is no sure process for fixing such pastels, they are made to go to posterity."[105] Diderot, writing in his review of the 1767 Salon exhibition, predicted that little more than "a flap of time's wings" would erase La Tour's pictures: "The precious powder will fly from the canvas, half dispersed in the air, half attached to old Saturn's long feathers."[106] La Tour had succeeded in making works that were as delicate as the lives that they portrayed, which was now simultaneously regarded as his primary achievement and his greatest shortcoming.

As this disconnect grew, pastel gradually lost its allure as an instrument of artistic ambition. Though artists would continue to produce pastel portraits through the second half of the eighteenth century, the medium was no longer understood to constitute a serious threat to the preeminence of oil painting. Already in 1754, Friedrich Melchior Grimm declared: "Everyone agrees that pastel is almost unworthy of being touched by a great painter."[107] By 1788, the amateur pastellist Paul-Romain Chaperon lamented that the medium's fragility had led to its undoing among professional artists: "They preferred oil painting as being more proper for transmitting their works to posterity."[108]

But it would be a mistake to conclude that La Tour had blazed a path that led only to a historical dead end. The model of worldly sociability through which he had achieved his success may have lost its credibility, but the aesthetic principles that La Tour derived from that culture had a lasting legacy. The playful and extemporaneous sensibility that he extracted from the realm of courtly conduct would become central to a new understanding of art, one that emphasized an improvisatory responsiveness to the present moment. Even as Enlightenment artists and philosophers rejected what they regarded as the commercial artifice and ephemerality of polite society, they never turned their backs on the notion that artistic inspiration drew much of its force from the contingencies of temporal experience. What was needed, by the second half of the eighteenth century, was a way to integrate these principles with a growing concern for art's historical status. Pastel had shown itself incapable of bridging the divide, but other materials and techniques would soon emerge from the desire to achieve an everlasting delicacy.

Wax, Fire, and the Fashion for Permanence

For a brief moment in eighteenth-century France, it seemed as if the future of painting would be in wax. Word of a startling discovery began to circulate in November 1754, when the painter Joseph-Marie Vien put the finishing touches on a work that he claimed to have created using a forgotten ancient technique known as encaustic (fig. 40).[1] Details remained scarce, but the process reportedly involved some combination of wax and fire (the word "encaustic" is derived from the Latin *encaustica* and the ancient Greek ἐγκαίειν, meaning "burn in"). Vien's painting depicted Minerva, the mythic Roman protector of the arts, and the ambition behind it matched its august subject. Vien had executed the work under the guidance of the comte de Caylus, who heralded their achievement as a turning point in the history of painting.[2] Among the many supposed virtues of encaustic paintings, Caylus emphasized one in particular: "Neither air nor years should cause them any alteration."[3]

In the months that followed, encaustic became the subject of frenzied speculation.[4] Vien and Caylus initially refused to divulge the details of their process, bestowing upon it an air of mystery. Diderot publicly demanded that they reveal their secret, and he published his own treatise on the technique while working in collaboration with the painter Jean-Jacques Bachelier.[5] Artists soon sought to capitalize on the controversy, creating works using one or a combination of the three principal methods that Caylus and Diderot had devised for transforming wax into a suitably fluid painting medium: heating it over fire, emulsifying it with alkaline substances, and dissolving it in turpentine.[6] When the Salon exhibition opened in Paris that summer, the walls were lined with more than a dozen paintings in one version of the process or another.[7] One critic hyperbolically exclaimed that the exhibition hall was "filled with paintings in this manner."[8]

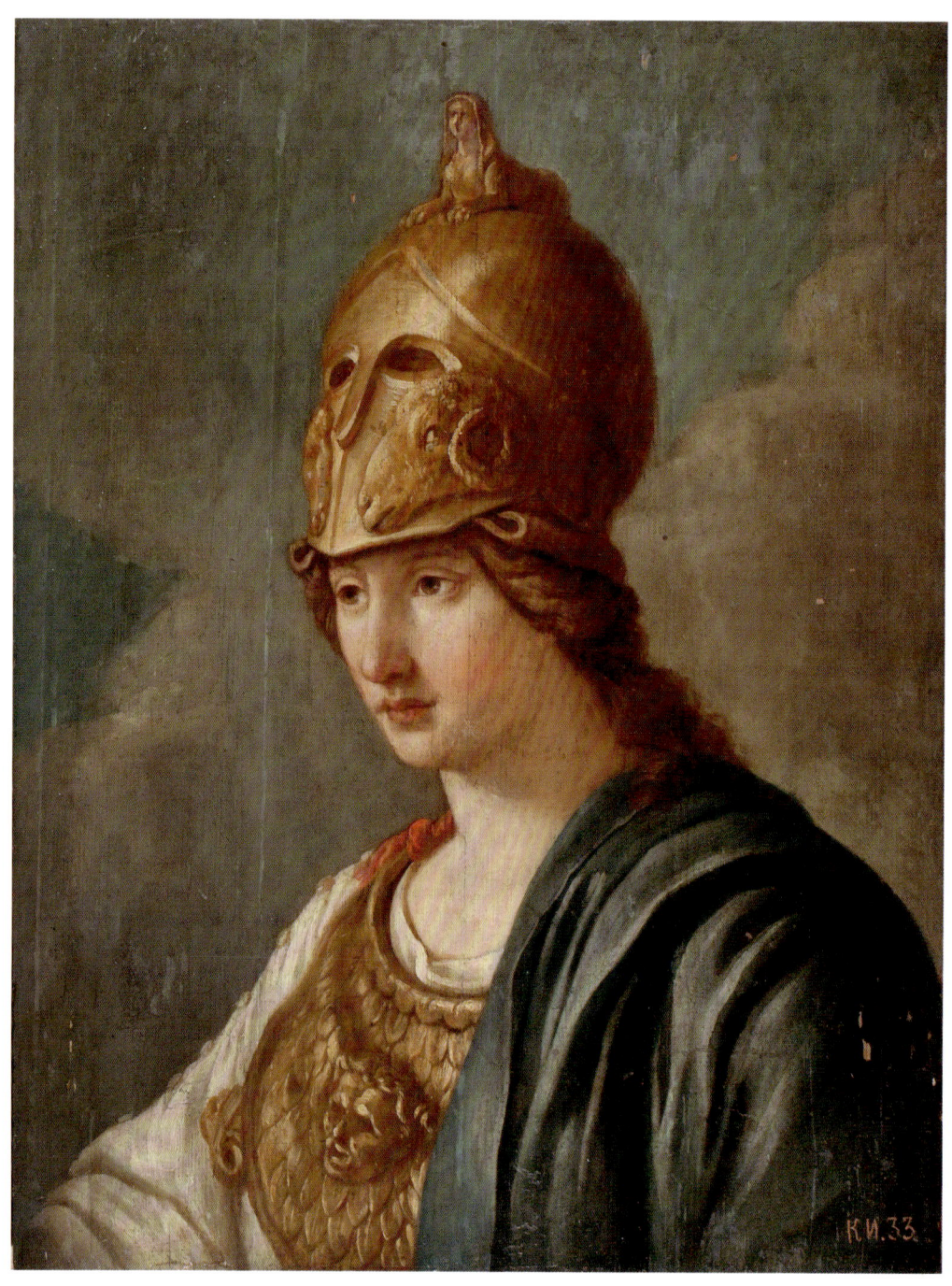

FIG. 40 Joseph-Marie Vien, *Minerva*, 1754. Oil and wax on wood panel, 94.5 × 81.5 cm. State Hermitage Museum, Saint Petersburg. ГЭ 3688. Photo © The State Hermitage Museum / Svetlana Suetova.

The encaustic revival has often been understood as part of the reform movement enacted by the French royal arts administration in the 1750s.[9] In the wake of the anti-Rococo attacks launched by La Font in the late 1740s, the Academy attempted to distance itself from the taint of commercial ephemerality. Caylus took the opportunity to assume a position of greater leadership within the Academy, reviving its tradition of regular lectures and launching a pedagogical program organized around the Classical tradition.[10] Taking inspiration from the newly rediscovered remains of Herculaneum, Caylus and his circle sought to remedy the deleterious effects of the *goût moderne* with a healthy dose of antiquity.[11] Encaustic painting extended this initiative to the level of material practice, demonstrating a commitment to posterity through painting's very substance.

Left out of this narrative, however, is the degree to which the encaustic craze was itself a product of the temporally unstable market forces that it was purportedly designed to restrain. The flood of publicity surrounding the medium and its rapid adoption among prominent artists and collectors underscored how quickly the French art world could be captivated by the latest trend. The high prices generated by encaustic paintings—Vien's *Minerva* was rumored to have sold for the elevated sum of 1200 livres—also made clear the fortunes that artists could derive from such novelties.[12] The connection between encaustic and ephemeral consumption was further highlighted when the medium failed to deliver on its promises. Within a few years, some encaustics started to change color or turn cloudy. Others became brittle and flaked.[13] Their process of production turned out to be only distantly related to ancient practices, and the mixture of wax with modern materials like turpentine proved unstable.[14] French artists and collectors soon lost interest in the medium, and prices for wax-based paintings precipitously declined.

It is tempting to dismiss this fleeting episode in the history of French painting as a mere curiosity. Yet the short-lived notoriety and subsequent failure of the encaustic revival is precisely what makes it indicative of the broader structural forces governing the French art market at the time. As scholars in the emerging discipline of media archaeology have emphasized, it is often in the technological graveyard that we find the clearest evidence of the historical pressures that defined an era.[15] Discarded inventions, through the unrealized expectations that once surrounded them, betray the conflicting demands and impossible desires of their time.[16] It is in these chimerical dreams, not merely in the technical details, that the full significance of the encaustic revival becomes apparent. When we consider the commercial fervor and outsized hopes that accompanied the medium, encaustic's supposed durability and its ultimate ephemerality reveal more than an irony of history. They stand, instead, as a microcosm of a deeper problem that artists and critics began to face in the 1750s and 1760s: the power of the commercial sphere to co-opt any attack against it, commodifying the very objects that were meant to transcend the temporally unstable values of the marketplace.

Durable Delicacy

In some respects, the links between encaustic painting and the commercial sphere were present from the outset. Proponents of encaustic painting may have presented themselves as purifiers of French taste, but these men were more attached to the sensuous delights of the private art market than their rhetoric of reform would suggest. Caylus, after all, had been a devotee of Watteau, and he eagerly collected Rosalba Carriera's fragile pastels.[17] Diderot, too, mixed his admiration of antiquity with a more modern sensibility, willingly succumbing to the thrall of painting's flickering and ethereal surface effects.[18] These inclinations did not disappear when these men turned their attention to encaustic painting. The great promise of the medium, they believed, was to give delicate pleasure a more durable form, one that would cleanse it of any association with ephemeral consumption.

Caylus, in his manuscript papers on encaustic, provides a glimpse of these aspirations. The writings describe his efforts to reconstruct the ancient methods of encaustic painting based on a close reading of Pliny the Elder's cryptic commentary on the topic. Caylus's larger motivations, however, become clear when he explains the visual effects that he believed these techniques could produce. Most notably, he suggests that the bright colors and unlabored appearance of encaustic paintings would resemble the eighteenth century's most notoriously fragile medium, displaying the "freshness that is presented to us by pastel."[19] Pastel, by this time, had become an emblem of commercial ephemerality, which may explain why Caylus chose not to repeat this analogy in print. The comparison, though, is central to the potential that Caylus saw in reviving the ancient medium. If the great shortcoming of pastel was that its airy lightness came at the expense of durability, then wax promised all its benefits without any of its costs. Caylus believed that wax, like pastel, would allow the artist's hand to move unencumbered, recording touch with infinite subtlety. But unlike pastel, he imagined that it would eternalize the traces of the hand in their pristine state: "It furnishes greater facility than the practice of oil painting . . . [but] years will not cause it any alteration."[20]

Encaustic, then, would be *délicat* in the courtly sense of seemingly effortless charm, but not in the literal, degraded sense of material impermanence. Diderot expressed similar hopes in his treatise on the medium. Encaustic, he argued, obviated the need for art restoration, which inevitably destroyed the delicate traces of the artist's hand:

> whatever attention one brings to [the cleaning of paintings], these precious molecules that constitute the truth, the *délicatesse*, the freshness and the originality of touch, that soul of the artist, this breath of life that he has so lightly spread across the canvas, this vapor that sometimes appears separate from it as if scattered and suspended in the air between the painted objects and the

eye of the spectator, will it not be removed? This tender and delicate veil, will it not be violated? These flowers, will they conserve all their vivacity and all their brilliance? This powder so fine that colors them, will it not dissipate? These fruits, will they not lose any of their downy skin? The plushness of that cloth or its nap, will it not be grazed? This flesh so firm, so round, so young, so brilliant, so fresh, will it conserve all its charms?[21]

The unapologetically sensual language makes evident that Diderot, like Caylus, remained devoted to the sensorial pleasures of painting's material effects even as he pursued a program of artistic reform.[22] Sensualism and reformism were not easy to integrate at a time when perishable surface effects increasingly connoted commercial decadence, but Diderot and Caylus both attempted to reconcile these interests. To do so, they sought to restore a distinction that the commercial sphere had eroded, a dividing line between the charming *délicatesse* of subtle yet unlabored expression and the base fragility of the disposable commodity.

What might this distinction look like in artistic practice? The reception piece that Vien submitted for admission to the Academy in 1754 offers some answers (fig. 41).[23] The work itself is an oil painting, having been completed shortly before Vien and Caylus had succeeded in recovering what they believed to be the forgotten technique behind encaustic. The themes and form of the painting, however, functioned as an extended commentary on their aspirations. The painting depicts Daedalus fabricating the wings of Icarus with feathers and wax. It was an unusual subject. The story of Daedalus and Icarus had typically served as a cautionary tale about the dangers of hubris; its meaning was generally derived from the climactic moment when Icarus flies too close to the sun, causing his waxen wings to melt, plunging him into the ocean.[24] Vien's picture, by contrast, shifts the focus of the story away from the hubristic flight and toward the feat of engineering that preceded it. Icarus holds a bundle of feathers in his hand as his father works to fasten them. In the foreground of the composition, Vien shows us the bowl of wax that Daedalus uses to attach these feathers and the smoldering cauldron with which he heats his wax. These details undoubtedly alluded to Vien's own experiments with wax—a connection that would have been all the more obvious when Vien exhibited the work together with his encaustics at the Salon of 1755.[25] By establishing this link with Daedalus, the preeminent artisan of ancient Greece, Vien positioned himself as the inheritor of an ancient and illustrious tradition of craftsmanship.

On a formal level, though, the painting presents a more complex picture, one that shows how Vien sought to reconcile the sound workmanship of the ancients with the sensual seductions of the moderns. The austere setting, restricted palette, and orderly composition are all in keeping with the theme of Classical solidity, but they belie the airy pleasures at the painting's center. Icarus's nubile body, bathed in light and surrounded

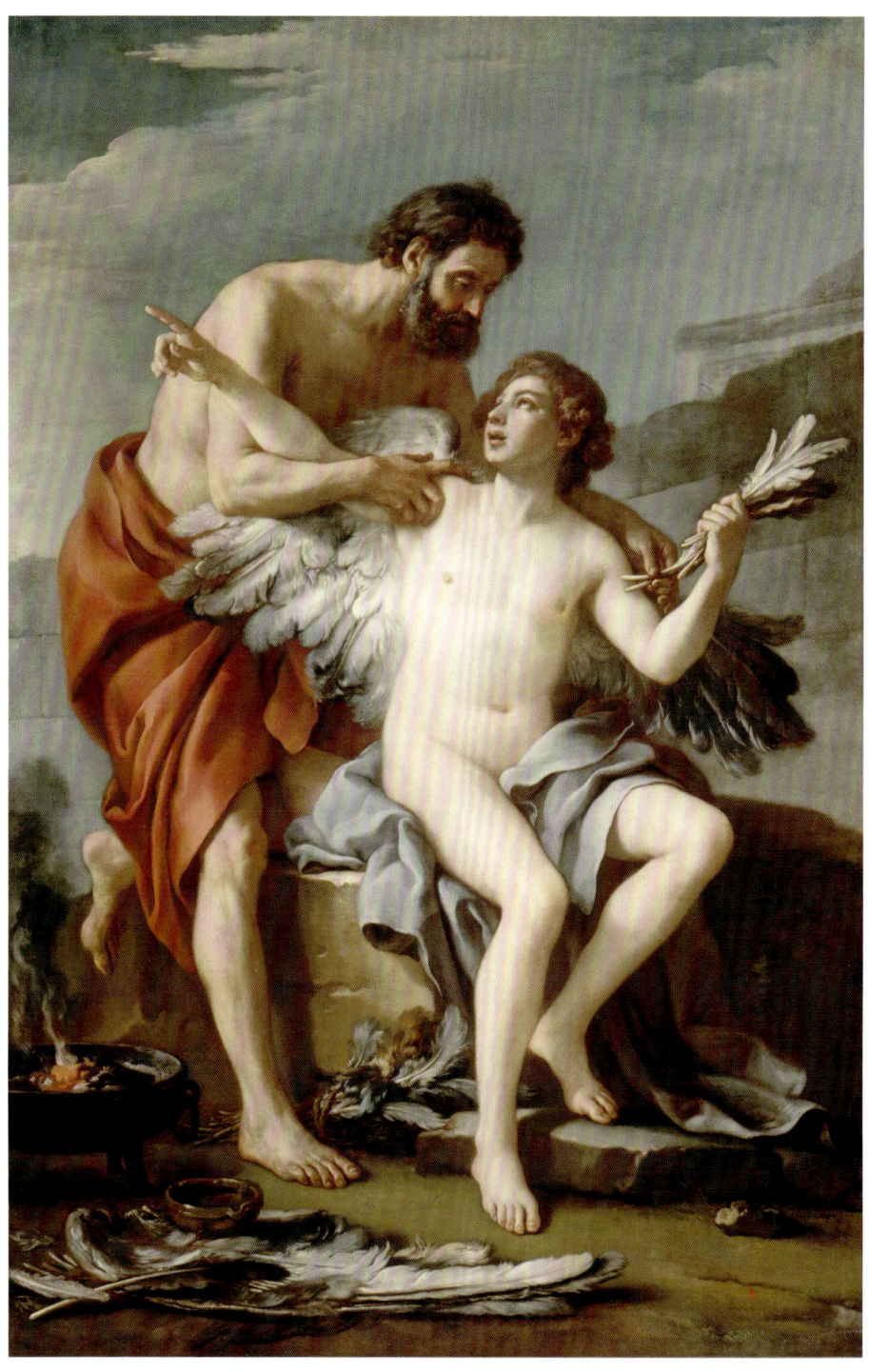

FIG. 41 Joseph-Marie Vien, *Daedalus Attaching the Wings of Icarus*, 1754. Oil on canvas, 198 × 132 cm. École Nationale Supérieure des Beaux-Arts, Paris. INV 8418. Photo © RMN-Grand Palais / Art Resource, NY (Gérard Blot).

by gauzy plumage, captivated critics with "the tenderness of the skin tones."[26] Daedalus gently caresses his son's shoulder, encouraging us to consider the feeling of feathers and flesh, their soft textures set in contrast with the hard stone of the background. Through these material effects, Vien invites us to luxuriate in the lightness of his brushstrokes, which have all the ethereality of the nearly weightless feathers that they depict. These passages of the painting literalize what Caylus termed "lightness of touch," a property to which he devoted an entire lecture at the Academy a little more than a month after Vien's painting had gone on view at the Salon.[27] Drawing from the language of courtly sociability, Caylus defined this quality as a "harmony that the great master expresses in conserving truth with a seductive *délicatesse*."[28] An artist who conveys this lightness is, in Caylus's words, "a man of the world who speaks with charm, to whom one listens with pleasure." Referring again to the conversational arts, he states that lightness of touch "originates in seduction, or charm produced by the turn of phrase, the tone, and the apropos."[29]

This invocation of courtly "lightness" underscores the larger strategy behind the reforms that Caylus and the artists in his circle sought to enact. Rather than give up on the pleasures of *délicatesse*, they attempted to legitimize them through an appeal to an older, established social order. Metaphors of "lightness" played an important role in these efforts. While lightness could function as a pejorative term denoting insubstantiality, many French writers in the middle decades of the eighteenth century appropriated it as a badge of honor, one that reflected a distinct national identity constructed around civility and refinement.[30] "Our jealous neighbors may call us, if they like, light, frivolous, inconsequential," the novelist Jacques-Antoine-René Perrin observed in 1762, before concluding, "This lightness, this frivolity is the source of our amusements and our pleasures; it is to *délicatesse* and gallantry itself that we owe our happiness; they are virtues for us."[31] As David Bell has argued, such comments reinforced an emerging French narrative of civilizational progress; to be "light" was to stand at the final stage of social evolution, far ahead of barbarous cultures abroad.[32]

Lightness, though, still had troubling associations with commercial ephemerality, particularly when materialized in the visual arts. How could artists and collectors ensure that airy lightness did not devolve into material decay, that Vien's feathery brushstrokes would not turn into Watteau's cracked paint? As the story of Daedalus and Icarus makes clear, airy pleasures can go too far. Vien's depiction of Daedalus may emphasize the artisan's technical proficiency, but the outstretched finger of Icarus reminds us, proleptically, that lightness has its dangers. Caylus, at the conclusion of his lecture on "lightness of touch," also alludes to peril. Turning his attention to material instability, he acknowledges that the areas of a painting that exhibit the greatest lightness are generally the most susceptible to damage: "Time has often destroyed a part of it."[33] He goes on to observe that even the most careful art restorer will inevitably harm this aspect of a painting, which he metaphorically describes as the "flower" of the work: "It is out of respect for this flower that one must touch paintings as little as possible."[34] The final line of the lecture emphasizes the impossibly precarious state of painting's most ineffable properties: "Virginity is delicate; the slightest thing can injure it."[35] Here was the problem that encaustic was meant to remedy. By allowing artists to work with unimpeded ease while preserving their brushstrokes in waxy suspension, the medium promised to protect lightness of touch, in all its "virginal" delicacy, from corruption.

The Virginal Surface

Caylus's invocation of virginity is worth probing in more detail because it reveals the important function of sex and misogyny in the eighteenth-century discourse on material fragility—a function that encaustic painting would bring to the fore. Libidinal metaphors provided male critics and collectors with a way to reconcile the contradictions in their own attitudes toward fragile objects. When French writers wished to denounce commercial ephemerality as a sign of moral corruption, they turned to the language of female seduction and prostitution, presenting transient commodities as the purview of licentious *coquettes* and *grisettes* who trafficked in fleeting pleasures.[36] If these same commentators wished to redeem fragile sources of delight, however, they could rely on the language of virginity—an analogy that reframed perishability in terms of moral purity rather than corruption. Metaphors of chastity therefore granted artists and collectors a way to maintain an interest in the pleasures of *délicatesse* without defiling their reputations. The language of virginity was not unique to encaustic painting, but practitioners in the medium had a particular appreciation for its power as a means of moral absolution. By drawing upon virginity as both a material and iconographic symbol, they could present themselves as protectors of delicacy in its unadulterated form.

The materiality of encaustic painting was well suited to this purpose. Wax had long-standing associations with virginity. Bees, in Classical tradition, had been regarded as unusually chaste organisms, as Virgil attested: "They indulge not in conjugal embraces, nor idly unnerve their bodies in love."[37] Christian writers, building upon this idea, adopted both bees and beeswax as symbols of virginal purity.[38] By the eighteenth century, "virgin wax" had entered secular parlance, and Caylus himself explained that the term was commonly used in reference to the purest form of beeswax, which he recommended for all encaustic paintings.[39]

Encaustic painters chose subject matter that played upon these virginal associations. Of the ten known works that Vien undertook in encaustic, four of them represent either virgins or chaste priestesses (fig. 42).[40] Vien was not alone in his preference for

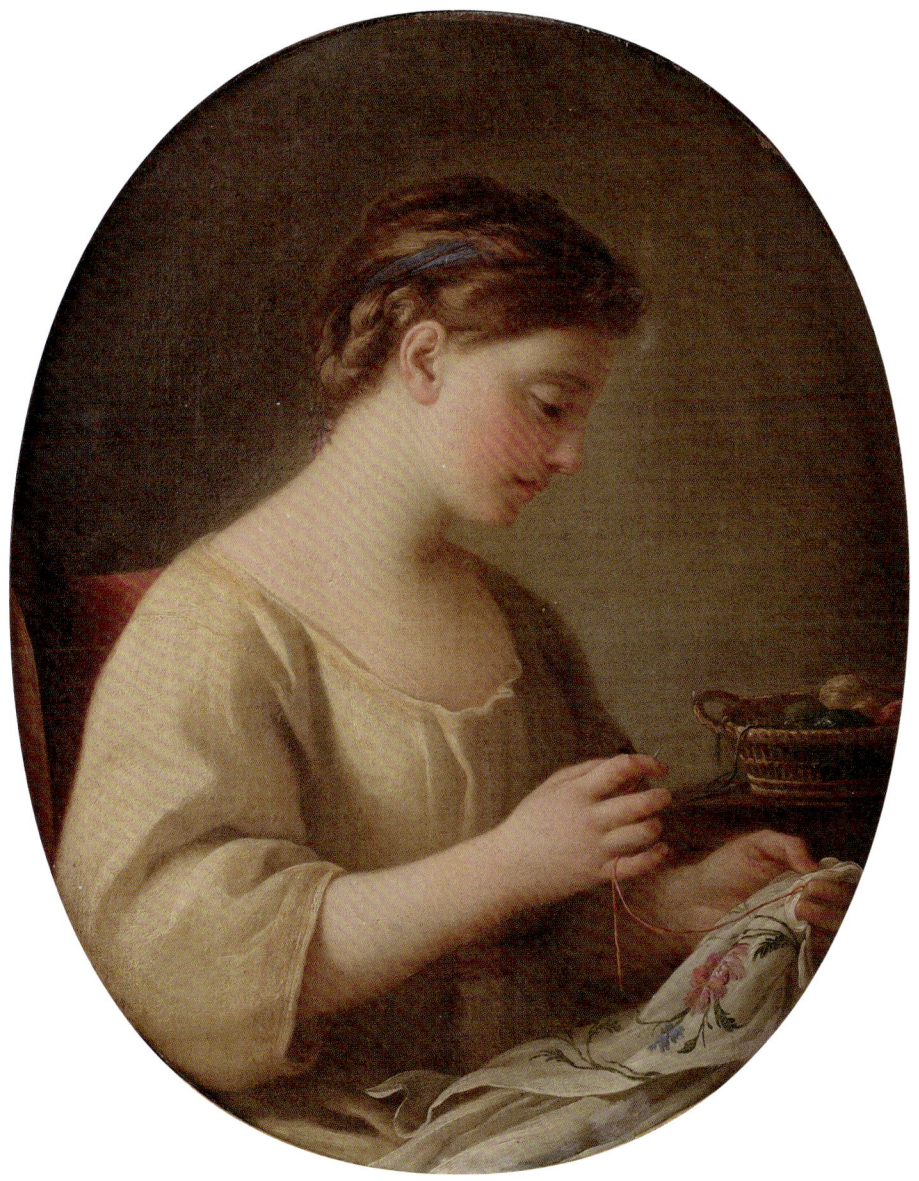

FIG. 42 Joseph-Marie Vien, *Priestess Embroidering Temple Decorations*, 1755. Oil and wax on canvas, 57 × 46 cm. Private collection. Photo © Osenat.

this subject matter. According to sale catalogs and collection inventories, virgins were common subjects for many encaustic painters during the period.[41] Oil painters had treated similar subjects before; allegorical portraits of women in the guise of vestal virgins had recently become fashionable among female patrons, who used the genre as a means of self-consciously performing their virtuousness.[42] But this fashion alone does not explain the exceptional pervasiveness of virginal subject matter among encaustic painters. Carle Van Loo is an instructive example. Of the nine encaustic paintings listed under his name in eighteenth-century sale catalogs, six are described as "vestals."[43]

The prevalence of these subjects in encaustic can be understood, in part, as an extension of a longstanding artistic fascination with virginal complexions. The skin of virgins was widely understood to be exceptionally subtle, and artists throughout the early modern period had regarded the Virgin Mary as an ideal subject for demonstrating their technical prowess in representing skin color.[44] Since at least the seventeenth century, French art theorists had extolled Raphael, Parmigianino, and other Italian Renaissance painters for their talent in capturing the virgin mother's skin.[45] When encaustic painters set out to establish the subtle effects that they could achieve with their medium, they knew that depictions of virgins would strike collectors and connoisseurs as a suitable proof of concept. The Virgin Mary was an anachronistic subject for showcasing a waxen medium whose origins predated Christianity, but pagan virgins served much the same purpose, allowing artists to display their facility with refined complexions.

Moreover, virgins spoke to the sexual politics of the French art world in the 1750s. Anti-Rococo art critics such as La Font relied on the broader misogynistic rhetoric surrounding women and fashion, ascribing the literal and figurative degradation of art to feminine immorality.[46] "It is principally the ladies whom one must hold responsible if our productions often fall into the small and the trifling," La Font wrote in his review of the 1753 Salon.[47] Madame de Pompadour, in her dual capacities as royal mistress and powerful patron of the arts, personified the union that anti-Rococo critics saw between female sexuality and cultural decline. In truth, men supported the *goût moderne* in great numbers, and the fleshy female nudes that La Font took to be a sign of decadence attracted a predominately male viewership.[48] In a rhetorical sleight of hand, however, La Font and his compatriots conflated the seductive female subjects of modern painting with the coquettish flirtation of an imagined female audience.

If the hypersexualized woman functioned as an emblem of artistic degeneration, then the virgin was, according to the masculinist logic of the period, an obvious icon around which to organize a program of reform. The virgin was especially useful because she allowed the process of cultural purification to be enacted on the level of both iconography and technique. The two were closely linked. In the eyes of anti-Rococo critics, the beguiling surfaces of modern oil paintings were akin to the cosmetics-laden faces of seductive women such as Pompadour (fig. 43).[49] Virginal women, according to

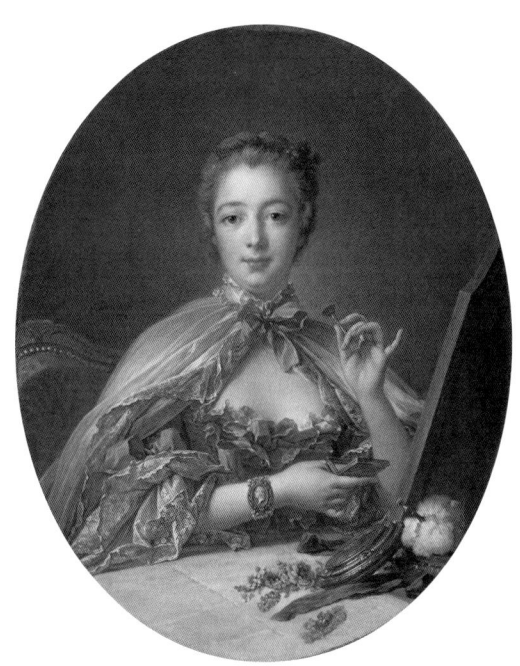

FIG. 43
François Boucher, *Jeanne-Antoinette Poisson, Marquise de Pompadour*, 1750 (with later additions). Oil on canvas, 81.2 × 64.9 cm. Harvard Art Museums / Fogg Museum, Cambridge, MA. Bequest of Charles E. Dunlap. 1966.47. Photo © President and Fellows of Harvard College.

Christian tradition, had no need for such deceptive embellishment, nor would they dare modify their God-given appearance.[50] The matte texture of encaustic paintings echoed this principle of virginal honesty; while the sheen of a varnished oil painting called attention to its own materiality, glittering like a mirror, the surface of an encaustic painting appeared to provide an unmediated window onto its subject.[51] Diderot explicitly contrasted this feature of wax-based painting with cosmetic duplicity, asking whether French collectors who had been entranced by the glossiness of oils would accept the unadorned appearance of wax: "It is a matter of knowing if we would want our paintings to be made-up like our women."[52]

The supposed virginal purity of encaustic was, of course, still a sexualized understanding of painting, even if it was less explicitly prurient than the Rococo paintings that Diderot decried. To see painting as a virgin was a way of asserting its moral elevation while keeping it within the realm of erotic desire. Caylus, in fact, repeatedly described his attachment to ancient culture in such sexual terms in his private correspondence: "I took antiquity for a mistress: I caress her, I look at her, I study her."[53] A short time later he wrote, in a similar vein, "antiquities are female; for this reason, do not go looking for them—they will look for you."[54] Such comments make obvious that the *goût antique* did not expunge the sensual and libertine ethos of the *goût moderne* but often simply disguised it beneath the surface—a surface that was all the more convincing because it appeared not to be concealing anything at all.

WAX, FIRE, AND THE FASHION FOR PERMANENCE (75)

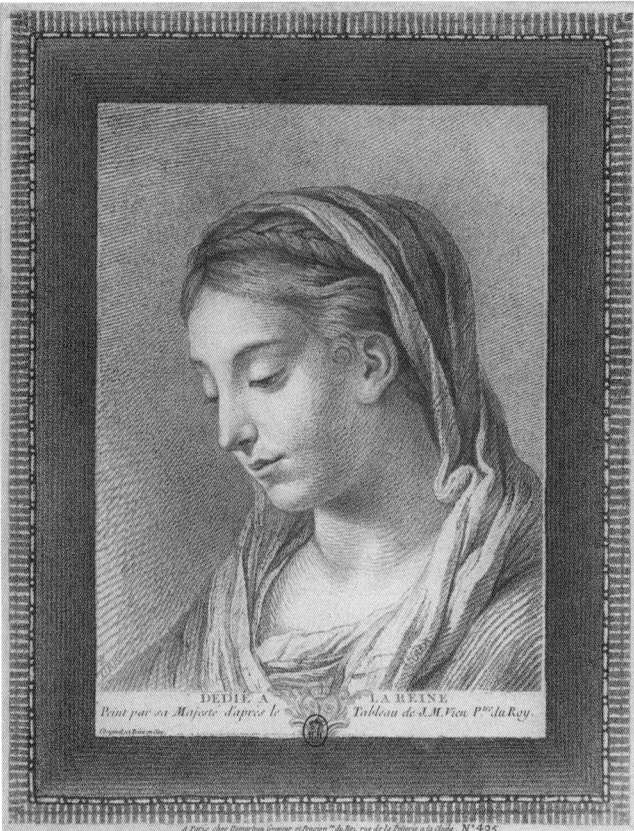

FIG. 44
Jean-Charles François and Gilles Demarteau after Joseph-Marie Vien, *The Virgin*, second half of eighteenth century. Crayon manner print, 28 × 22 cm. Bibliothèque nationale de France, Paris. EF-9 (13)-FOL. Photo: gallica.bnf.fr / BnF.

The social function of these surface effects becomes clearer when we consider the collectors to whom such works appealed. Encaustic virgins could be found in a variety of collections in the second half of the eighteenth century, but they appeared with particular frequency in the homes of the merchants and financiers who now needed to protect themselves against charges of commercial excess. Jean de Jullienne and Ange-Laurent de La Live de Jully, for example, both held wax paintings of virgins within their collections.[55] Female patrons, too, gravitated toward waxen portraits of chaste women, perhaps in an effort to shield themselves from the moral condemnation and sexual shaming of anti-Rococo critics. Madame Geoffrin, for instance, came to Vien's studio in 1755 and purchased an encaustic *Virgin*—a work that is now known only through a print (fig. 44).[56] Geoffrin, as a bourgeoise whose standing in worldly society depended upon her association with respectable taste, had cultivated a reputation as a benefactor of reform-minded artists such as Vien.[57] She allowed Caylus to preside over the Monday dinners that she hosted for artists and amateurs, and it was rumored that she was responsible for ameliorating the taste of Pompadour's brother, the future arts minister Abel François Poisson.[58]

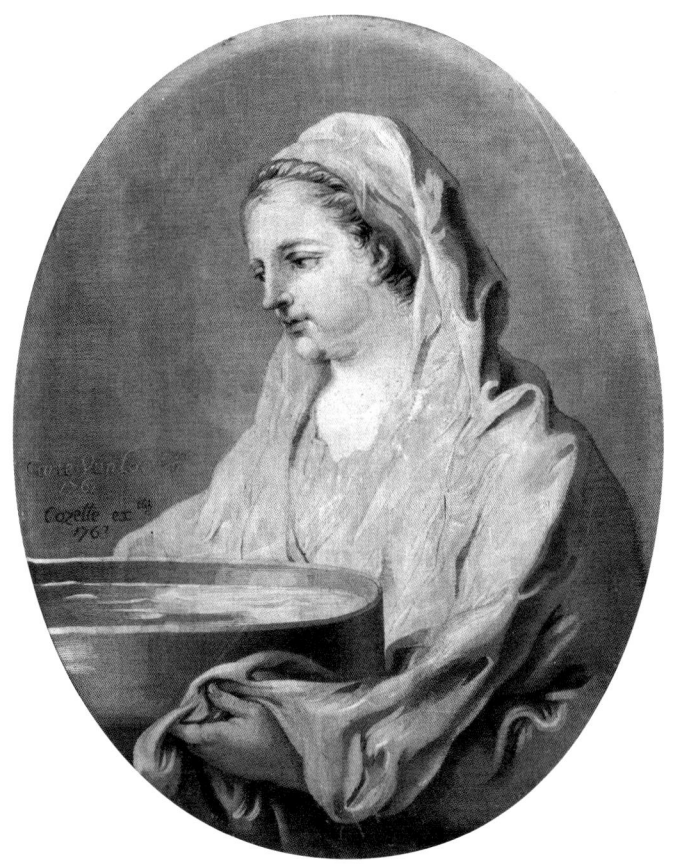

FIG. 45
Pierre-François Cozette after Carle Van Loo, *The Vestal Tuccia*, 1763. Wool and silk tapestry, 87 × 69 cm. Mobilier national, Paris. GMTT-1225-000. Photo: Mobilier national (Isabelle Bideau).

Perhaps the most notable buyer of a waxen virgin, though, was Pompadour herself, who commissioned one from Van Loo in 1761.[59] The original is now lost, but a faded tapestry copy of it (fig. 45) shows that it depicted the vestal virgin known as Tuccia performing the miracle that proved her chastity: aided by the gods, she carries water in a colander without spilling a drop. Pompadour, who was now a lady-in-waiting to the queen after her liaison with the king had ended, may have regarded the object as a means of projecting penitence. More likely, though, this newfound devotion to chastity from a woman famous for her sexual affairs was meant to convey a hint of irony. The fact that Pompadour commissioned a copy of the work in tapestry, a notoriously light-sensitive medium, also underscores that she had hardly become a devoted defender of cultural preservation. Pompadour's simultaneous engagement with the durable and the ephemeral is perhaps better understood, as Susan Wager has argued, as a performance of identity, a means of responding to her critics without succumbing to them.[60]

What these savvy appropriations of encaustic underscore is the self-consciousness with which the medium's collectors deployed its moral symbolism. For such buyers,

WAX, FIRE, AND THE FASHION FOR PERMANENCE

the ephemerality of flirtatious artifice and the enduring virtue of delicate virginity were not so much opposites but two sides of the art market's common currency. If the two were sometimes difficult to distinguish, then this was part of the point. The purified delicacy of encaustic was no less determined by the contingencies of commerce than the degraded transience of the media it was meant to displace—a truth that would become more apparent as demand for the medium began to plummet.

Fashionable Permanence

Were the collectors of encaustic painting simply following the latest fashion? The fact that the medium's boosters included people who had gravitated to the ephemeral pleasures of the *goût moderne* invites speculation about their true motivations. Their nearly complete abandonment of encaustic by the late 1760s, too, suggests that their interest in the medium stemmed as much from its novelty as from its supposed durability. But it would be unfair to conclude that the rapidly fading enthusiasm for encaustic painting in France proves that the initial interest in the medium was disingenuous. Fleeting commitments are not necessarily insincere. One of the defining facets of eighteenth-century consumer culture was the way heartfelt preferences changed with surprising alacrity, seemingly of their own accord. Diderot himself commented on the issue in his 1769 "Regrets on Parting with My Old Dressing Gown," in which he playfully bemoaned his *tact délicat* (delicate sensitivity) because it drove him into a pernicious spiral of consumption that he felt powerless to resist: "Fatal instinct for tasteful conformity! Delicate and ruinous sensitivity! Taste! Sublime taste that changes, that rearranges, that builds things, that knocks them down, that empties the coffers of fathers, that leaves daughters without dowries, sons without education, that makes such beautiful things and such great misfortunes, you who substituted in my house the fateful and precious bureau in place of the wooden table."[61] Consumer desire, according to Diderot's self-satirizing description, is no less authentic for being mutable. The source of the humor lies, instead, in the irony that compulsions can be both ephemeral and deeply felt. Fleeting yet all-consuming predilections, Diderot suggests, are the inevitable product of a social identity that has come to depend on getting and spending.[62] When examined in the context of these systemic pressures, the rapid rise and fall of encaustic says less about the intentions of its enthusiasts than it does about the capacity of the market to turn anything, including the pursuit of permanence, into an ephemeral phenomenon.

Scholars have long recognized that Neoclassicism was, at least in part, defined by fashion and commercial interest.[63] What requires greater scrutiny is the conflicted temporal consciousness generated by the fusion of antiquity's supposedly timeless values and the marketplace's unending turbulence. Caylus, writing in 1763, complained that collectors of antiquities only prized what they believed others valued, which meant that demand for objects could reverse itself nearly instantaneously: "Everything is fashion in Paris, and when one has not seen something, one does not want it. *Such a person has it?* I want to have it, etc."[64] Art inspired by antiquity, no less than antiquities themselves, was subject to these sudden changes of fortune. In the 1764 catalog of his collection, La Live de Jully defensively explained that his possessions, which included Vien's encaustics, had been at the forefront of what was now a ubiquitous and debased fashion: "It is in the time since the creation of this cabinet that the taste for works *à la grecque* spread to the point that one ridiculously uses it for everything, for dishes, jewelry, fabrics, hairstyles . . . up through the shops whose signs are now nearly all *à la grecque*."[65] La Live was not exaggerating. By the early 1760s, merchants of every sort promoted their products with names that evoked Classical antiquity, from *vinaigre romain* for whitening teeth to *eau grecque* hair dye.[66]

La Live wished to distinguish his collecting habits from those of consumers who followed the latest fashion, but the difference between them was not as clear as he desired. The taste for antiquity, from its very inception, could be understood as part of an endless cycle driven by collective social dynamics; already in 1752, the architect Pierre Vigné de Vigny described the process: "We destroy the antique to make room for the modern, then we abandon the modern to go study the ruins of antiquity, as if the latter did not have any faults, and the former had no beauty."[67] French artists and writers had been complaining about the temporal instability of fashion for decades, but what was novel about Vigny's sentiment was the sense of fashion's inescapability. Antiquity could no longer be assumed to represent a bulwark protecting timeless values from the forces of commercial ephemerality, and fickleness could no longer be understood as the exclusive purview of those who favored the *goût moderne*.[68] In the eighteenth-century commercial sphere, no aesthetic existed outside the capricious tyranny of the market.

For artists and writers of the period, the fervor over encaustic painting became a preeminent example of the temporal incongruities surrounding the renewed interest in Classical antiquity. Because the explosion of publicity surrounding encaustic was framed so explicitly in terms of the medium's permanence, it made obvious the paradox of a fashion premised on durability. Almost from the moment that the medium was announced, satirists called attention to the apparent contradiction. In May 1755, for example, the enamel painter Jean André Rouquet published a parody of encaustic entitled *The New Art of Painting in Cheese, or in Ramequin, Invented in Pursuit of the Laudable Project of Gradually Finding Manners of Painting Inferior to Those that Exist*.[69] The text outlined a method similar to Bachelier's technique of encaustic painting, but Rouquet replaced wax and turpentine with cheese and eggs. The treatise came complete with an ancient origin story for the medium, which Rouquet claimed to have rediscovered. He explained that he had hoped to enlist "learned men to give it a name with a Greek or Arab origin," but did not have time to do so because he had heard that someone else was about to reveal the secret behind his method, forcing him to rush to publication.[70] He berated himself for announcing his technique without yet having an ancient name for it because, in his words, "one must always give things that one wants to make fashionable a remarkable name that has an air of erudition and importance."[71]

Perhaps the most mordant critique of encaustic's fashionable permanence came in a 1755 essay published by the artist Charles-Nicolas Cochin entitled "Advice for Ladies."[72] The article's pretext was that recent inventions for making permanent paintings might also be useful for fashionable women who grew tired of constantly reapplying makeup. Cochin wrote that these techniques could save women tremendous amounts of time, "rendering them as red as they desire, in little time and in a permanent manner, which will spare them the trouble of beginning anew every day."[73] He suggested, for example, that the various recipes for fixing pastel portraits might be useful for permanently attaching makeup to the face: "One could seek out one of the pastel painters, with which Paris is teeming, and then fix this color, in such a manner that nothing can alter it."[74] Encaustic painting, he went on to say, constituted "the most important" of the new inventions. He offered instructions on its potential use, noting how a wax solution should be placed on the skin, then a hot iron brought near the face to bond the colors, giving them an "immutable solidity." The technique, he admitted, came with some risk of injury: "This difficulty may restrict the use of this colored wax to so few people that even those who are the most sure that it can be used safely will have reason to fear that others will accuse them of trying to distinguish themselves in society."[75] If partisans of encaustic painting had hoped to present the medium as an antidote to cosmetic artifice and effeminate fashion, then their campaign had apparently been less than persuasive.

These dismissals of encaustic as a passing trend contributed to its declining fortunes, and in this respect the satires were self-fulfilling prophecies. By August 1755, when the first group of encaustic paintings went on display at the Salon, critical enthusiasm for the medium had already begun to cool.[76] One of the more generous critics concluded, "We are not able to deny that this manner of painting in wax has apparent advantages over painting in oil; it is up to time to make known whether they are real."[77] Another reviewer offered a similar note of caution: "The proof of time is still necessary for their works, in order to know if the colors will change, and if the wax will not melt or crack."[78] Others were more openly pessimistic in their predictions. "I do not envision a great fortune for them," one declared.[79] Some critics wondered whether any more time was really needed to judge encaustic, arguing that oil painting remained superior for the breadth and subtlety of its colors: "What need is there for new discoveries when we possess better ones?"[80]

Encaustics appeared only sporadically on the Salon wall in subsequent exhibitions, and their market value precipitously declined.[81] The burning expectations that French audiences once held for the medium briefly spread to neighboring countries, most notably England and Italy, then fizzled (painters have periodically rekindled interest in wax in the time since).[82] The dynamics that had given rise to encaustic, however, remained in place. The explosion of publicity that initially surrounded its rediscovery revealed the potential interest that existed in a novel, purportedly everlasting medium. Simply the promise of such an invention, it was now clear, was enough to attract significant public attention. As a result, a cottage industry emerged to satisfy demand. Inventors and entrepreneurs came forward with their own supposedly indestructible materials and techniques, freshly invented or newly rediscovered. Many of these methods were direct descendants of encaustic, such as the supposedly odorless and inalterable wax-based wall paint developed by Théodore Odiot, a color merchant who had purchased the rights to Bachelier's encaustic technique.[83] A housepainter by the name of Dandrillon soon promoted a competing invention, which he dubbed paint *à la grecque*, and which came with similar promises of endurance.[84] Dandrillon followed this announcement with his discovery of gilding *à la grecque*, a technique that reputedly preserved woodwork in its pristine state, and which Caylus endorsed.[85] Around this time the German antiquarian and amateur painter Johann Friedrich Reiffenstein sent word to France that he had developed a method for integrating pastel with encaustic, which he called *pastel en cire*, declaring that it rendered pastel resistant to damage.[86]

The sheer volume of these now-forgotten inventions underscores the degree to which encaustic painting had established a model for marketing artistic techniques that endured well after the medium itself fell out of favor. The essential features of encaustic's legacy become clear when we consider, by way of conclusion, just one of these inventions in greater detail: a peculiar method of oil painting promoted in the 1760s and 1770s by an obscure artist-entrepreneur named Arnaud Vincent de Montpetit.[87] His invention had all the elements that had become a winning formula for attracting attention, including promises of endurance and vague associations with Classical antiquity. Montpetit dubbed his technique "eludoric" painting, a term he invented by combining the Greek words for oil and water.[88] According to his own account, he executed his eludoric works in oil paint submerged beneath a layer of water; when finished, he drained the water and immediately sealed the picture behind a pane of glass.[89] The guiding principle of the process, he explained, was that at every phase the painting remained protected from the corrosive effects of air, which he asserted was the primary cause of art's physical decay.[90] Claiming to have definitively triumphed over this problem, he declared that an eludoric painting would "endure with all its freshness for posterity."[91]

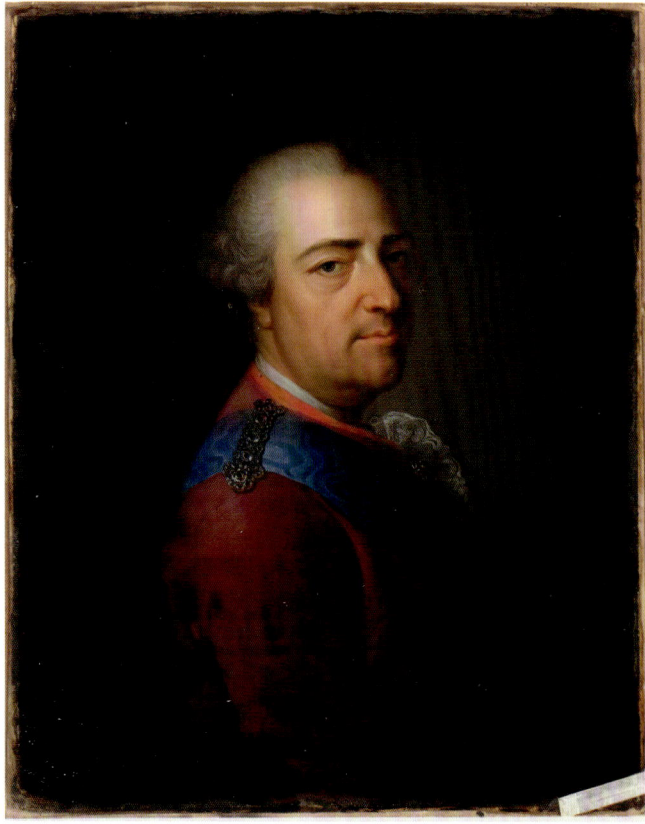

FIG. 46
Arnaud Vincent de Montpetit, *Louis XV*, 1774. Oil on canvas fixed under glass, 74 × 61.2 cm. Châteaux de Versailles et de Trianon, Versailles. MV 8452. Photo © C2RMF / Pierre-Yves Duval.

His arguments were apparently compelling enough to earn him the patronage of Louis XV, who modeled for one of the few eludoric paintings known to survive (fig. 46).

Montpetit, though, had greatly overstated the durability of such works. The portrait of Louis XV remains in presentable condition, but other examples of his eludoric paintings have suffered from flaking and discoloration.[92] A portrait of the poet and dramatist Alexis Piron, for example, exhibits significant losses where the painting separated from the glass around the perimeter, particularly in the lower right corner (fig. 47).[93] Montpetit, of course, had little way of knowing whether his claims about the permanence of his medium were true (any pronouncement about the permanence of a new invention, after all, is inherently speculative). What Montpetit did understand, however, was a strategy for legitimizing his unverifiable assertions. Echoing the refrain of anti-Rococo critics, he positioned his invention in opposition to what he described as the hasty and short-sighted methods of profit-minded artists: "Whether out of laziness or self-interest, they love to make a lot in little time; they sketch, they varnish, they glaze, they daub . . . and here is a painting that creates the effect, that seduces for

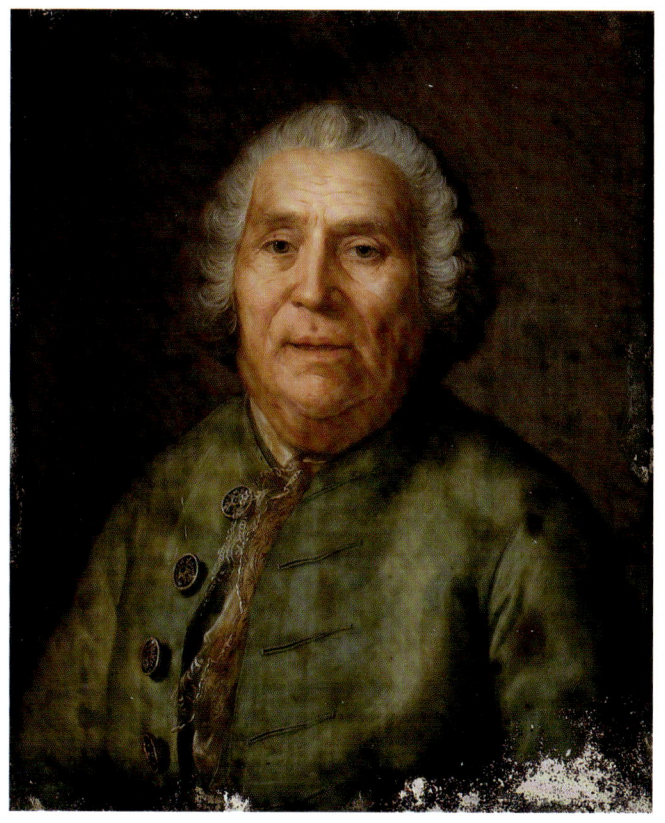

FIG. 47
Arnaud Vincent de Montpetit, *Alexis Piron*, 1777. Oil on canvas fixed under glass, 84.3 × 73.5 cm. Musée Antoine Lécuyer, Saint-Quentin. Photo © C2RMF / Pierre-Yves Duval.

the moment, but that destroys itself in little time and no longer offers anything to see but hard and disagreeable touches. This prompt manner is attractive to those who do not know the consequences. It is in this way that paintings can proliferate to infinity without many passing favorably to posterity."[94] The comments harkened back to the rhetoric that La Font had deployed to dismiss Watteau thirty years earlier. But in an ironic inversion, Montpetit appropriated this anti-commercial discourse in order to sell the public on his own unstable productions.

This was a key lesson derived from the encaustic revival: the condemnation of commerce was now, paradoxically, a prerequisite for the promotion and sale of any new artistic technique. When the chemist and lawyer Louis-Bernard Guyton de Morveau presented a new and supposedly inalterable zinc white pigment in 1781, for example, he emphasized that the pursuit of permanence transcended commerce: "One does not haggle over immortality."[95] Within a year, however, his assistant had set up distribution of their pigment through shops in Dijon and Paris, where they offered their product at different price points depending on quality.[96] Artists may not have been able to negotiate over immortality, but permanence still had a price.

None of these facts should be taken as an indictment of these men. In a market economy, artists and inventors support themselves by selling their wares. With the exception of Caylus, who belonged to a family of military nobles, most of the men who promoted these new materials and techniques came from bourgeois backgrounds and lacked sinecures to fund their activities.[97] Their decision to market their products through anti-commercial rhetoric may contain a whiff of false virtue, but the hypocrisy was less a personal failing than a product of circumstance: the commercial sphere had, by now, fully assimilated the charges of ephemeral consumption that had been brought against it. Permanence was the fashion of the day and an essential feature for marketing any new product.

The commercial co-optation of permanence as a means of product differentiation represented, on the surface, a further sign that the encaustic revival had failed to achieve its purpose. On a deeper level, however, it constituted the fulfillment of a principle that was already tacitly understood by encaustic painting's adherents, who had themselves benefited from the promotional potential that existed in novel claims of temporal transcendence. Whether they had capitalized on this opportunity willingly or reluctantly is of little consequence. What the encaustic revival made clear, whether its proponents wished it to be true or not, was that there was no such thing as art that existed outside the marketplace. For the ambitious artist, even for one who dreamed of posterity, the question was no longer whether to engage with commerce, but how.

4

Clodion's Fragile Monuments

"Here lies Fifi. Born May 3, 1767. Died April 7, 1772." So reads the inscription on a miniature mausoleum, dedicated to the memory of a pet canary (fig. 48). The object was created by the sculptor known as Clodion, and it typifies the insouciance that became a hallmark of his work. Sculpted for an unknown patron shortly after Fifi's demise, it is less a monument than an anti-monument, parodying the conventions of memorialization.[1] Standing at a modest thirteen inches tall, it apes the form of an ancient cenotaph, trivializing it through miniaturization. Three birds lie strewn over the crosshead. At the bottom of the pile, a shrouded bird wields death's scythe. Another bird attempts to fend off death, clutching the torch of glory in its talons. Atop its wings lies the deceased canary, its belly turned unceremoniously toward the sky.

Clodion's work, in its lighthearted engagement with the tradition of sculptural commemoration, encapsulates the tensions and contradictions of French art in the second half of the eighteenth century. On the one hand, the era revived the Classical rhetoric of heroic eternalization, giving rise to the modern Pantheon, the cult of "great men," and the triumphant erection of statues dedicated to the era's intellectual achievements.[2] Monumental sculptures provided a material corollary to the Enlightenment's philosophical devotion to posterity, serving as objects of worship for a secular age.[3] On the other hand, these initiatives emerged against the backdrop of a private market with a more playful sensibility and shorter temporal expectations. In contrast to the staid solidity of marble monuments commissioned by the state, private buyers increasingly gravitated to small-scale, delicate ceramics.[4]

Clodion built a career at the intersection of these competing tendencies. He spent nearly nine years training at the French Academy in Rome, developing a deep appreciation for the Classical tradition and the capacity of sculpture to communicate across time. And yet, after returning to France in 1771, he devoted himself to sculpture with a very different temporal register, producing sprightly works in the newly fashionable and

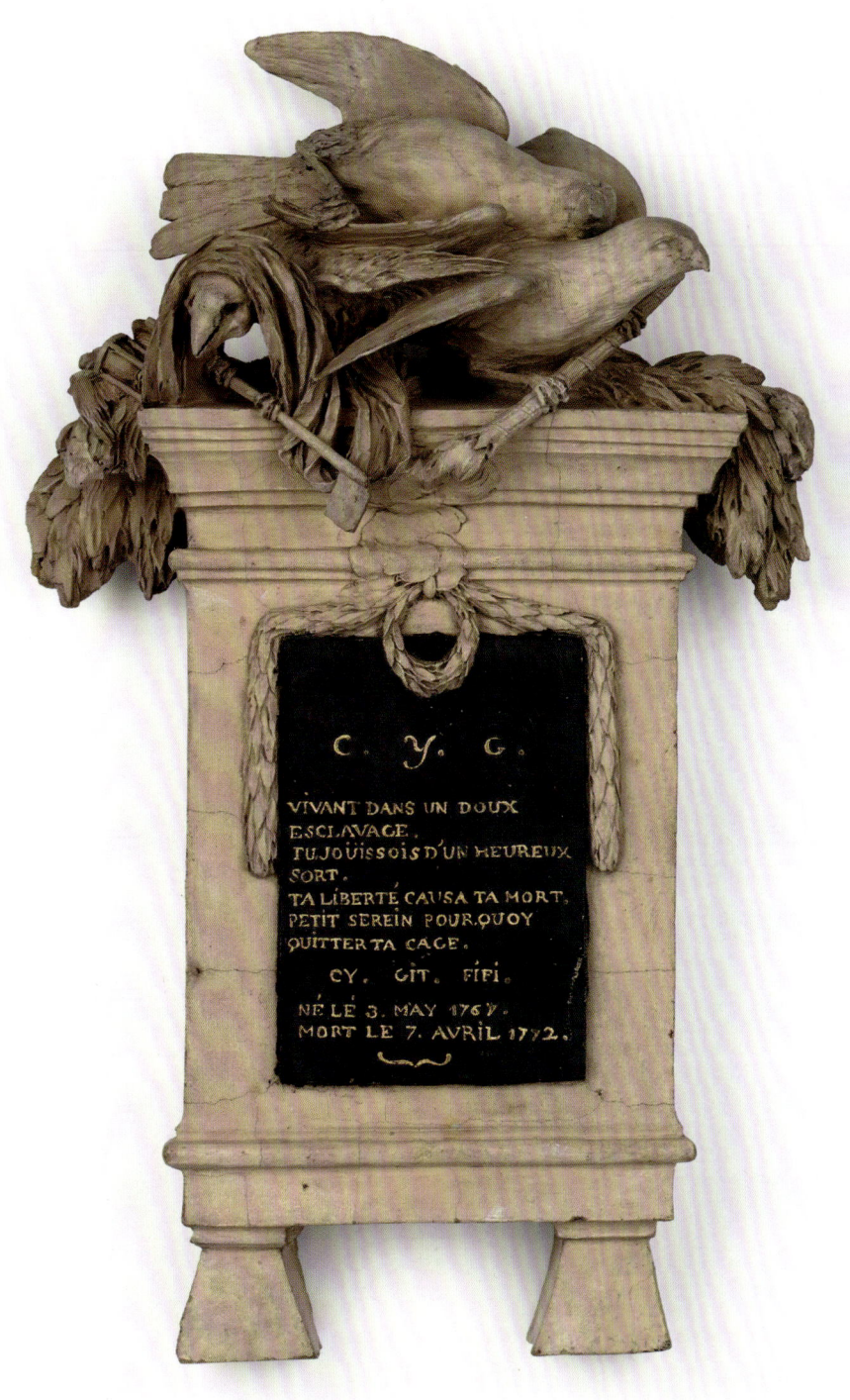

FIGS. 48 & 49 (*opposite*) Clodion (Claude Michel), *Mausoleum of Fifi*, ca. 1772. Terracotta, 32.5 × 20.5 × 9.4 cm. Musée des Beaux-Arts et d'Archéologie, Besançon. DB.994.1.1. Photo © Besançon, Musée des Beaux-Arts et d'Archéologie (P. Guenat).

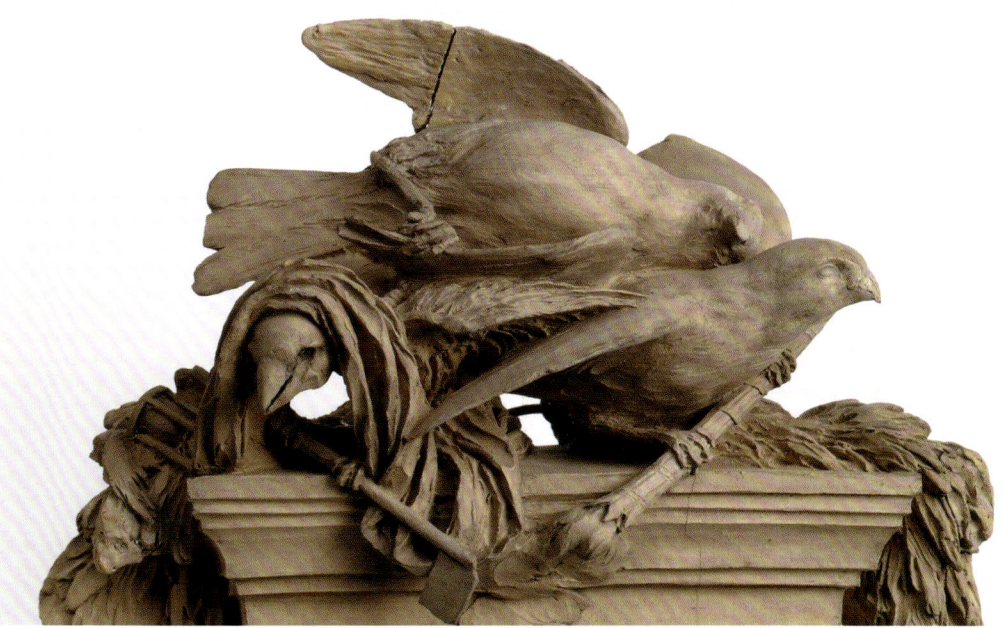

famously fragile medium of terracotta. Clodion's monument to Fifi makes the medium's vulnerability clear. Only a truncated stub remains of death's scythe, and, until a recent restoration, a pronounced crack cut across the deceased bird's wing (fig. 49). Restorers have used colored wax to replace other parts of the sculpture that broke off at various points, including the tips of several wings and the entirety of Fifi's head.[5]

Such objects, despite their fragility, proved lucrative. During the 1770s and 1780s, the market for delicate, small-scale sculpture thrived, while opportunities for monumental works in marble or bronze were comparatively limited.[6] As the state became increasingly mired in debt from costly wars to defend its overseas colonies, royal purse strings tightened.[7] Sculpture of more modest dimensions provided artists with an alternative source of income, attracting financiers and speculators who collected art in growing numbers.[8] These collectors enjoyed ready access to financial capital at a time when credit markets expanded, real estate speculation soared, and the volatile Paris stock exchange generated new fortunes.[9] Art itself became a vehicle for such "chimerical speculation," as the dealer François Charles Joullain described it in 1786. Joullain explained how the art market was now dominated by those who, "not having a particular taste for anything, are attracted to everything with a spirit of speculation, buying and selling in order to buy and sell."[10]

We might be inclined to see this exuberant, cash-flush market for terracotta sculpture as the final flourish of the Rococo, a brief revival of the same sensibility that had given rise to Watteau at the beginning of the century. Art historians have tended to make sense of Clodion in these terms, describing his work as "a last grace note of *douceur de vivre*" before the Revolution dealt these ephemeral pleasures a fatal blow.[11] But the demand for terracotta sculpture in the second half of the eighteenth century arose from something more complex than a momentary resurgence of ephemeral consumption and frivolity. Collectors of the period remained sensitive to the anti-luxury discourse that dominated the public sphere, and artists such as Clodion understood that they needed to guard themselves against charges of commercial decadence.[12] Terracotta sculptures met these requirements. Their breathtakingly sensuous and fragile forms satisfied impulses that had guided collectors since Watteau's time, while the terrestrial simplicity of their buff and russet surfaces could be plausibly presented as an antidote to Rococo artifice.

Clodion, as we will see, was exceptionally adept at striking this balance, producing works whose earthen candor provided cover for their embrace of commercial ephemerality. But Clodion did not simply mask his participation in the production of fragile commodities. He also transmuted it, linking the temporal instability of the marketplace to the capriciousness of artistic inspiration. The resulting objects came with no claims of immortality, tending instead to poke fun at such grandiose pretensions. And yet, in reconciling the supposedly degraded short-sightedness of the market with the purportedly transcendent spontaneity of the artist, Clodion established what would become, paradoxically, one of the era's most lasting legacies. Clodion's fragile sculptures, when understood as embodiments of artistic genius in the age of consumer capitalism, were not the dying breaths of the *ancien régime* but the birth of something new.

A Happy Medium

How did a medium as fragile as terracotta attract widespread admiration during a period when the culture of ephemeral consumption faced heightened suspicion? One possible explanation is that the private art market was not subject to the same critical scrutiny as public exhibitions or state-sponsored commissions, permitting greater indulgence of transient pleasure. Clodion, like his contemporary Fragonard, largely turned his back on the Salon exhibitions organized by the Academy, and he could therefore avoid the most hostile attacks of anti-Rococo critics.[13] But the popularity of terracotta, which found abundant support within the confines of the Academy, cannot simply be reduced to a distinction between the public virtue of the royal arts administration and the private vice of the art market. What made terracotta special was the fact that its unusual technical properties could offer something to please each of these audiences.

The medium itself was an ancient one, consisting simply of clay that has been fired in a kiln.[14] Its name, derived from Italian, provides an even more succinct definition: cooked earth. Iron oxide in the clay gives terracotta its distinctive colors, which range from grayish tan to reddish brown depending on the atmosphere and temperature in the kiln during firing (the whiteness of porcelain, by contrast, derives from its low iron oxide content).[15] Sculptors throughout the early modern period used terracotta both for finished sculptures, which were frequently painted, and for preparatory models. The difference between a study and a finished work could sometimes be unclear, such as when Bernini produced loosely modeled sketches that collectors prized as autonomous productions.[16] By the middle of the eighteenth century, collectors commonly expressed greater admiration for the improvisatory appearance of such terracottas than for fully realized large-scale statues in marble or bronze.[17] "These models," explained the amateur La Live de Jully, "often have advantages over marbles because one better finds in them the fire and true talent of the artist."[18]

The "fire" of inspiration became central to the mythology of terracotta, and not simply because it evoked the heat of the ceramics kiln.[19] Flames linked terracotta to a Promethean rhetoric of masculine creation.[20] The masculinization of artistic inspiration through the language of fire was common in writing from the late eighteenth century, but it was especially important for a medium such as terracotta, whose notorious fragility might easily conjure the supposedly feminine domain of ephemeral consumption.[21]

The medium's fragility was not a hypothetical matter. While fired clay is more durable than unfired *terre crue*, it is nonetheless much more vulnerable to breakage than carved stone or bronze. Problems can begin even before the work enters the kiln. The modeling of terracotta requires exacting techniques to prevent cracking while drying (fig. 50).[22] Sculptors must carefully calibrate clay thickness, the hollowing of larger masses, joining methods, and the regulation of drying through strategic use of damp cloths.[23] Armatures can provide structural support for clay while an artist works, but they can also cause cracks because they do not shrink with the terracotta as it dries.[24] After firing, even the most carefully constructed terracotta objects remain vulnerable to clumsy handling and accidental collisions. As a result, the objects that we see on display in museums today are sometimes a combination of their original material and modern interventions—torsos of eighteenth-century clay adorned with modern appendages.[25]

Eighteenth-century artists and collectors were well aware of terracotta's fragility. Clodion acquired a firsthand appreciation for the perils of his medium early in his career. He spent nine days restoring a number of terracotta and plaster sculptures by his uncle, Lambert-Sigisbert Adam, after the sculptor died in 1759.[26] Throughout his career, Clodion was also charged with overseeing the repair of his own work when collectors

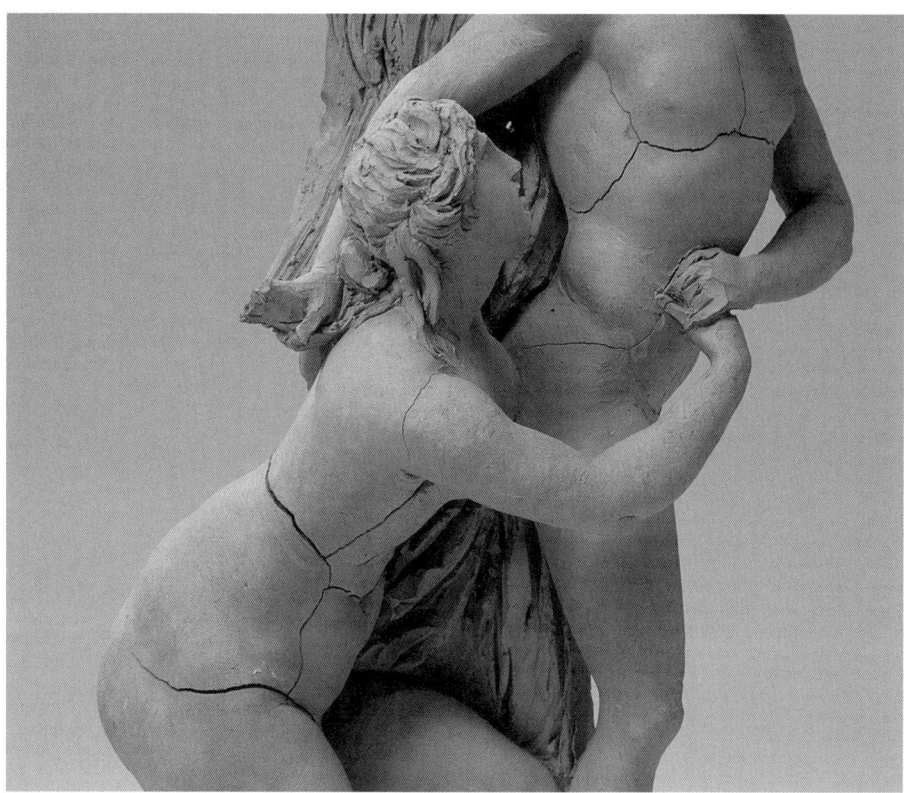

FIG. 50 Johan Tobias Sergel, *Amor and Psyche* (detail), ca. 1770–72. Terracotta, 28 × 16.7 × 15 cm. Nationalmuseum, Stockholm. NMSk 488. Photo: Nationalmuseum.

reported that it had sustained damage—a Clodion vase in a 1785 sale catalog, for example, specifies that it was "preciously repaired under the eyes of this artist."[27] Sale catalogs from the late eighteenth and early nineteenth centuries offer additional glimpses of how fragile Clodion's work could be. An 1809 entry for a terracotta group with four figures includes the vaguely inauspicious condition note: "A little mutilated."[28] To avoid such damage, collectors commonly placed Clodion's work under protective vitrines.[29] The glass was not only meant to shield the object from accidents but also to prevent it from accumulating dust, which would be difficult to remove without endangering the work.[30] The glass itself, of course, was fragile and sometimes broke, as sale catalogs testify.[31]

These risks were not enough to sully the medium's reputation, but terracotta's admirers still felt the need to address them. When Caylus outlined a program for reforming taste in sculpture in a lecture to the Academy in 1749, he argued that terracotta could be used as a means of influencing "rich people" who would be attracted to the medium's fragility: "We would gradually accustom them to terracottas; their fragility could

(90) A DELICATE MATTER

become a merit in their opinion."[32] Fragility, Caylus suggested, was a necessary sweetener to get tasteless *arrivistes* to improve their cultural diet. At a time when French consumers spent extravagantly on fragile porcelain objects imported from China, Caylus hypothesized that terracotta might provide French sculptors with a tool for catching their distracted eyes: "How do we know that some day good models would not take the place of grotesque porcelain figures [*magots*] and pagodas of China?"[33] The distinction that Caylus draws between terracotta and popular, imported porcelain makes clear the way xenophobia and elitism could shape the perception of fragile consumer goods.[34] Mariette similarly suggested that appreciation for terracotta was a measure of discernment and good taste, marking those "who deserve to carry the title of true connoisseur."[35] He conveniently framed the medium's fragility as a manifestation of the artist's genius, which was itself delicate: "Fine and enlightened eyes discover in [terracotta] all the spirit of the master, that creative spirit, that sparkling and entirely divine fire that emanates from the soul, and that an instant of reflection is so ready to extinguish and make disappear."[36]

Terracotta's virtues, then, were not always so different from the qualities that defined the supposedly debased and disposable products of consumer society. Much of the medium's appeal resided in the fact that it provided a vehicle for themes and forms that might otherwise be politically inconvenient. Clodion's many borrowings from Boucher, for example, show the degree to which terracotta could redeem subjects that were increasingly perceived as decadent and artificial in the realm of painting. Among Clodion's earliest works is a terracotta vase (fig. 51) that closely corresponds to one that Boucher depicted in a drawing (fig. 52) and several paintings.[37] The two artists were mutual admirers. Boucher acquired the vase along with at least one other work by Clodion.[38] Clodion, in turn, would come to own at least three paintings by Boucher, and he would borrow motifs from the artist's work for much of his career.[39]

It might seem surprising that Clodion would continue to take Boucher as a model long after the painter's reputation—and the market value of his work—suffered from charges of superficiality and commercial excess, but terracotta had a way of mollifying the most acerbic anti-Rococo critics.[40] Boucher's chief antagonists, in fact, were among the medium's greatest boosters. La Font, for example, admired terracottas "where the clay is handled with great *esprit*," observing that the material conveys an artist's "fire and genius."[41] For Diderot, the appeal of terracotta similarly lay in the direct access that it provided to a moment of inspired creation.[42] "The artist throws his fire into the clay," he wrote in his *Salon de 1765*.[43] Like the sketch for a painting, terracotta allowed the viewer to glimpse artistic ideation in its purest form. Marble statues, because they simply imitated the clay sketch, left Diderot cold. "Marble, as we know, is only a copy of terracotta," he repeatedly reminded his readers.[44]

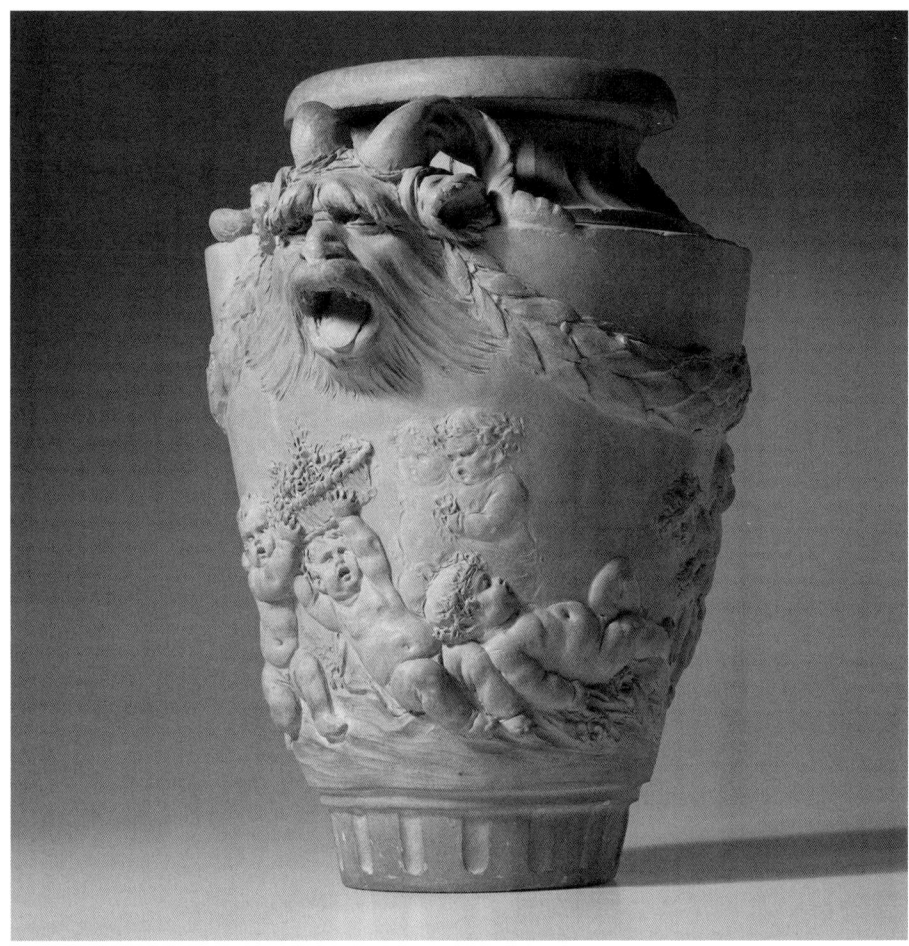

The description of marble as a copy and terracotta as the original work became axiomatic in theoretical writing on sculpture in the second half of the eighteenth century, and it is consistent with the period's growing preoccupation with the autographic traces of the artist's hand.[45] But the appeal of terracotta's sketch-like originality went deeper, assuaging anxieties about the increasingly mediated nature of art in a commercial age. For critics such as Diderot and La Font, the dangers of commerce lay in its dizzying array of copies and imitations that unmoored representation from reality, destabilizing social order through a profusion of simulacra.[46] They condemned Boucher as a purveyor of artificial surfaces and ersatz reproductions, which turned art into a vehicle of subterfuge.[47] Terracotta, by contrast, appealed to them as a medium that had nothing to hide, privileging substance over surface, original over copy. The direct quality of unglazed clay allowed artists such as Clodion to draw heavily upon Boucher's imagery while escaping his critical misfortunes.

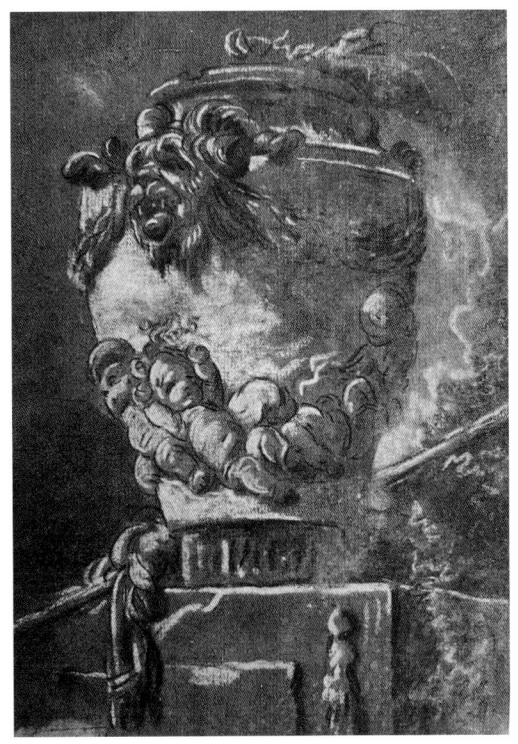

FIG. 51 (*opposite*) Clodion (Claude Michel), *Vase with Putti*, 1760s. Terracotta, 24 × 22 cm. Private collection. Photo © Christie's Images / Bridgeman Images.

FIG. 52 François Boucher, *Drawing of a Vase*. Chalk on paper, 26 × 18 cm. Untraced. From Guillaume Marie Étienne de Gontaut-Biron, *Collection de marquis de Biron* . . . (Paris, Imprimerie G. Petit, 1914).

It is worth emphasizing that Clodion's work was no less commercial than Boucher's. Clodion worked at the height of what Patrick Michel has described as the "speculative phase" in the French art market, when collectors bought and sold work at an unprecedented pace, often seeking to profit from their purchases.[48] Clodion's work was actively traded in this market, and the vase that he sculpted after Boucher's design is a case in point. An item closely matching the object's description appears in no fewer than ten different sale catalogs between 1771 and 1783.[49]

Some of these sale records may refer to copies of the original object—a reminder that terracotta was hardly as spontaneous or unmediated as its proponents claimed. The ductility that made clay responsive to the artist's touch also made it suitable for shaping in molds, opening opportunities for replication.[50] Artists of the period commonly sold clay reproductions of their work, and Clodion pushed the practice to an extreme.[51] At the same time, Clodion was sensitive to potential charges of producing nothing more than commercial copies, and he took care to invest each object with the semblance of originality. Consider, for example, a small sculpture depicting the goddess Erigone (fig. 53). Consider, too, a nearly identical version (fig. 54). Both objects were likely created in Clodion's studio in the early 1780s. Each loosely corresponds to a much larger plaster statue that Clodion produced for the comte d'Artois around this same time.[52] The

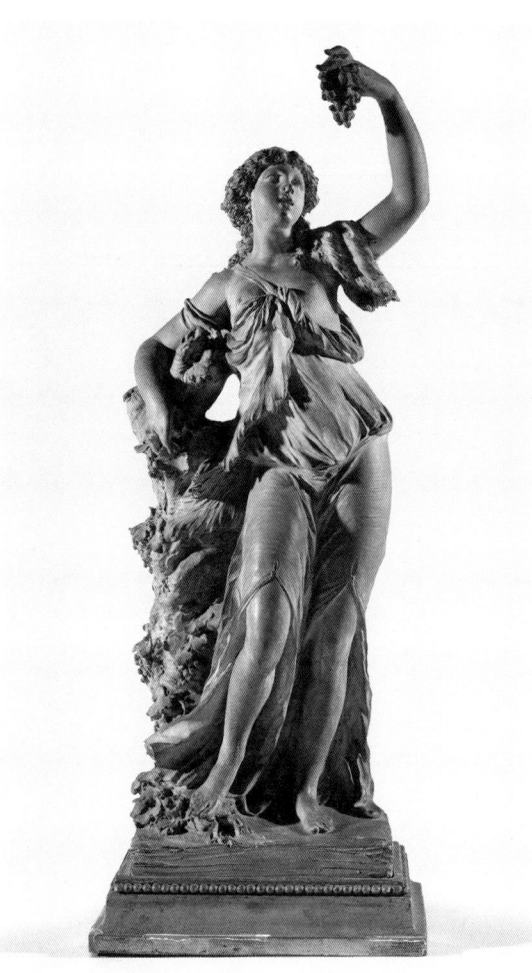 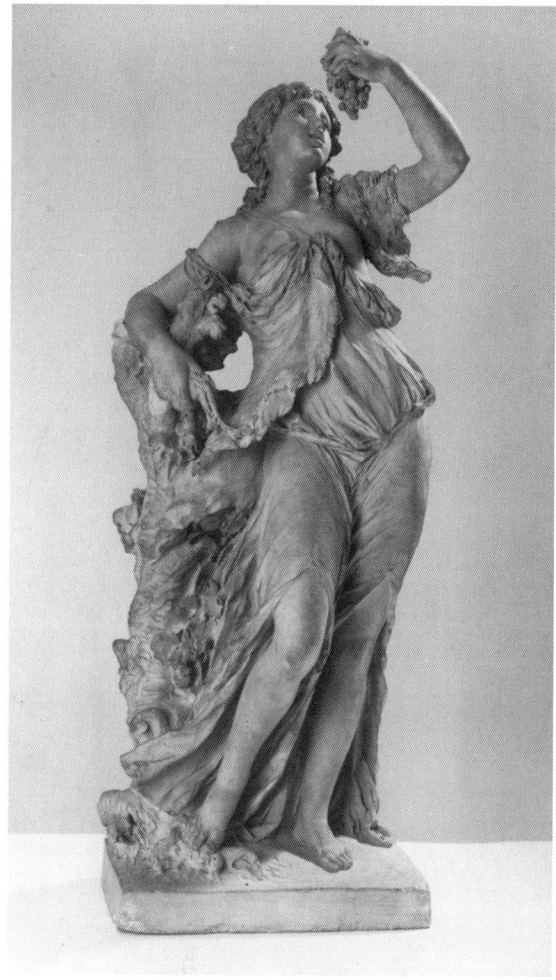

FIG. 53 Clodion (Claude Michel), *Erigone*, ca. 1783. Terracotta, 51 × 18 × 12 cm. Private collection. Photo courtesy of Sotheby's.

FIG. 54 Clodion (Claude Michel), *Erigone*, ca. 1783. Terracotta, 52.5 × 18 × 12.5 cm. Nationalmuseum, Stockholm. NMSk 1676. Photo: Nationalmuseum.

terracottas might, on first inspection, appear to be preparatory studies for the plaster version. Perhaps Clodion used the clay models to draft his work on a smaller scale, relying on terracotta's malleability to produce spirited sketches. Closer examination, however, reveals that they served a different purpose. In each object, the figure holds the same pose, suggesting that Clodion was not using them to work out ideas but was reproducing an already finished design. The statuettes are identical in size, and elements of them may have been made from the same molds. Any trace of mechanical reproduction has been carefully hidden, however, by details that give each object a unique

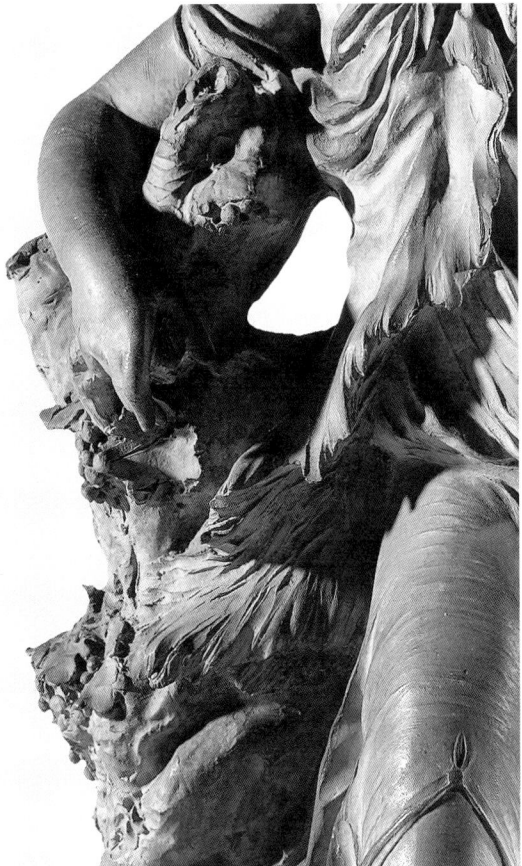 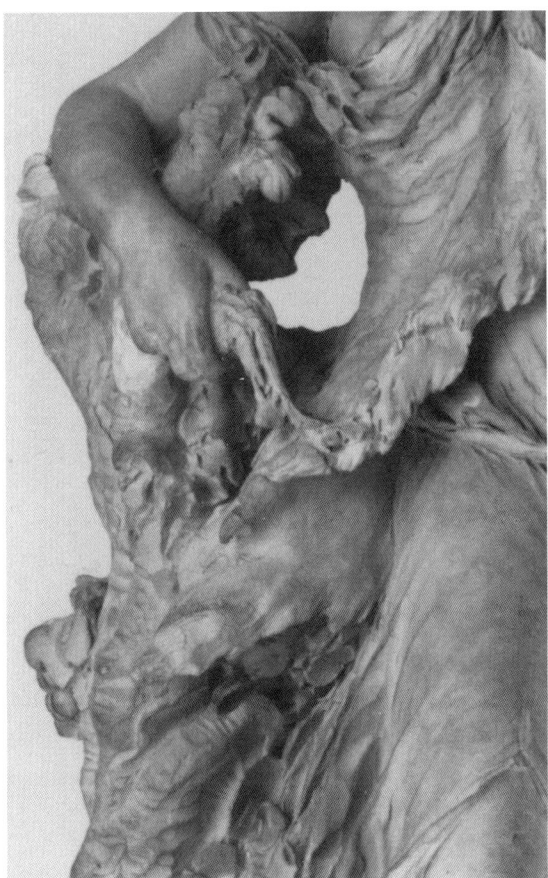

FIG. 55 Clodion (Claude Michel), details of *Erigone* (figs. 53 and 54). Left: private collection, courtesy of Sotheby's. Right: Nationalmuseum, Stockholm.

character. The folds of Erigone's tunic have a life of their own, each ripple having been reworked by hand. The animal skin that Erigone holds in her right hand provided further opportunities for improvisation with a sculptor's modeling tool, becoming a platform for energetic lines specific to each statue (fig. 55).[53]

This calculated extemporaneity typified the production system of Clodion's studio. Clodion oversaw a team of workers, which included his brothers and anonymous assistants, who all helped reproduce his work.[54] Clodion expanded the practice in 1781, when he set up shop close to the queen's porcelain factory, likely seeking to attract nearby workers with experience replicating ceramics.[55] We can infer some aspects of the production process within Clodion's studio from a posthumous inventory of his possessions, which describes numerous molds along with entire lots of limbs and torsos.[56] Clodion and his assistants likely assembled such body parts into complete sculptures, creating new works from molded pieces of previous ones. The practice would become known in the early nineteenth century as "marcottage," a term borrowed from botany where it referred to the propagation of plants through clippings that sprout new roots.[57] After Clodion's team pieced together body parts into full figures, specialists in accessories such as fruit and vegetation would typically add any necessary details. Before firing, the surface of the model would be reworked by hand to create the impression of the artist's animated gesture, and Clodion would add his signature.[58]

Sculptors, of course, had long distributed labor among assistants and apprentices, but Clodion's methods responded to a novel problem that artists confronted in the eighteenth century: on the one hand, collectors and amateurs increasingly fetishized the unique character of the artist's touch; on the other hand, artists needed to market their work efficiently to a widening group of consumers. Clodion successfully reconciled these competing interests, producing work through partially mechanical methods while still earning praise for the inimitable qualities of his hand. Critics and collectors regularly remarked upon the distinctive impression that Clodion left on his clay. An anonymous Salon critic in 1773 set the tone, admiring Clodion's work for "a lightness of touch [*une légèreté d'outil*] that leaves nothing to be desired."[59] Mariette similarly commended Clodion for the "suppleness" with which he sculpted.[60] The publisher and printmaker Pierre-François Basan extolled Clodion for his "touch full of fire and spirit," while the dealer Jean-Baptiste-Pierre Lebrun praised Clodion for his "spiritual and easy touch."[61]

This sense of the artist's ineffable imprint helped enhance a sculpture's value—autographic works commanded a significantly higher price than copies—but it also served to protect the object from the perception that it was nothing more than a disposable commodity.[62] The key point was for the delicacy of the object to evoke the ethereal soul of the artist without conjuring the insubstantiality of a consumer society entranced by ephemeral luxuries. If the balancing act was executed successfully, the extraordinary number of objects that emerged from Clodion's studio would appear not as products of commercial reproduction but as evidence of the artist's prolific imagination. "His fecund genius," his friend Antoine Dingé asserted, "multiplied pleasing subjects, without repeating itself, nor copying itself."[63] Fawning and misleading as this language was, it nonetheless pointed to a real effect of Clodion's work. By integrating the methods of commercial production with the signs of artistic originality, Clodion could turn fragile ceramics into emblems of a fertile mind.

Fertility, Propagation, and the Aesthetics of Earth

The perceived fertility of Clodion's imagination was not simply a product of his techniques. It was also a function of the relation between his techniques and his subject matter. Boucher had offered him a useful precedent—as Katie Scott has argued, the painter's endless depiction of putti allegorized the process of artistic invention while perhaps also providing a winking acknowledgment of the reproductive processes that had allowed him to disseminate his work.[64] The many babies who populate Clodion's sculptures suggest that he also appreciated the tradition of deploying putti as emblems of creation.[65] But Clodion's iconography of fertility differed from Boucher's in ways that reflected the changed cultural climate in which he operated. Here, too, sexual fecundity, bound as it was to women's bodies, took on a vexed status as critics condemned what they regarded as the ephemeral products of an overly effeminate consumer society.[66] Clodion understood the dilemma, and he also recognized alternative metaphors to evoke his fertile imagination. At a time when critics of luxury consumption were elevating agriculture as a remedy for a society sick on commerce, agrarian fertility presented itself as an especially viable option.[67] And for a sculptor whose earthen objects appeared to grow from the richness of the soil, the analogy would prove all the more fitting.

At first glance, Clodion's choice of subject matter would appear to represent little more than an extravagant exploration of sensual pleasure. He showed a particular proclivity for followers of Bacchus, depicting bacchantes and satyrs carrying bundles of grapes, pouring wine, dancing, and playing music (fig. 56). These subjects appear continually in sale listings for Clodion's work from the mid-1770s through the beginning of the nineteenth century.[68] By a significant margin, they constitute Clodion's most prevalent subject in sale records from this period, which contain references to over fifty unique examples.[69] In producing these works, Clodion tapped into a broader enthusiasm for Bacchic subjects among French collectors during the 1770s and 1780s. Poussin's *A Bacchanalian Revel Before a Term* (fig. 57), for example, sold for the astonishingly high price of 15,000 livres in 1777—more than fifteen times the amount that Poussin's paintings typically garnered during this period.[70] These sale records underscore the disconnect that existed between the rhetoric of the Academy and the tendencies of the marketplace. At a time when the Academy sought to elevate Poussin as a paragon of gravity and austerity, private collectors reserved their highest admiration for his most libertine subjects.[71]

We might take this market for Bacchic imagery as evidence that the inebriated and present-minded spirit of the *mondain* remained alive and well almost a half-century after Voltaire wrote his ode to the transient pleasures of worldly existence. Bacchic figures, though, were not solely emblems of hedonism, and Clodion's embrace of these subjects spoke to more complicated demands than the debauched inclinations of the private market. While Bacchus exemplified drunken revelry for many viewers throughout much of the early modern period, antiquarians had granted him deeper significance, paying particular attention to his association with fertility in pagan tradition.[72] Poussin, in fact, was likely already attentive to these subtleties in the seventeenth century,

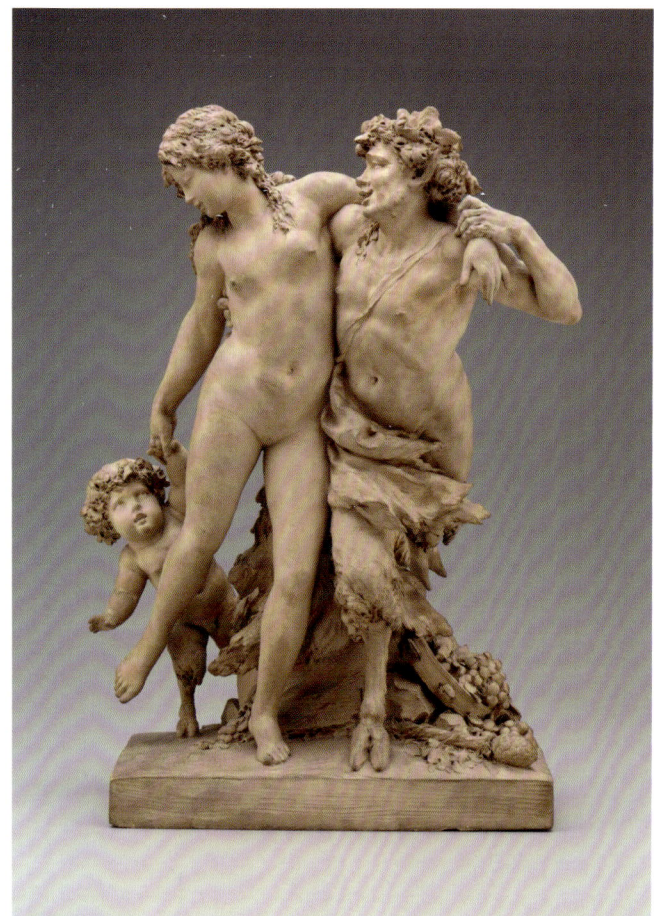

FIG. 56
Clodion (Claude Michel), *Bacchante and Satyr with Young Satyr*, ca. 1775–80. Terracotta, 47.6 × 30.5 × 22.2 cm. Detroit Institute of Arts, Detroit. 71.173. Photo © Detroit Institute of Arts, USA / Bequest of Mrs. Horace E. Dodge in memory of her husband / Bridgeman Images.

infusing his bacchanalia with references to the sun cults of antiquity.[73] Such antiquarian considerations surely still resonated for Clodion's more erudite viewers, steeped as they were in the period's abundant literature on ancient iconography.[74] But by Clodion's time, awareness of pagan fertility rituals extended beyond antiquarian circles. The key disseminators of this knowledge were advocates of economic reform, who argued that France's declining fortunes stemmed from its failure to recognize that agriculture constituted the foundation of thriving civilizations.[75] These *économistes*—or Physiocrats, as they came to be known—routinely cited pagan fertility gods as evidence that the great societies of antiquity revolved around their religious devotion to agriculture.[76] In his foundational Physiocratic essay *L'ami des hommes* (1756), the marquis de Mirabeau explained: "The first men were all farmers, shepherds, etc. They scarcely deified anyone but those who had taught the use of nature's gifts, Ceres, Bacchus, Triptolemus."[77] Mirabeau lamented that the sculptors of his time failed to honor such

(98)   A DELICATE MATTER

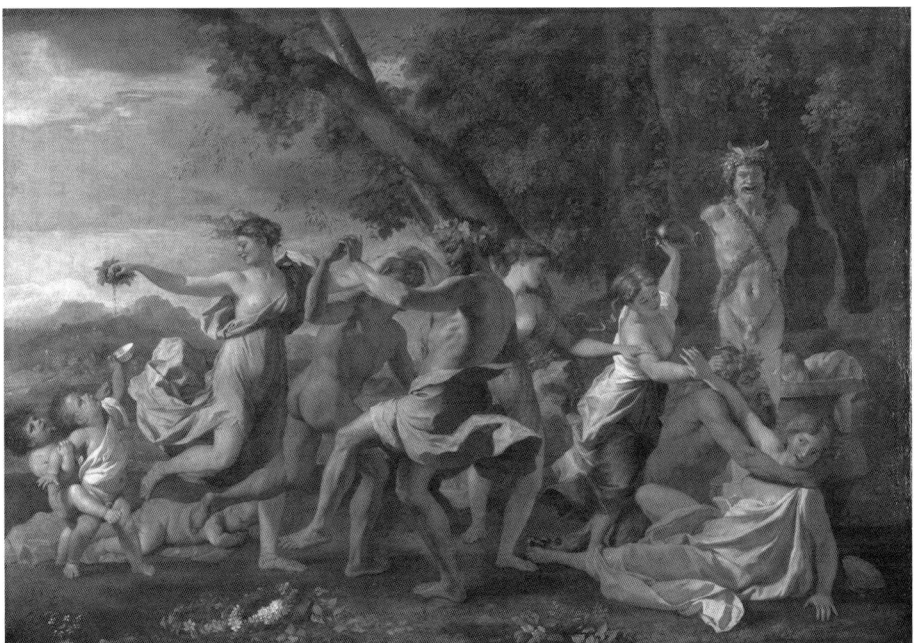

FIG. 57 Nicolas Poussin, *A Bacchanalian Revel Before a Term*, 1632–33. Oil on canvas, 98 × 142.8 cm. National Gallery, London. NG 62. Photo © National Gallery, London / Art Resource, NY.

figures, and he proposed that statues should be created depicting "the philosopher of our time who dedicates his leisure and his studies to the perfection of agriculture." At the corners of such a statue, Mirabeau would place figures representing "the era's most famous laborer, gardener, shepherd, and winegrower."[78]

In the decades that followed, other writers would elaborate on these themes, often presenting Bacchic iconography as a sign of devotion to agricultural abundance. The most extensive treatment of Bacchic tradition during this period is found in the work of the Physiocratic writer and linguist Antoine Court de Gébelin, who devoted a thirty-page essay to the story of Bacchus in his monumental study of ancient language and culture, *Le monde primitif*.[79] Building on the Physiocratic assumption that agronomy was the guiding principle of early civilization, Court de Gébelin sought to prove definitively that Bacchus originally "was not envisaged simply as the god of the vine" but instead was "an illustrious personage" who represented "the powers of the sun relative to the artificial productions of the earth, flour and wine."[80] Clodion likely knew Court de Gébelin personally; both were members of the masonic lodge known as the Amis Réunis, as were several of Clodion's patrons.[81] Not all of these men shared Court de Gébelin's Physiocratic leanings, and it would be simplistic to see Clodion's work as an illustration of Physiocratic precepts (he certainly never produced anything as

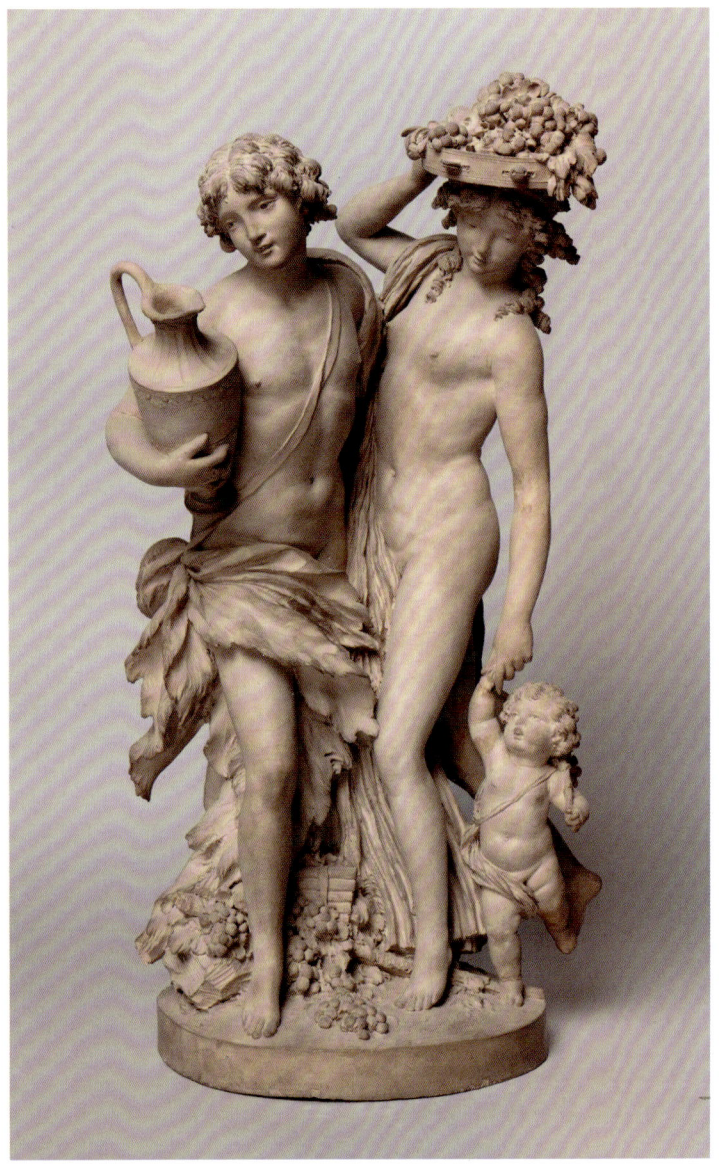

FIG. 58
Clodion (Claude Michel), *Votaries of Bacchus*, early 1780s. Terracotta, 51 × 28 × 26 cm. Waddesdon Manor (National Trust), Aylesbury. Bequest of James de Rothschild, 1957. Acc. no. 2457. Photo: Waddesdon Image Library.

FIG. 59
Clodion (Claude Michel), *Votaries of Bacchus* (detail), early 1780s. Terracotta, 51 × 28 × 26 cm. Waddesdon Manor (National Trust), Aylesbury. Bequest of James de Rothschild, 1957. Acc. no. 2457. Photo: Waddesdon Image Library.

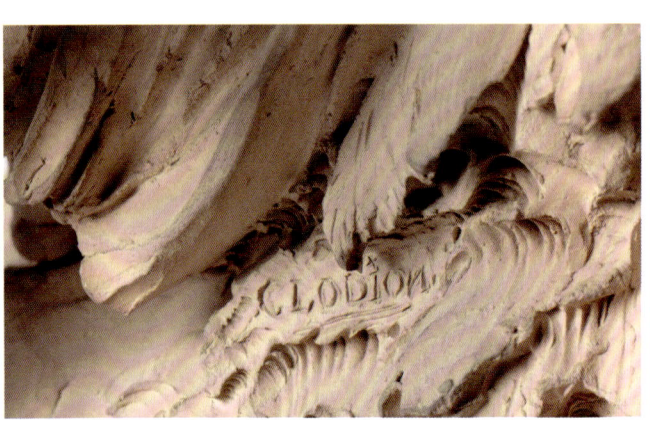

didactic as Mirabeau's imagined monument to agriculture). But the agronomic rhetoric that dominated the discourse on commerce in the second half of the eighteenth century provided a way for artists such as Clodion to cast Bacchic pleasure in a more dignified light, presenting sensual indulgence through the prism of agrarian virtue.

Take, for example, a typical terracotta by Clodion depicting followers of Bacchus (fig. 58). By 1780, Clodion was producing many objects like these, making slight variations to bestow upon each work the semblance of originality.[82] In this example, a young man and woman stroll together, his arm around her back. On her head, the woman steadies a tambourine overflowing with grapes—a traditional attribute of bacchantes—while the man carries an ewer under his arm. The putto at their side holds a thyrsus, a sacred staff used in rituals honoring Bacchus. The Bacchic status of the figures is unmistakable, but the work hardly represents drunken depravity. The woman looks upon the putto with maternal affection, and the entire scene could be interpreted as a celebration of domestic unity. The young man's ewer presumably contains wine, but Clodion gives no hint that the figures are intoxicated, instead emphasizing their bountiful harvest of fruit. A pile of grapes appears at the couple's feet, along with the flute of Pan, god of shepherds. These signs of agricultural devotion emerge from the earthen matter of the statue's base. Clodion leaves some of his marks visible in rendering these details, burying his signature in a thicket of vegetation and non-signifying traces (fig. 59), as if the work were the product of both fertile soil and the artist's equally bountiful imagination.

The original buyer of this sculpture remains unknown, but sale records for comparable works give a sense of the audience to whom such objects appealed. Owners of Clodion's Bacchic subjects included financiers such as Jean-François Le Roy de Senneville, as well as members of old aristocratic families such as Marie-Joseph-Louis d'Albert d'Ailly, duc de Chaulnes.[83] These worldly Parisians might seem unlikely adherents to the cause of rural agronomy, but as John Shovlin has argued, the patriotic turn to the land provided members of the urban elite with a form of "image management in a cultural climate increasingly hostile to plutocracy."[84] The Physiocrats themselves made this alliance possible, arguing that their principles were not incompatible with commerce or even the sale of luxury goods.[85] Agricultural production, they maintained, depended on commercial exchange, allowing a society to move beyond subsistence farming and to transmit the wealth of the land throughout a nation.[86] It was in this spirit that Diderot would write in his *Salon de 1767* that "painters, poets, sculptors, musicians, and the crowd of adjacent arts are born from the earth."[87] By the 1770s, writers on commercial affairs increasingly distinguished between harmless luxuries that stemmed from the free flow of goods in an agricultural society and destructive luxuries that came from nothing more than privilege and abuse of power.[88] The problem with commercial society, they argued, was not that it involved trade or consumption but that it detached money from reality, creating a system of free-floating signs that could be manipulated

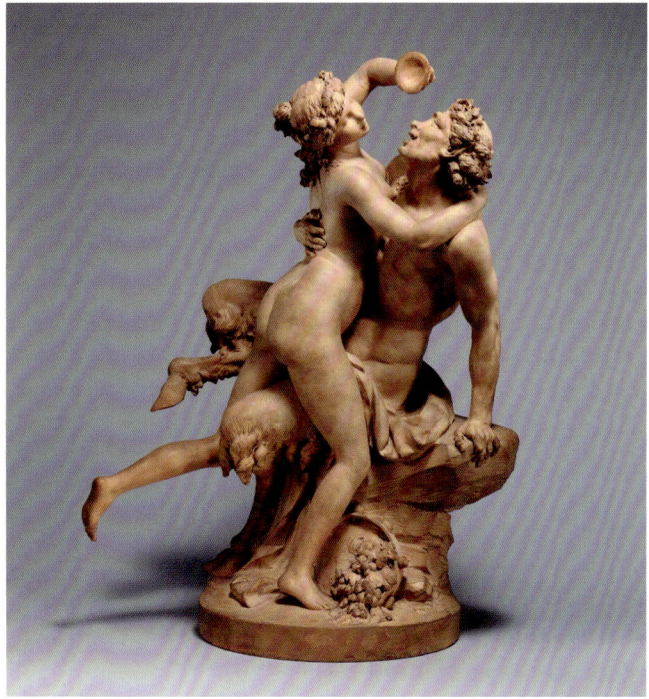

FIG. 60
Clodion (Claude Michel), *The Intoxication of Wine*, ca. 1780–90. Terracotta, 58 × 43 × 29 cm. Metropolitan Museum of Art, New York. Bequest of Benjamin Altman, 1913. 14.40.687.

for personal gain.[89] By rooting the marketplace in the *terra firma* of agriculture, agronomic reformers sought to rid commerce of its association with unstable and arbitrary value.

In pointing out the connection between Bacchic iconography and Physiocratic rhetoric, I do not mean to minimize the sybaritic aspects of Clodion's work. At times, his sculptures could be explicitly lubricious. *The Intoxication of Wine*, for example, presents a young woman straddling the leg of a satyr, pouring wine into his open mouth (fig. 60). A market clearly still existed for such unapologetic displays of sensual excess long after anti-Rococo critics had condemned them as decadent expressions of wasteful consumption. Where Clodion truly excelled, though, was in sublimating this intemperate sensibility into a more innocuous guise, creating sculptures that could function as paeans to the fecundity of earth without depriving collectors of the pleasures that had long guided their consumption habits. Bacchic subjects, far from simply being allegories of overconsumption, could simultaneously function as emblems of commitment to the virtuous commerce of the earth.

Ancient fertility cults offered a socially acceptable way of exploring many of the same ephemeral delights that had charmed Voltaire's *mondain* a generation before, but without the liability that came from patently artificial luxury. Where the *mondain* lived among glittering surfaces and delighted in novel luxuries such as champagne, his earthly successor could find refuge in the organic products of the soil and vine. What this new generation of consumers required, then, was plausible deniability for their participation in a culture of ephemeral consumption. Clodion's work provided it, allowing his patrons to have their wine and drink it, too.

Monumental Fragility

Clodion's abundant work for private patrons makes clear that sculpture in the final decades of the *ancien régime* did not solely consist of civic-minded monuments dedicated to posterity. A thriving commercial sphere provided sculptors with projects whose sensibility and temporal horizons differed markedly from those of the statues commissioned by the state. For the most part, these two different systems of sculptural production could coexist alongside each other. Clodion and his many imitators could happily cater to private buyers while sculptors seeking institutional recognition could search for commissions on a larger scale. Yet Clodion himself did not entirely shy away from opportunities to produce monumental sculpture. His most staggering work in terracotta, in fact, is the product of these efforts: a nearly four-foot-tall model for a royal monument to balloon flight (fig. 61). The monument itself was never built, and it is easy to imagine why—Clodion's swirling composition, teeming with putti, is a far cry from the Neoclassical austerity that defined state-sponsored monuments during this time. More puzzling is why Clodion would have bothered to submit such a proposal for consideration at all, given the improbability of its success. The question is worth considering in detail because it speaks to a fundamental aspect of both Clodion's work and the cultural climate in which he operated. At a time when the royal arts administration sought to promote a conception of sculpture as a staid art that immortalized virtuous men, Clodion put forward an alternative paradigm defined by the temporality of the marketplace. Though his approach would not receive official recognition, it would prove no less consequential, establishing a model of the artist as commercial showman that had an enduring afterlife.

It would be difficult to imagine a grander display of commercial spectacle than the balloon craze of the late eighteenth century. The dream of flight had long fascinated inventors, but it was not until 1783 that Joseph-Michel and Jacques-Étienne Montgolfier, affluent paper manufacturers from southern France, brought the fantasy to fruition.[90] The brothers unveiled their invention in their hometown of Annonay, where a small crowd of local dignitaries watched as an enormous globe made of paper and cloth swelled with hot air from a vigorous fire, then rose into the sky for a miraculous ten minutes. Word quickly traveled to Paris, where the Montgolfiers soon demonstrated their invention, and other inventors quickly developed competing versions, including

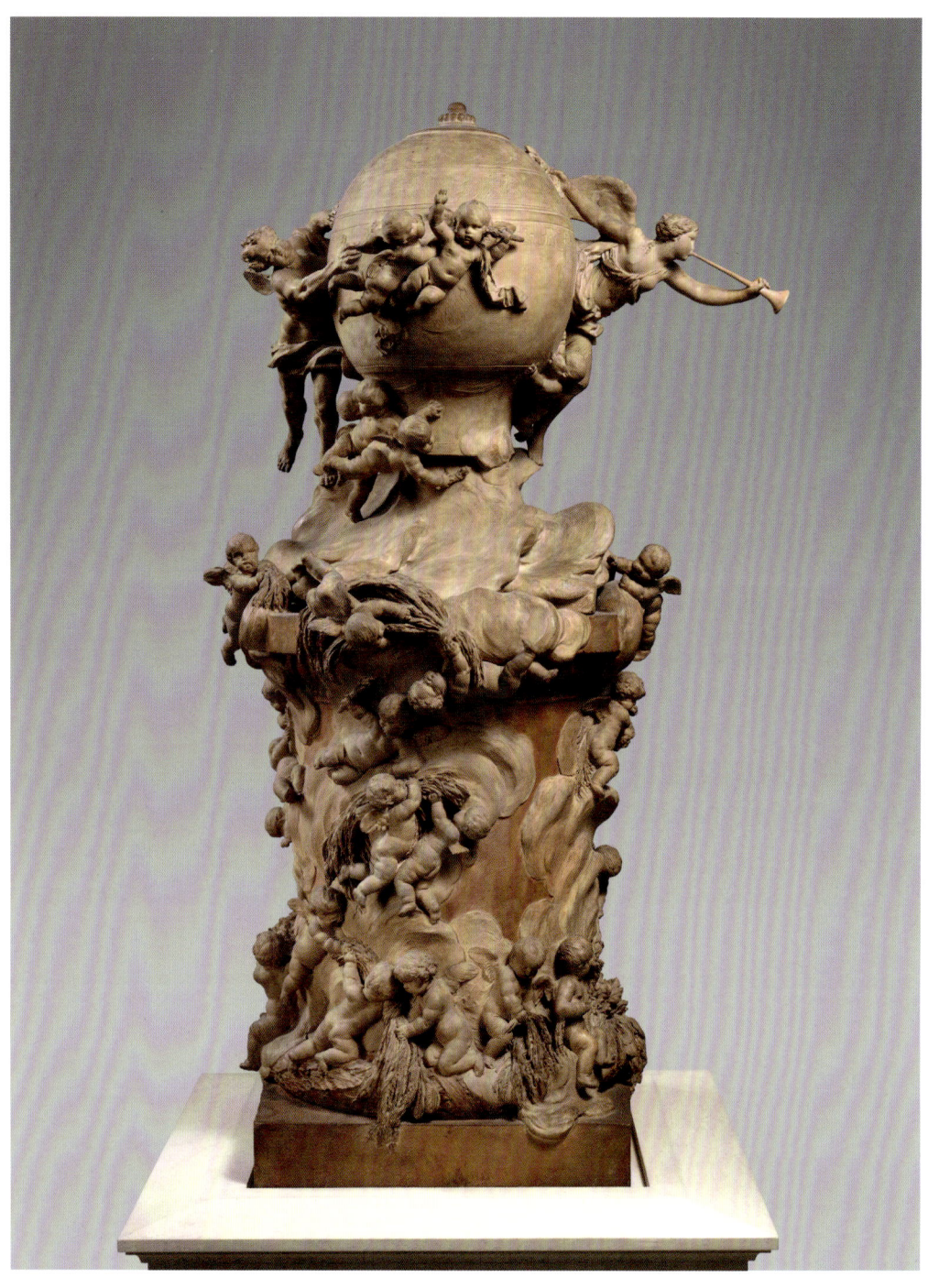

FIG. 61 Clodion (Claude Michel), *Model for a Proposed Monument to Commemorate the Invention of the Balloon*, ca. 1784. Terracotta, 110 × 63 × 52 cm. Metropolitan Museum of Art, New York. Purchase, Rogers Fund and Anonymous Gift, 1944. 44.21a, b. Image © The Metropolitan Museum of Art.

the first hydrogen balloon. By late November, the Montgolfiers succeed in launching the first human passengers aboard a balloon, which traveled to an altitude of 3,000 feet while drifting across most of Paris.[91]

The rapid development of the technology was a commercial achievement as much as it was a scientific one. While the balloonists received funds from the traditional channels of court patronage, they also pursued novel means of financing their projects, notably capitalizing on ticket sales for their demonstrations.[92] The balloons also presented marketing opportunities for paper manufacturers such as the Montgolfiers, who collaborated with the wallpaper designer Jean-Baptiste Réveillon to turn their "aerostatic machines" into lavishly decorated objects that implicitly served as advertisements for their paper products (fig. 62). As public fascination with ballooning swelled, so did opportunities for artists and merchants to profit from it: balloons soon appeared across the decorative arts, adorning snuffboxes, fabrics, tea sets, and fans (fig. 63).[93]

The royal arts administration, however, sought to present ballooning with greater gravity. At a moment when the crown needed to defend itself against charges of frivolous expenditure, it was essential for state sponsorship of balloonists to be perceived as a patriotic endeavor. Newspaper accounts, which were carefully managed by royal censors, consistently downplayed the entrepreneurial aspects of ballooning while presenting the Montgolfiers as selfless citizens devoted to the glory of the nation.[94] A competition for a royal monument commemorating the invention of balloon flight provided an ideal opportunity to reinforce this message, tethering the balloon to the weighty concept of posterity. The king's director general of royal buildings, the comte d'Angiviller, announced the initiative in a letter to the Academy in December 1783, describing the "aerostatic machine" as an invention that "will bring the greatest honor to this century and to the nation."[95] Emphasizing future honor over present interest, the king expressed his desire "to transmit to posterity the memory of this discovery."[96]

Clodion's decision to compete for the project is, in some respects, surprising. His relationship with the royal arts administration had long been a tenuous one. After winning the Academy's prestigious Prix de Rome, he never bothered to submit the reception piece necessary to become a full member of the Academy. His limited experience with royal patronage was also inauspicious. The one sculpture that the state had commissioned from him—a statue of Montesquieu for the series of royal monuments to great men—proved troublesome for everyone involved. Clodion fell behind on the project after prioritizing work for his private clients, resulting in a stern reprimand from the administration.[97] The plaster model that he produced for the statue—which is known only through a sketch by Gabriel de Saint-Aubin (fig. 64)—received widespread ridicule for its off-balance, animated pose, which struck critics as inappropriate for monumental sculpture.[98] The *Mémoires secrets* derided the work as overly commercial in its conception, comparing Montesquieu's demeanor to "that of a charlatan who

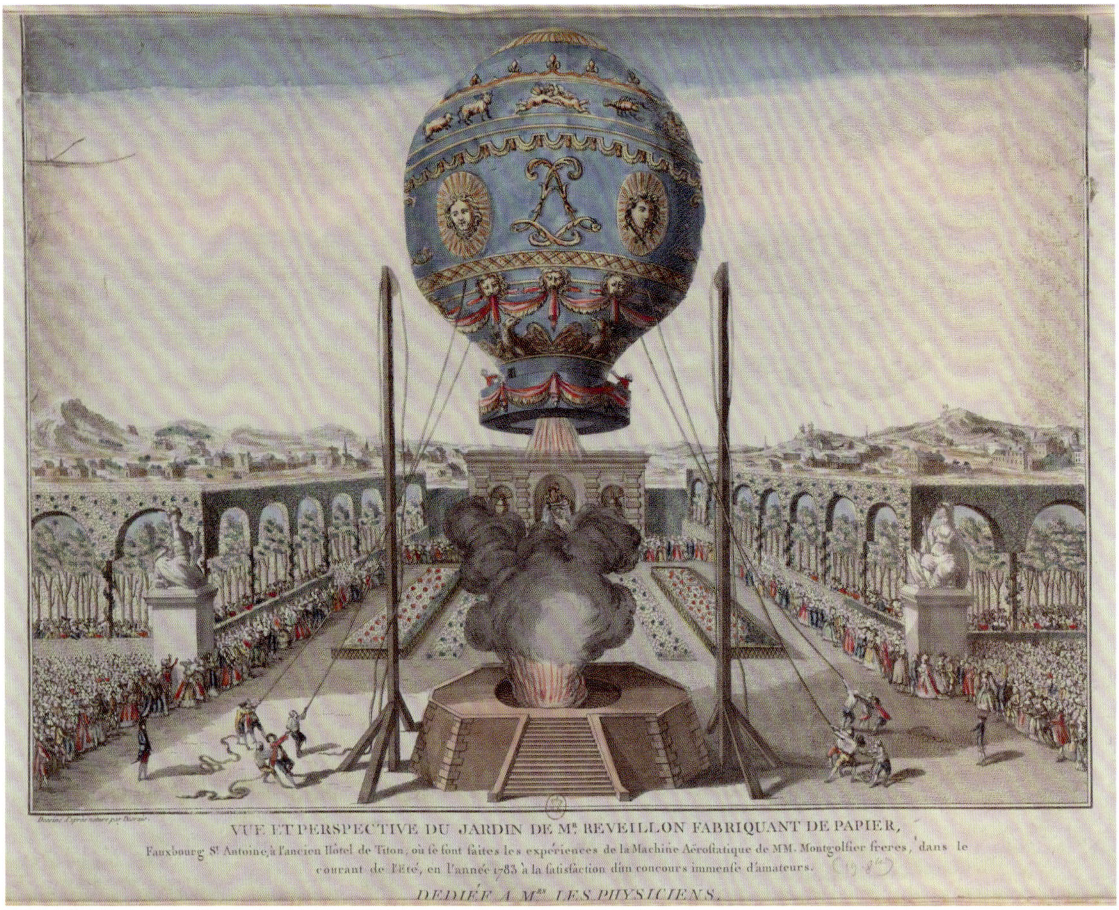

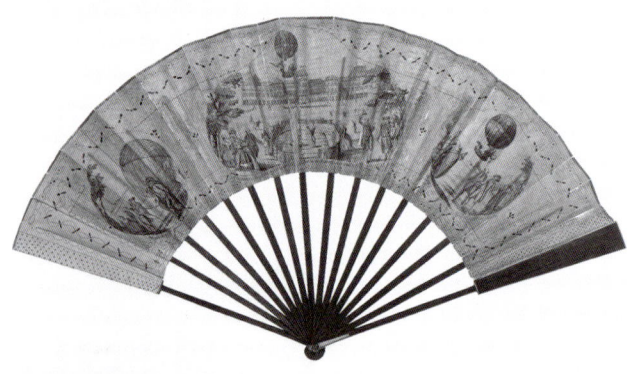

FIG. 62
Claude-Louis Desrais (print after), *Vue et perspective du jardin de Mr. Réveillon fabriquant de papiers, Fauxbourg St Antoine, à l'ancien Hôtel de Titon, où se sont faites les expériences de la Machine Aërostatique de M.M. Montgolfier frères, dans le courant de l'Eté, en l'anné 1783*, ca. 1783. Engraving, 34.9 × 46.7 cm. Bibliothèque nationale de France, département des Estampes et de la photographie, Paris. FOL-IB-1. Photo: gallica.bnf.fr / BnF.

FIG. 63
Anonymous, *Ascension of Charles and Robert at the Tuileries*, 1783. Fan (etching, rosewood, ivory), 27.6 × 12.5 cm. Musée Carnavalet, Paris. EV0998.

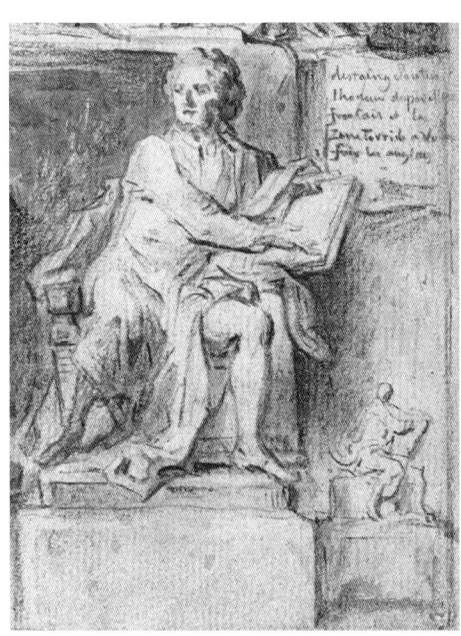

FIG. 64
Gabriel de Saint-Aubin, *Clodion's Montesquieu at the Salon of 1779*, 1779. Black chalk with watercolor. In *Philotanus, poëme, en forme de dialogue, ou l'histoire de la constitution unigenitus* (annotated manuscript), Royal Library, Stockholm. Reproduction: National Library of Sweden.

sells his quackery" and describing the sculpture's airy forms as those of a *colifichet*—a pejorative term for knick-knacks such as figurines, crystal vases, and other luxuries that were seen as evidence of bad taste.[99] Clodion capitulated to the critics for the final work (fig. 65), producing an uncharacteristically restrained statue in which Montesquieu sits in placid repose.

Given this track record, it is hard to imagine why Clodion would have shown interest in pursuing another commission from the crown. He had little need for more business at the time, which came at the height of commercial demand for his work. He also must have known that his chances of winning the competition were exceedingly low. He was not among the artists whom the administration invited to compete, and it would have been remarkable if the Academy passed over its full members for a sculptor who had never even submitted his reception piece.[100] Paradoxically, though, the unlikelihood that Clodion would win the competition may explain his eagerness to participate. Clodion could take the opportunity to produce an imaginary monument without fear of being dragged into the same difficulties that had consumed his Montesquieu commission. The target audience for the work, then, may not have been the Academy at all, but Clodion's private clients, who could see in the model the full range of his technical abilities.[101]

Clodion's treatment of the subject also suggests that he directed the work more to private clients than to the state. The official competition was meant to celebrate the invention of the "aerostatic machine" as a general category, allowing the arts

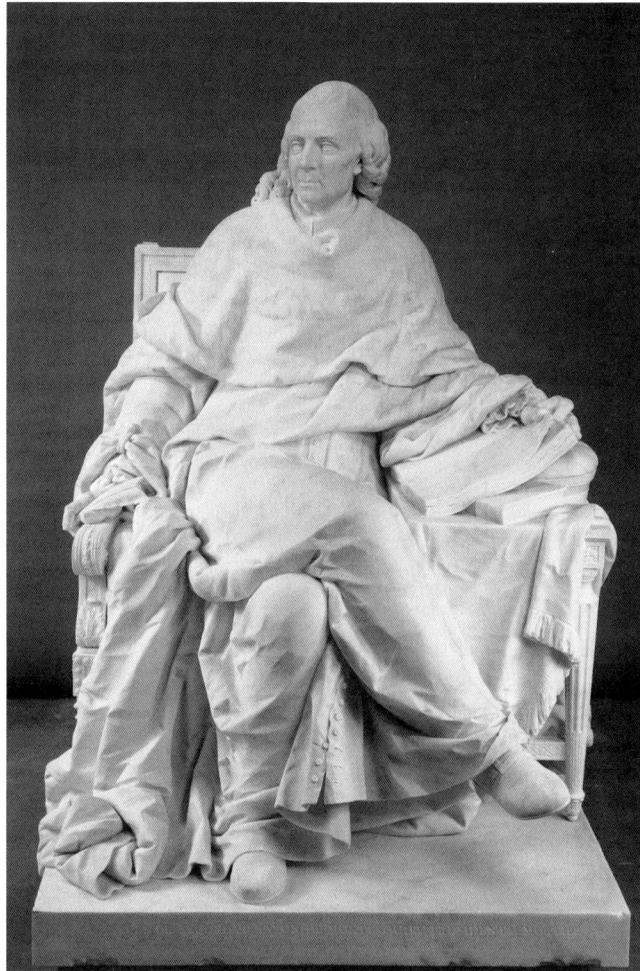

FIG. 65
Clodion (Claude Michel), *Charles-Louis de Secondat, baron de La Brède et de Montesquieu*, 1783. Marble, 164 × 122 × 122 cm. Musée du Louvre, Paris. ENT 1987.02. Photo © RMN-Grand Palais / Art Resource, NY (Christian Jean).

administration to remain neutral in the rivalry between the Montgolfiers' hot air balloon and the hydrogen variant developed by their competitors.[102] Clodion, however, elected to focus entirely on the hot air balloon, perhaps recognizing that its incendiary launch provided a much richer subject for showcasing his techniques. Fire, after all, was central to the mythology of terracotta sculpture, offering an opportunity to link the hot air balloon to both the burning kiln and the larger fiery metaphors of artistic invention. A smaller version of Clodion's monument—now known only through a photograph (fig. 66)—focuses on the moment of ignition. Two putti present a medal of the Montgolfier brothers while a winged figure holds a torch beneath the balloon, which rises from a cloud of smoke.[103]

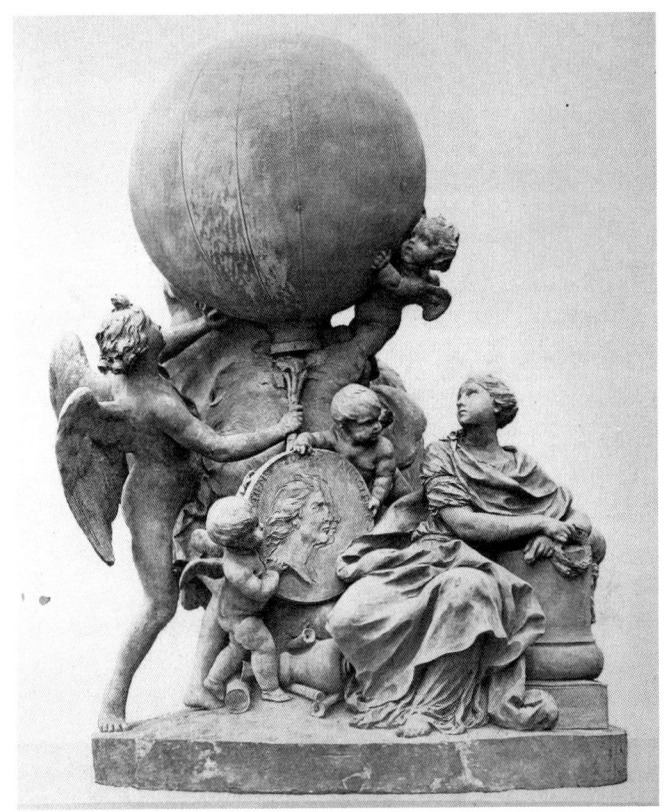

FIG. 66
Clodion (Claude Michel; photograph after), *À la gloire des frères mongolfier* [sic], in Gaston Tissandier, "Curiosités aérostatiques de l'origine des ballons, collection Tissandier," *Le Bulletin des Beaux-Arts* 3 (1885–86): 17–32. Photo: gallica.bnf.fr / BnF.

In Clodion's larger model (fig. 61), the pyrotechnic imagery becomes much more elaborate. In fact, the majority of the towering sculpture does not depict the balloon at all, but the process of fueling it. At the base of the monument (fig. 67), putti are hard at work gathering bundles of hay, recalling the abundant harvests found in Clodion's agrarian subjects. The many winged infants—approximately thirty appear in all—were likely created through Clodion's habitual use of molds, though none appears identical to any other.[104] They swirl around the cylindrical column, carrying the hay through clouds of smoke to feed the raging fire.

More smoke billows from beneath the balloon, which appears nearly weightless as it hovers above. The floating figures of Aeolus—god of the wind—and Renown amplify the anti-gravitational illusion, their bodies extending precariously into the open air (fig. 68). The limbs of the figures would have been nearly impossible to reproduce in marble without the addition of supporting trusses, had the royal arts administration called Clodion's bluff and awarded him the commission.[105] The translation of the work into another material would also have ruined much of its effect. What unifies the sculpture, above all, is the elemental theme that connects the subject with the materiality of

CLODION'S FRAGILE MONUMENTS (109)

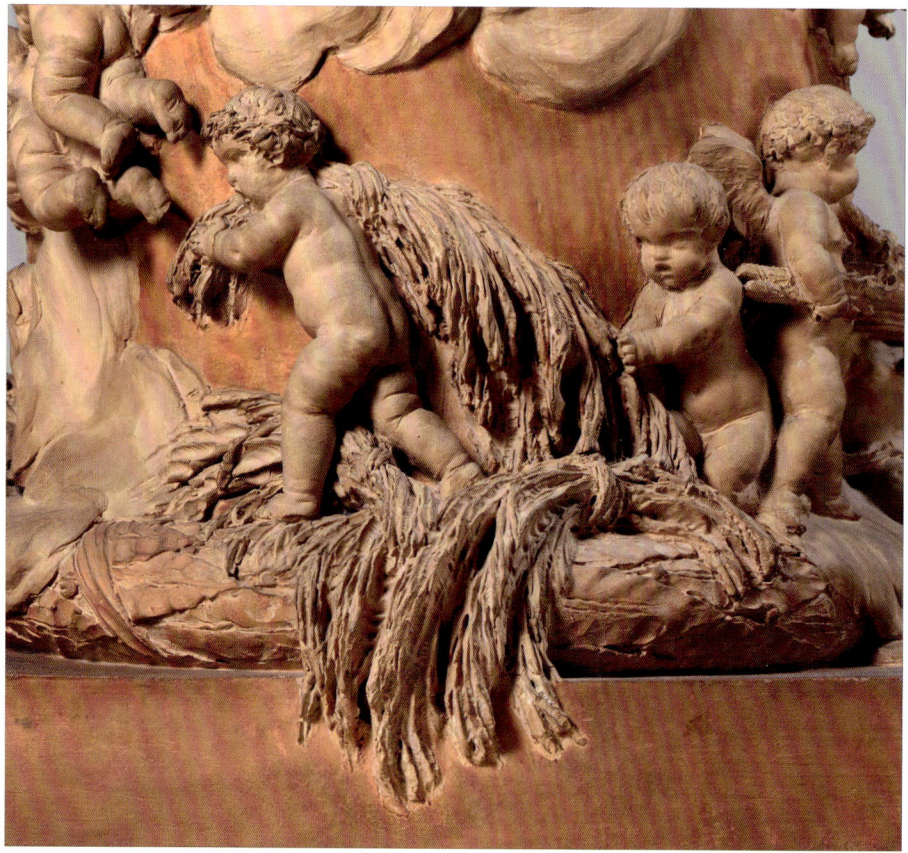

FIGS. 67 & 68 Clodion (Claude Michel), *Model for a Proposed Monument to Commemorate the Invention of the Balloon* (details), ca. 1784. Terracotta, 110 × 63 × 52 cm. Metropolitan Museum of Art, New York. Purchase, Rogers Fund and Anonymous Gift, 1944. 44.21a, b.

the object: Clodion constructs a monument to air travel using little more than earth, water, and fire.

There was no reason for Clodion to fear the prospect of winning the competition. His spectacularly fragile and sensuous terracotta model represented the antithesis of the austere and enduring virtues that the administration wished to associate with the invention of balloon flight. Clodion's competitors, whose models are unfortunately lost, almost certainly came closer to satisfying the terms of the assignment. None of them, however, would receive the commission, which ultimately went unrealized. Scholars have speculated that the increasingly commonplace nature of ballooning in the mid-1780s caused the administration to lose interest in the project, perhaps deeming the subject insufficiently notable to warrant a monument.[106] In fact, the opposite may have been the case—ballooning's notoriety only increased in the years following

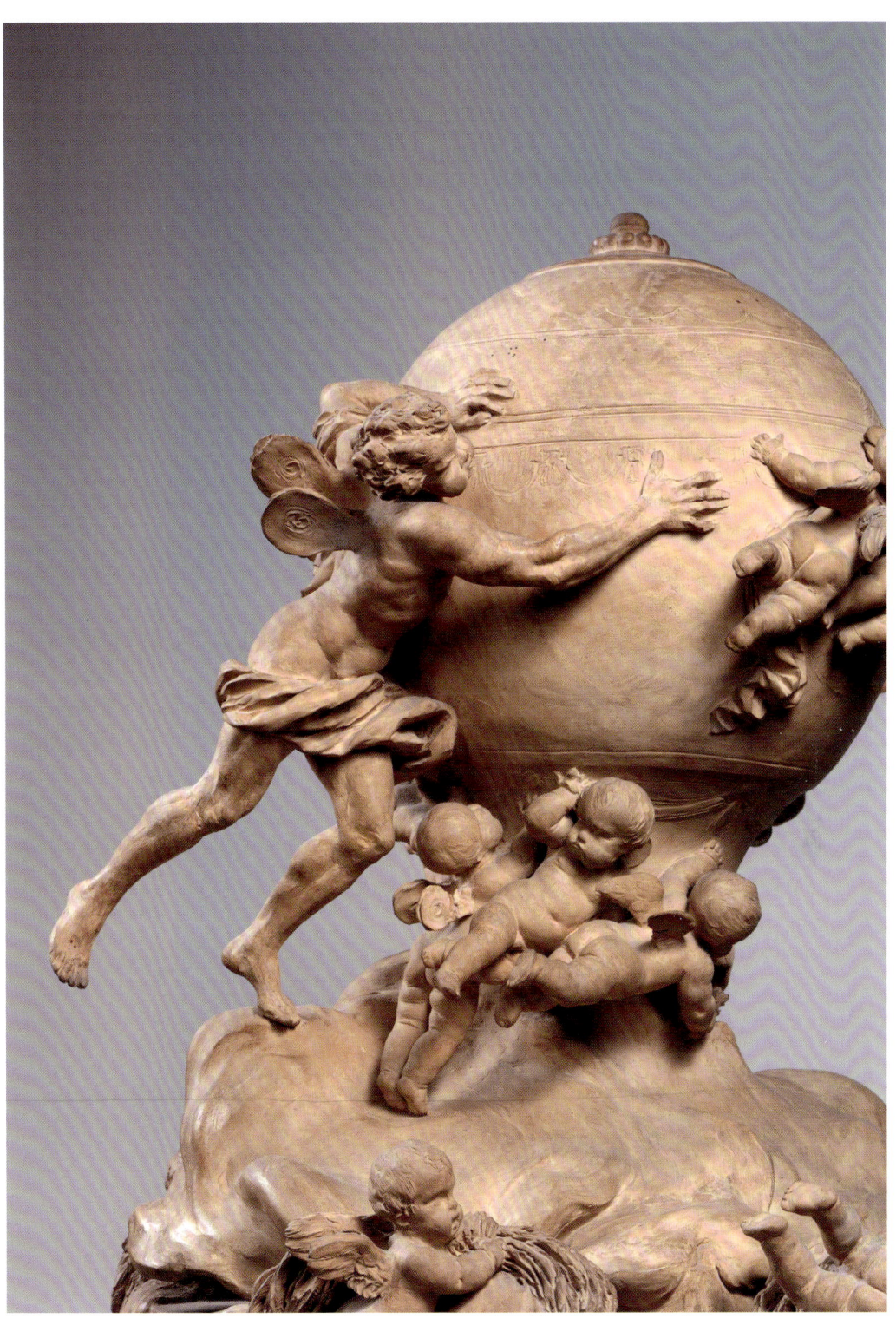

the initial launch, but its recognition was precisely the kind that the crown wished to avoid. A series of sensational ballooning accidents turned the invention into a symbol of ephemeral commerce and its dangers.[107] Public opinion took a decisive turn in July 1784 when two aspiring balloonists—the printmaker Jean-François Janinet and an amateur physicist known as the abbé Miolan—attempted to launch a hot air balloon in the Luxembourg gardens. Janinet and Miolan had widely publicized the event and generated enormous revenue from sale of advanced tickets, which they offered at different prices depending on proximity to the launch site.[108] On the day of the event, thousands of spectators watched as Janinet and Miolan struggled to inflate their balloon. The crowds, after standing for six hours in the summer heat, grew furious and began tearing the flaccid carcass of the balloon to pieces as Janinet and Miolan fled the scene (fig. 69).

Satirists seized upon the event, portraying ballooning as an art of charlatans who trafficked in hot air. A verse published in the aftermath played upon the double significance of the word "voler," meaning both to fly and to steal, noting that Janinet and Miolan had succeeded in at least one sense of the word.[109] Prints soon connected the balloon craze to the supposed excesses of effeminate fashion and consumption. One such example depicted a "coquette phisicienne" in sexually suggestive aeronautical attire who, according to the inscription, charmed men with her "balloons" (fig. 70). The public image of ballooning as a dangerous, seductive, and ephemeral fashion almost certainly led the arts administration to conclude that the subject no longer lent itself to immortalization in sculpture. Even the most sober and solid monument could not possibly redeem an invention that so perfectly embodied the supposed hollowness and insubstantiality of the commercial sphere.

It is ironic that the only surviving model from the state-sponsored competition is Clodion's terracotta, which highlighted precisely the aspects of ballooning that the administration wished to strike from the historical record. Clodion's dazzling and ethereal sculpture, in spite of its fragility, endured through the dedicated care of private collectors and museum curators who saw in it something worth preserving.[110] Ironic as this outcome may be, it also contains within it a larger lesson about the legacy of eighteenth-century art. The efforts of "reformers" such as the comte d'Angiviller to resuscitate the immortal, selfless, and patriotic art of monumental sculpture in the waning years of the *ancien régime* was hardly an unqualified success.[111] Marble statues of Enlightenment "great men," of course, still stare down upon us from pedestals in municipal buildings and public squares, but the manner of artistic production that they exemplify was losing its relevance from the outset. The comte d'Angiviller himself appears to have recognized as much. Looking back on his career in 1790, he explained that he sought to combat the effects of commerce on the arts by supporting "little lucrative" work in history and sculpture.[112] He then conceded the limits of what he accomplished: "I did

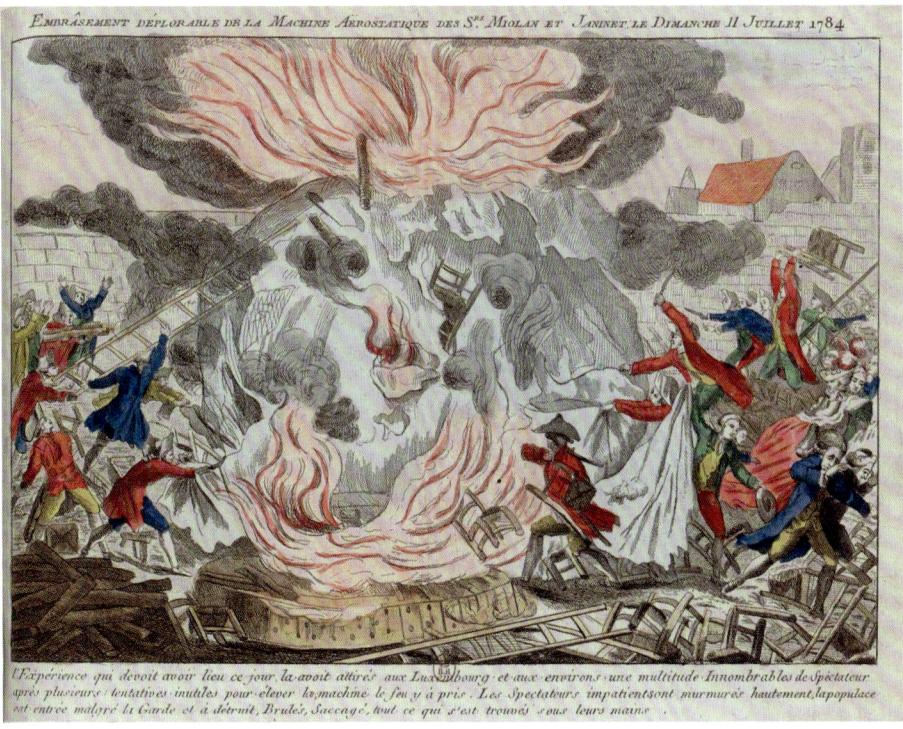

FIG. 69 J. Chéreau, *Embrâsement Déplorable de la Machine Aërostatique des S.rs Miolan et Janinet, le Dimanche 11 Juillet 1784*, 1784. Hand-colored etching, 25 × 35 cm. Bibliothèque nationale de France, département des Estampes et de la photographie, Paris. FOL-IB-2. Photo: gallica.bnf.fr / BnF.

not do everything that I would have desired, but I did what I could."[113] The commercial sphere may have generated ephemeral fashions and disposable luxuries, but the forces governing this system were far too resilient for d'Angiviller to subdue. The Academy's attempts to eliminate from art any trace of the fragile, time-specific forms that had defined private consumption proved to be a futile exercise.

The survival of Clodion's balloon monument, then, testifies to the endurance of the artistic values that it enshrines. I do not simply mean that Clodion ensured the survival of his sculptures through his ability to market his work. The longevity of Clodion's art stemmed from a related but subtler skill, a capacity to give the present-minded ethos of the commercial sphere the appearance of something more socially acceptable, even venerable. Rather than resist the temporally unstable norms of the marketplace, Clodion wedded them to the transcendent virtues of artistic spontaneity and imagination. Upon Clodion's death in 1814, a friend would sum up this aspect of his art in terms of "the *délicatesse* and verve of his genius."[114] The word choice is telling. *Délicatesse*, which had become increasingly tainted by association with ephemeral consumption

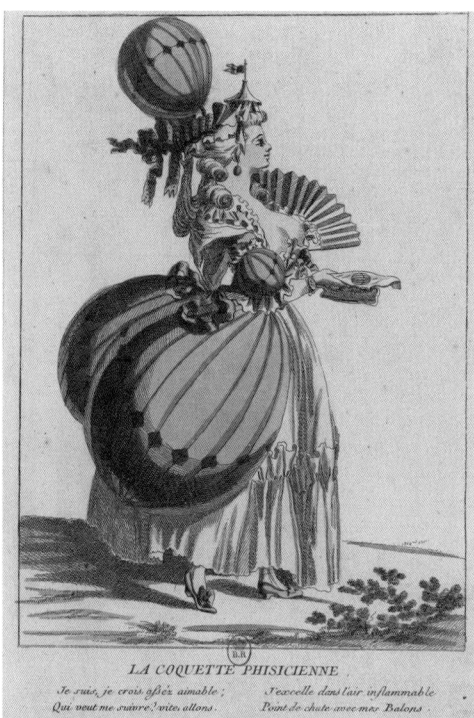

FIG. 70
Anonymous, *La coquette phisicienne*, 1784. Hand-colored etching, 22.7 × 16.5 cm. Bibliothèque nationale de France, département des Estampes et de la photographie, Paris. FOL-IB-4 (3). Photo: gallica.bnf.fr / BnF.

over the course of the eighteenth century, here found a form of redemption. The artifice and unpredictability of fashionable commerce was, in Clodion's hands, transformed into the volatile spark of artistic genius. The difference between the debased instability of the marketplace and the lofty delicacy of transcendent art was, of course, not always easy to determine. Clodion's art was no less a product of the marketplace than the spectacular balloon launches that attracted crowds to the Luxembourg gardens. The major difference was Clodion's knack for presenting the temporality of eighteenth-century consumer culture through the lens of artistic creation. Whether this talent constituted a form of deception or a sign of inspiration is, perhaps, beside the point. In the expanding art market, the ability to transmute commerce into art was fast becoming the ultimate mark of genius.

Epilogue
This Is So Contemporary

It is 2005 and I am visiting the 51st Venice Biennale. I enter a room, empty aside from three gallery attendants. They dance merrily while repeating an incantation in singsong tones: "Oh, this is so contemporary! Contemporary! Contemporary!" I resist the urge to take a photograph because the artist, Tino Sehgal, prohibits any documentation of his work. I try, instead, to be present in the moment, to accept the artist's stated aim of "creating further presents instead of an orientation towards eternity."[1] Eventually I leave, and the Biennale ends. The work exists only in my memory, in the minds of others who experienced it, and in the publicity that the event generated.

When art historians consider the legacy of eighteenth-century French art, Tino Sehgal is not typically among the first artists to come to mind. Much has been written in recent years about the "neo-Rococo" movement among artists from Jeff Koons to Yinka Shonibare, who have self-consciously appropriated formal motifs and subject matter from the eighteenth century.[2] The aesthetic maximalism of their work evokes Rococo extravagance in a way that Sehgal's comparatively spartan art does not. He works solely in ephemeral configurations of body and voice to produce what he describes as "constructed situations." His choreography has occasional Rococo resonances—Sehgal has expressed his admiration for Watteau's languorous arrangements of bodies in space—but his relationship with eighteenth-century art is both deeper and more subtle than this, manifesting itself less in style and iconography than in an attitude toward time, materiality, and above all, money.[3]

Transience can be monetized. This principle constitutes the essential link between eighteenth-century French art and Sehgal. Unlike many performance and conceptual artists of the 1960s who regarded the ephemerality of their work as a means of resisting its commodification, Sehgal describes himself as "pro market."[4] He willingly sells his work for prices upwards of $50,000, and institutions from the Museum of Modern Art to the Tate Modern now count themselves as owners. "By circulating the situations through museums and selling them, I'm critiquing the naive, anti-market romanticism of the '60s," he told one interviewer.[5] Even in commercial exchange, Sehgal resists attaching his situations to any stable material object. Purchases are negotiated entirely through oral contracts, which generally bar the buyer from producing physical documents related to the work. "Cash is the only object involved," he has said of the sale process.[6] When institutions acquire his work, they designate staff members as stewards who commit the attributes of the situation to memory.[7] The work is conserved insofar as its memory is maintained, whether by restaging it or transmitting its reputation through oral tradition. Sehgal himself has suggested that if his work falls out of fashion for an extended period, it will cease to exist as recollections of it fade.[8]

In some respects, this total dematerialization of the art object represents an affront to the eighteenth-century fetishization of art's materiality. Yet materiality was always a means to an end, serving as a vehicle for the sensorial stimulation of the viewer. For the eighteenth-century amateurs who deeply engaged with the surface effects of objects, the pleasures of this experience were themselves defined by their temporal delimitation. The men and women who pore over the oval canvas in Watteau's shop sign (fig. 17) enter, as we have seen, into a process of courtship with the object they examine, understanding the attraction of art to be as mercurial as love between people. Such rituals of inspection combined the temporal subjectivity of empirical philosophy with the cycle of pleasure and boredom that served as a motor for the period's emerging consumer culture.[9] The collector Louis Robert de Saint-Victor captured the time-sensitive mentality of the consuming subject nicely in 1778 when describing the process of arranging newly acquired objects in his home: "This delight of amateurs is one of the most lively after unpacking; it is a shame that these sweet pleasures are of the same nature as others, which is to say too short."[10] These fluctuating rhythms of cultural consumption were, as I have argued throughout this book, implicated in the temporal instability of art itself, pushing artists toward ever more experimental techniques in an effort to seduce viewers. Sehgal takes these dynamics to their logical conclusion, synchronizing the evanescent existence of art with the viewer's time-based experience of it until the two become coextensive. The resulting works commodify experience itself, selling a set of sensorial and emotional encounters.

By linking Sehgal's constructed situations to the materially unstable work of eighteenth-century artists, I do not mean to put forward a teleological narrative in which art ineluctably moves toward greater degrees of ephemerality. Teleology assumes a goal-oriented conception of history, ignoring the contingencies of context and circumstance. What interests me about the connection between Sehgal and the other artists in this book is, on the contrary, what it reveals about their respective contexts, highlighting both their divergences and commonalities. Scholars and critics of contemporary art have rightly emphasized the way Sehgal's work responds to historical conditions that have emerged only recently, most notably the rise of the "experience economy" in which consumption organizes itself around the pursuit of emotional gratification rather than the acquisition of material goods.[11] The experience economy derives much of its power from the rise of digital technologies, which have simultaneously normalized the purchase of non-tangible commodities and fueled a countervailing desire for real-life experience as an antidote to an otherwise screen-based existence. Installation and performance artists have capitalized on these developments, building on what has sometimes been described as an "experiential turn" in contemporary art.[12] Museums have become the clearinghouses for the purchase and sale of these experiences, relying on artists such as Sehgal to attract visitors with the promise of immersive encounters that no digital simulation can replicate. But these recent changes in the technological and museological context for artistic production take place against the backdrop of a more fundamental, structural transformation whose historical origins lie in the eighteenth century—namely, the competitive marketplace for public attention.

Among art historians, the commodification of attention has typically been understood as a phenomenon that dates back to the nineteenth century, and Jonathan Crary's foundational scholarship on the topic has highlighted how artists from Manet to Seurat were enmeshed in the broader technological conversion of vision into a marketable product.[13] Crary is careful to avoid technologically deterministic claims; he subtly analyzes nineteenth-century technologies of vision from photography to the moving image as both a means of producing new forms of human subjectivity and as a response to broader epistemological transformations. The fractured temporal consciousness that he locates in nineteenth-century economies of vision is likewise understood to be as much a cause as an effect of the period's expansive technological changes. Crary's argument nonetheless leaves us with an account of marketable attention whose origins are inextricable from European industrialization and the mediation of vision through the mechanical devices of mass entertainment.

Throughout this book, I have put forward a different set of foundations for the commercialization and concomitant temporalization of visual attention. We have seen how the diminishing power of the church and state in the cultural arena gradually transformed artists into economic free agents who needed to appeal to the desires of an increasingly diffuse audience of consumers. Operating through new sites of public display from the shopfront to the exhibition hall, artists devised novel technical and material practices to hold viewers in their thrall. The tools that they used, from pastel to terracotta sculpture, did not have the same reach as a flickering projection on a cinema screen, but they shared with such later technologies an emerging understanding of audience attention as a scarce and temporally contingent economic resource. Moreover, precisely because artistic media appealed to a restricted viewership, they preserved an aura of exclusivity that could confer status. Art, in its dazzling and delicate materiality, thus provided a forum for social distinction within the burgeoning marketplace for public attention.

To see pastel or even oil paint as a technology for managing viewer attention allows us to appreciate the pivotal position of the eighteenth century in establishing the modern economy of visual experience. The style and subject matter of the period are, to be sure, alien to the visual sensibilities that followed, and it is therefore understandable that the French Revolution is often taken as the starting point for artistic modernity and its associated sense of temporal contingency.[14] Only by granting materiality the same interpretative weight as iconography and form can we recognize that the fall of the old regime represented a less decisive rupture than has been assumed.

In fact, much of the eighteenth-century discourse on the instability of art and its relationship with market pressures continued to reverberate through the nineteenth century and beyond. In part, these concerns stemmed from the growing reliance of artists on pre-prepared materials from color merchants, whose commercial motives had elicited suspicion since the rise of the profession in the second half of the eighteenth century.[15] The growing prevalence of industrially and synthetically manufactured paints in the nineteenth century only exacerbated the sense that the materiality of art was increasingly corrupted by business interests.[16] More fundamentally, though, nineteenth-century artists and critics expressed misgivings about the commercial pressures on artists themselves. The painter Jehan Georges Vibert complained in his 1891 treatise on technique that the modern artist "paints haphazardly, without care for the next day, having no other preoccupation than following fashion, because fashion interferes!"[17] Vibert lamented that artists needed to generate business by attracting the attention of critics, who pushed artists toward an ever-changing array of unstable surface effects: "Agate flesh, marbled transparencies, muted mattes, crepuscular modeling etc.: it is not enough, it is lacking, the journalists demand it!"[18] The painter and writer Charles Moreau-Vauthier elaborated on many of these same themes in his 1912 study of artistic processes, providing a revealing if somewhat hyperbolic explanation for the declining durability of painting over the preceding hundred years: "Public exhibitions put a premium upon charlatanry. How is an artist to attract attention among the crowd of competitors? The artist must be independent, must prove it, and attract attention. Handling is a means to this end, and so is color."[19] The idea that public exhibitions had become commercial showrooms where artists competed to generate business and publicity was a well-established theme in commentary on the arts throughout the nineteenth century.[20] Moreau-Vauthier goes a step further by linking these competitive forces to the corruption of art's very materiality. He offers a synopsis of all the technical trends that had gripped painting in recent decades before concluding: "The object of all these technical obsessions is to dazzle, and not to build up solidly. This is evil. Adopted imprudently, without any care for the health of the picture, but with a desire to awaken curiosity and to rivet attention, they end, as a rule, in disaster."[21]

The attribution of all technical failures in nineteenth-century painting to the fashions and rivalries of the private art market is, of course, reductive. Delacroix, for example, produced some of his most unstable work for publicly commissioned murals, resorting to unorthodox materials in a misguided search for more durable painting media.[22] The somewhat simplistic narratives of Vibert and Moreau-Vauthier are nonetheless instructive for the way that they position art's technical properties within the context of a broader economy of attention, building on claims that had first emerged in the eighteenth century. More than one hundred and fifty years had passed since La Font bemoaned how the "charming" and "seductive" pleasures of Watteau's paintings had been achieved at the expense of their durability. What remained consistent was the idea that the technical practices of artists existed within a system of much broader economic interests, ones that subjected the materiality of art to the temporal dynamics of consumer capitalism.

The significance of these continuities between the eighteenth century and later developments in the history of art is not simply a matter of establishing when art truly became modern—a question whose answer will always depend on semantic disputes over the meaning of the word "modern" itself. What I want to emphasize, instead, is the way the discourse on material instability that accompanied the commercialization of art during the eighteenth century is part of an ongoing history of cultural efforts to process the temporal effects of capitalism. The implications of this larger history go beyond the realm of art. In recent years, everyone from business consultants to environmental activists have questioned the capacity of capitalism to encourage long-term projects that benefit future generations.[23] The tyranny of "short-termism," as management theorists describe it, has become all the more apparent in an age of climate crisis, when quarterly earnings statements and fast fashion thwart any collective effort to confront an existential threat to the habitable world.[24] In the face of looming catastrophe, art history might appear to offer little more than a diversion. Yet, for the artists and audiences in this book, art became a heuristic for working through a question that remains urgently relevant in our time: to what degree can markets support values that transcend the interests of the immediate moment?

Art history, too, can provide a forum for taking up this same question. In fact, a vulgarized form of art history has already entered the popular discourse on the climate crisis as CEOs and climate activists alike have called for a return to "cathedral thinking," the intergenerational mindset that went into the centuries-long construction of the temples whose towering spires still stand at the center of European capitals.[25] What gets left out of these well-intentioned references to the architectural achievements of the middle ages is any analysis of the economic and political conditions that enabled such undertakings, which emerged from anti-democratic societies in which long-term planning was inseparable from the concentration of power in the church and crown. A more rigorous version of this art-historical approach to our contemporary predicament would take seriously the concerns of the artists and critics who first grappled with the decline of royal and religious authority and the temporal uncertainties that it entailed. For them, the link between temporal consciousness and the political and economic structure of society was not so easily ignored, and the reconciliation of economic liberalism with a commitment to future generations was all the more elusive.

Sehgal, for his part, has argued that his situations, in their dematerialized existence, provide a model for sustainable capitalism because they do not depend on the extraction and waste of the planet's finite resources. Modern consumption, he maintains, has unduly linked the construction of the self to the acquisition of physical goods: "If you buy a pair of sneakers ... you buy subjectivity, you buy a differentiation of who you are."[26] By eliminating the material product from the equation, he proposes to sell what he calls "a pure service" that provides "more sustainable and interesting ways to respond to this demand for a differentiation of our subjectivity."[27] Sehgal has further declared his commitment to the preservation of the natural environment by avoiding planes when he travels for work, favoring trains and ships whenever possible.[28] Of course, these laudable tributes to sustainability conveniently ignore the carbon footprint of the jetliners that transport gallerists, curators, and tourists to the art fairs and museums where Sehgal shows his work. Sehgal's insistence that his situations can only be experienced live and in person necessitates exactly the resource-intensive travel on which so much of the modern experience economy depends. In fact, without this requirement, his work would lose the cachet that comes from limited access. By imposing spatial and temporal restrictions on the dissemination of his art, Sehgal produces the artificial scarcity that grants his work market value and social prestige, notionally elevating it above the reproducible products of mass culture.

It is tempting to view these contradictions as a sign of hypocrisy. Another possibility, however, is that Sehgal sees no other choice than to operate within the conditions of a market economy whose long-term impact he implicitly understands to exist beyond his control. Asked about alternatives to capitalism, he has responded that he can envision few other options: "I don't see culture moving away from that, like back to a farming society. You couldn't do that with the amount of people we have."[29]

Political economists can debate the merits of the claim, but what art history can provide is a framework for understanding how artists and their audiences have grappled with such questions in the past. If art constitutes one of the primary means through which alternative futures are first imagined and constructed, then the answers that it offers—or fails to provide—should concern us all. The future expectations of artists and audiences from three centuries ago matter, then, not simply because they resonate with contemporary anxieties but because they represent one of the earliest responses to the temporal conditions of a market-based economy whose underlying structure we have come to inherit. If the horizon of expectation embedded within the fragile and unstable materiality of eighteenth-century art strikes us as too short, then we need to examine the systemic forces that made it so.

Notes

INTRODUCTION

1. "Louvre Plan/Information," n.p.
2. "Procès-verbaux des commissions de restauration," January 28, 1986, Centre de recherche et de restauration des musées de France, Versailles, no. 9530.
3. Lepavec, "Rapport d'intervention." See also Bergeon and Martin, "Fragonard."
4. For a more detailed discussion of these issues, see chapter 1. For specific warnings about drying oils at the Academy, see the comments of the comte de Caylus and Jean-Baptiste Oudry in Lichtenstein and Michel, *Conférences de l'Académie royale*, 5:94–96 and 6:66–78.
5. For the practices of collectors, see Ziskin, *Sheltering Art*; P. Michel, *Peinture et plaisir*; P. Michel, *Commerce du tableau*; Guichard, *Amateurs d'art*, 93–185; Tillerot, *Jean de Jullienne*. On dealers, see Glorieux, *À l'enseigne de Gersaint*; McClellan, "Watteau's Dealer"; Edwards, *Alexandre-Joseph Paillet*. See also the foundational research in Pomian, *Collectors and Curiosities*.
6. Étienne, *Restoration of Paintings*; Massing, *Painting Restoration*. Both build on Guillerme, *Atelier du temps*.
7. For the importance of touch as a mode of artistic individuation, see Lajer-Burcharth, *Painter's Touch*; Guichard, *Griffe du peintre*. For authorship's role in the historical desire to preserve the original materiality of art, see Nagel and Wood, *Anachronic Renaissance*, 14–16.
8. Oudry, "Sur la pratique de peindre," 77.
9. Barcilon and Marani, *Leonardo*, 328–426; Menu, *Leonardo da Vinci's Technical Practice*.
10. Haskell, *Rediscoveries in Art*, 22–38.
11. Diderot, "Le pour et le contre."
12. Gabriel Bouquier, "Manuscrits provenant de G. Bouquier" (n.d.), Ms. 141, Archives de l'Assistance Publique. Quoted in P. Michel, *Peinture et plaisir*, 254.
13. Kimball, *Creation of the Rococo*; Marcel, *Peinture française*.
14. Scott, *Rococo Interior*.
15. For the relationship between time and pleasure, see especially Kavanagh, *Esthetics of the Moment*; Caviglia, *History, Painting*, 60–73. For a discussion of time and subjectivity, see Lajer-Burcharth, "Drawing Time"; Padiyar, *Fragonard*. On risk, with an emphasis on credit markets, see Dubin, *Futures and Ruins*. On subject formation and gender, see Hyde, *Making Up the Rococo*.
16. For sixteenth- and seventeenth-century definitions of *délicat* and *délicatesse*, see Huguet, *Dictionnaire de la langue française*, 2:771; Nicot, *Thresor de la langue françoyse* (1606), 183; Richelet, *Dictionnaire françois* (1680), 1:224. For *delicatus*, see the *Oxford Latin Dictionary*, 509.
17. Bouhours, *Entretiens d'Ariste et d'Eugène*, 85.
18. Bouhours elaborates the point in Bouhours, *Manière de bien penser*, 157–59. For the other courtly shibboleths allied with *délicatesse*, see Viala, *France galante*; Scholar, *Je-Ne-Sais-Quoi*.

19. Furetière, *Dictionnaire universel* (1690), n.p.

20. Coquery, *Hôtel aristocratique*; Coquery, *Tenir boutique à Paris*.

21. Kwass, *Consumer Revolution*; Sewell, "Empire of Fashion"; Sewell, *Capitalism*. For the importance of credit markets to consumption, see Crowston, *Credit, Fashion, Sex*; Sargentson, *Merchants and Luxury Markets*, 26–33.

22. Kwass, *Consumer Revolution*, 71–74; Shammas, "Changes in English and Anglo-American Consumption," 191; Claverías, "Inégalité comme norme," 35; Roche, *France in the Enlightenment*, 632–34.

23. Roche, *France in the Enlightenment*, 632–34.

24. S. Levey, *Lace*, 35–37; Kraatz, *Catalogue des dentelles*, 133–55.

25. On consumption as a forum for competition between the old nobility and the financially ascendant, see the foundational claims in Elias, *Court Society*, 66–77; Elias, *Civilizing Process*, 421–35. More recent scholarship has nuanced Elias's argument, emphasizing that social competition coexisted with individual expression and personal pleasure as motivations for eighteenth-century consumption. See especially Kwass, *Big Hair*, 641–44; Kwass, *Consumer Revolution*, 99–104; Roche, *Culture of Clothing*, 42–43.

26. On the broadening demographics of luxury consumers, see Fairchilds, "Production and Marketing."

27. On "fausse délicatesse," see La Fevrerie, "En quoy consiste l'Air du Monde," 57–59.

28. Sorel, *De la prudence*, 67–68.

29. Le Noble, *École du monde*, 6:29.

30. The classic study is Bourdieu, *Distinction*, 11–96. For a recent attempt to complicate Bourdieu's binary opposition of social and economic capital, see Crowston, *Credit, Fashion, Sex*, 13–15.

31. La Font de Saint-Yenne, *Reflexions sur quelques causes*, 98 ("le peu de durée") and 17–19 (for glass and plaster).

32. For more on the efforts of artists to assert their intellectual status, see Heinich, *Du peintre à l'artiste*.

33. Bouhours, *Entretiens d'Ariste et d'Eugène*, 231.

34. See, for example, Desfontaines, *Apologie du caractère*, 3.

35. Dryden, *Satires of D. J. Juvenalis*, lxxxv. See his similar comments in Dryden, *Fables Ancient and Modern*, n.p.

CHAPTER I

1. Antoine La Roque, obituary published in *Le Mercure*, August 1721, republished in Rosenberg, *Vies anciennes de Watteau*, 5–6.

2. Gersaint, *Cabinet de feu M. Quentin de Lorangère*, 192.

3. Le Carpentier, *Galerie des peintres célèbres*, 2:113.

4. Bryson, *Word and Image*, 58–88.

5. On Watteau and *honnêteté*, see Plax, *Watteau*, 108–53; Vidal, *Watteau's Painted Conversations*, 99–142. Aaron Wile and James Elkins have both cited the social norm of *délicatesse* as an important reference point for Watteau's work: Wile, "Watteau, Reverie, and Selfhood," 329–30; Elkins, *Why Are Our Pictures Puzzles?*, 133–36.

6. Wile, in particular, has made this point: "Watteau, Reverie, and Selfhood," 330.

7. Marsy, *Dictionnaire abrégé de peinture*, 2:376.

8. Gersaint, *Cabinet de feu M. Quentin de Lorangère*, 187–88.

9. Mariette, *Abecedario*, 6:106.

10. Caylus, "Vie d'Antoine Watteau," 96.

11. Paintings by Watteau's imitators, such as Lancret and Pater, have proven more physically durable. Martin and Sindaco-Domas, "Technique picturale." Already in 1752, Dezallier d'Argenville placed Lancret's work above Watteau's in terms of durability. Dezallier d'Argenville, *Abrégé de la vie*, 3:292.

12. For the text of the original statutes, see Lespinasse, *Métiers et corporations*, 2:192–95. On the importance of material durability in the foundation of the guild, see Guiffrey, "Histoire de l'Académie de Saint-Luc," 6.

13. Lespinasse, *Métiers et corporations*, 2:195.

14. Heinich, *Du peintre à l'artiste*; Pevsner, *Academies of Art*, 82–100; Posner, "Concerning the 'Mechanical' Parts."

15. Félibien, *Recueil de descriptions de peintures*, 28.

16. For Félibien's technical recommendations to painters, see Félibien, *Entretiens*, 3:8–18.

17. The financial resources available to painters during this period were first given scholarly attention in Marcel, *Peinture française*, 121–54.

18. This point has been particularly emphasized in Schnapper, *Métier de peintre*; Schnapper, *Jean Jouvenet*, 71.

19. Schieder, *Jenseits der Aufklärung*, 145–52.

20. On the varied motivations of private collectors in Paris during the first half of the eighteenth century, see especially Ziskin, *Sheltering Art*. For an account more heavily weighted toward the second half of the century, see Bailey, *Patriotic Taste*.

21. See especially Tillerot, *Jean de Jullienne*, 111–58. See also Ziskin, *Sheltering Art*, 93–117.

22. Braudel, *Wheels of Commerce*, 60–75; Coquery, *Tenir boutique à Paris*, 21–22.

23. On the problem of dating the origin of a consumer consciousness, see Coquery, *Tenir boutique à Paris*, 261–66.

24. For the early provenances of Watteau's paintings, see the individual catalog entries in Grasselli and Rosenberg, *Watteau*, 246–458.

25. Ibid., 369.

26. On the family's investment in colonial commerce, which goes back to Jullienne's uncle Jean Glucq, see Lévy, *Capitalistes et pouvoir*, 2:320.

27. Tillerot, *Jean de Jullienne*, 135–36.

28. Ibid., 154.

29. On consciousness of permanence among Dutch artists during this period, see van Eikema Hommes, "Methods Used by Painters." The Dutch market did create demand for simpler and more rapidly executed works, but not less durable ones. On changes in Dutch painting techniques stimulated by commerce, see Montias, "Cost and Value."

30. On guild directives, see van Eikema Hommes, "Methods Used by Painters." See also the dated but classic W. Martin, "Life of a Dutch Artist."

31. A parallel can be found in England, where the waning influence of the Painter-Stainers' Company resulted in looser craft standards and growing conservation issues, notably in the work of Joshua Reynolds. R. Jones, "Introduction," 11; Hunter, *Painting with Fire*, 77.

32. P. Michel, *Peinture et plaisir*, 246–50.

33. Ibid., 248–50.

34. Economists have long scrutinized these behaviors. For an overview of the literature, see Frederick, Loewenstein, and O'Donoghue, "Time Discounting and Time Preference."

35. David Hume had already begun grappling with the problem of impulsivity in the market beginning in the 1730s.

Palacios-Huerta, "Time-Inconsistent Preferences."

36. For the links between colonial speculation and the *goût moderne*, see especially Ziskin, *Sheltering Art*, 93–117; Orain, *Politique du merveilleux*, 103–11. A similar tolerance for financial risk has been observed among the buyers for Joshua Reynolds's unstable paintings in England: Chu, "High Art and High Stakes"; De Marchi and Van Miegroet, "Ingenuity, Preference."

37. On the subjective dimensions of Law's "System," see especially Orain, *Politique du merveilleux*.

38. Van Eikema Hommes, "Methods Used by Painters."

39. For a survey of technical manuals from this period, see Massing, "French Painting Technique." See also Massing's indispensable annotated bibliography, "Painting Materials and Techniques."

40. De Piles, *Premiers élémens*, 61–62.

41. I base this description on the advice offered by de Piles, who provides one of the more detailed accounts of these cleaning procedures from the period. Massing ("French Painting Technique," 338) has situated his recommendations within the broader technical literature.

42. Caylus, "Vie d'Antoine Watteau," 94.

43. Ibid., 96.

44. *Huile grasse*, despite what its name might suggest, is not especially high in fat. It is prepared by heating oil with oxidized metals, which actually reduces the grease content of the oil. The resulting product is more brown and viscous than the oils ordinarily used in painting, which may explain the name. On the chemical composition of *huile grasse* and the problems involved in its translation, see Baumer, Koller, and Fiedler, "Fette Öle." On *huile grasse* and atmospheric halftones, see Oudry, "Sur la pratique de peindre," 77.

45. We find references to *huile grasse* as early as Pierre Le Brun's *Recueil des essaies des merveilles de la peinture*, first published in 1635, reprinted in Merrifield, *Original Treatises*, 2:815–17. For a survey of seventeenth-century recipes for *huile grasse*, see Massing, "French Painting Technique," 345–46.

46. Caylus, "Vie d'Antoine Watteau," 94.

47. Gersaint, *Cabinet de feu M. Quentin de Lorangère*, 187–88. For the definition of *très-alès*, see Gersaint, *Succession de M. Angran*, 243–44; Pernety, *Dictionnaire portatif de peinture*, 544–45. Both authors cite the cracks in Watteau's paintings as an example. See also Glorieux, *À l'enseigne de Gersaint*, 105.

48. Oudry, "Sur la pratique de peindre," 67.

49. The cracking effects of *huile grasse* have been well documented in the scientific literature. See, for instance, Bergeon, "Quelques points de technique picturale," 135–39; see, more recently, Martin and Sindaco-Domas, "Technique picturale," 32–33, and Wenders de Calisse, "Zur Maltechnik von Antoine Watteau," 77–78.

50. Mariette, *Abecedario*, 6:106; Gersaint, *Succession de M. Angran*, 265–66. Gersaint, Mariette, and Oudry suggest that the problems of *huile grasse* are not just a matter of cracking but also involve color and tone. To my knowledge, conservators have not fully explored the latter effects.

51. The painting has undergone multiple cleanings and restorations beginning in the eighteenth century. For an overview of its condition and historical treatment, see Volle, "Restaurations," and Bergeon and Faillant-Dumas, "Restoration."

52. The cracks in these figures show features of both "drying cracks" stemming from Watteau's excessive use of drying oil and "impact cracks" that result from some disturbance of the picture after completion. For

the classification of such patterns, see Bucklow, "Description of Craquelure Patterns," and Bucklow, "Description and Classification of Craquelure."

53. M. Levey, *Painting and Sculpture in France*, 34.

54. Goncourt, *Catalogue raisonné d'Antoine Watteau*, 134.

55. Restoration report quoted in Seidel, "Friedrich der Grosse als Sammler," 57; for the painting's provenance, see Vogtherr, *Französische Gemälde*, 123.

56. Restoration work may well have occurred while the painting was in private hands before 1750, but such interventions were rarely documented. For the multiple restorations that took place in the years following this date, see Vogtherr, *Französische Gemälde*, 125–26.

57. The precise number of paintings in Watteau's oeuvre has been the subject of some dispute. A body of 215 works was presented in Adhémar, *Watteau*; this number was subsequently reaffirmed in Camesasca, *Tout l'œuvre peint de Watteau*. A drastically reduced number was presented in Ferré, *Watteau*. Ferré's arguments were met with great skepticism and have not been widely accepted in the field. See Cailleux, "Strange Monument," and Posner, "*Watteau* by Jean Ferré."

58. On the few exceptions, see Eidelberg, "Watteau's Drawings."

59. For Watteau's drawing process and its relationship with temporal experience, see Lajer-Burcharth, "Drawing Time."

60. Caylus, "Vie d'Antoine Watteau," 96. Technical analysis of Watteau's paintings indicates that his practices may have been somewhat more varied than Caylus suggests. Glorieux, *Watteau*, 191.

61. On the ideal of *sprezzatura* in eighteenth-century French painting, see especially Sheriff, *Fragonard*, 122–27.

62. De Piles, *Cours de peinture par principes*, 159.

63. Ibid., 159–60.

64. Sheriff, *Fragonard*, 124–25. The subject particularly preoccupied Caylus, whose views on rapidity of execution have been sensitively analyzed in Démoris, "Comte de Caylus et la peinture," 31–43.

65. Coypel, "Le coloris et le pinceau," 83.

66. Ibid.

67. Ibid. The quotation is attributed to Zeuxis in Plutarch, *Moralia*, 2:55.

68. Candace Clements has called attention to the rise of personal speculation among artists during these years, focusing on the example of Coypel's son Charles Coypel, who became a member of the Academy in 1715. Clements, "Noble Liberality and Speculative Industry."

69. Coypel, "Les anciens et les modernes," 125.

70. Ibid.

71. Ibid.

72. Gersaint, *Cabinet de feu M. Quentin de Lorangère*, 182–83. Caylus confirms the point: "Il était encore moins consolé par le prix qu'on lui donnait; il n'aimait point l'argent et, assurément, il n'y était point attaché." Caylus, "Vie d'Antoine Watteau," 91.

73. A. Brejon de Lavergnée, *Inventaire Le Brun de 1683*, 45.

74. Commentators have generally assumed that the picture is being loaded into the crate, but as has sometimes been pointed out, nothing rules out the opposite action. Vogtherr and Wenders de Calisse, "Watteau's 'Shopsign,'" 304.

75. Neuman, "Watteau's *L'Enseigne de Gersaint*," 153–64. Some have gone so far as to see the entombment as an invocation of seventeenth-century *vanitas* imagery, a meditation on mortality and the transience of human endeavors. See, in particular, Banks, *Watteau and the North*, 241–42.

76. Vogtherr and Wenders de Calisse, "Watteau's 'Shopsign,'" 304. See also Nagel, *Medieval Modern*, 202–3.

77. The painting appeared in the 1715 description of the Academy: Guérin, *Description de l'Académie royale*, 99. See also Guicharnaud, "*Le progrès des arts du dessin*."

78. Gersaint, *Cabinet de feu M. Quentin de Lorangère*, 10–11.

79. Ibid.

80. On the audience for Watteau's work and their interest in the material surface, see Posner, "Concerning the 'Mechanical' Parts," 596–97.

81. Guichard, *Amateurs d'art*, 15–17.

82. Period dictionaries often define the amateur simply as "qui aime." See *Dictionnaire de l'Académie françoise* (1694), 1:22; *Dictionnaire universel* (1743), 1:363. For a succinct statement of the distinction between connoisseurs and amateurs, see Marsy, *Dictionnaire abrégé de peinture*, 1:140–41. See also Smentek, *Mariette*, 3; Gibson-Wood, *Studies in the Theory of Connoisseurship*, 46.

83. For the technical practices of amateurs, see Guichard, *Amateurs d'art*, 239–99.

84. For a number of personal accounts from amateurs who conflate these kinds of attraction, see ibid., 177.

85. See, for instance, McClellan, "Watteau's Dealer," 440.

86. Gersaint, *Cabinet de feu M. Quentin de Lorangère*, 3.

87. Diderot, *Salon de 1765*, 163.

88. For a broader history of the "temporalization of love" in early modern France, see Luhmann, *Love as Passion*; for its application to Watteau, see C. Michel, *Le célèbre Watteau*, 234.

89. La Font de Saint-Yenne, *Reflexions sur quelques causes*, 98.

90. Ibid., 98–99.

91. Ibid., 99.

92. Ibid., 76.

93. Ibid.

94. Ibid., 56.

95. Crow, *Painters and Public Life*, 122–26; Scott, *Rococo Interior*, 263–64. Complicating matters is the fact that La Font himself came from a family of ennobled silk merchants and could therefore easily be accused of being complicit in the commercial world that he denounced. On these contradictions, see Shovlin, *Political Economy of Virtue*, 43–44.

96. Massing, "French Painting Technique," 339.

97. McClellan, *Inventing the Louvre*, 18.

98. For the broad outlines, see Haskell, *Rediscoveries in Art*, 22–38. For a detailed, empirical analysis of changing market trends, see P. Michel, *Peinture et plaisir*, 153–328. See also Christopher Wood's discussion of how the eighteenth century's subjectivized understanding of taste destabilized artistic canons: Wood, *History of Art History*, 150–52.

99. On "charmant" and "séduisant" as terms affiliated with the courtly norms of *galanterie* and *délicatesse*, see Viala, *France galante*, 31–39; Scholar, *Je-Ne-Sais-Quoi*, 203–211.

CHAPTER 2

1. Alberti, *On Painting and On Sculpture*, 61.

2. For an overview of theoretical writing on the memorial function of portraits, see Pommier, *Théories du portrait*, 116–27.

3. Scholars have given wide-ranging estimates for the number of pastellists active in Paris at midcentury. Jeffares persuasively places the total at 200–300: Jeffares, "Prolegomena," 129n441. A frequently repeated count of 2,500 (Shelley, "Pastelists at Work," 109; Bury, *Maurice-Quentin de La Tour*, 8n2) is surely an exaggeration.

4. The technical properties of the medium have been most extensively examined in Burns, *Invention of Pastel Painting*. See also Jeffares, "Prolegomena," 14–51.

5. For scientific analysis of pastel's fragility and best practices for conservation, see Sauvage, "'De poudre et de papier'"; Kosek, "Heyday of Pastels"; Voßkamp, "Preservation of Pastels"; Herrenschmidt, "Prêt des pastels."

6. "Nos échos," *L'Intransigeant*, October 22, 1912, 2. Cited in Neil Jeffares, "Prolegomena," 57.

7. Sauvage, Wei, and Martinez, "When Conservation Meets Engineering."

8. Important studies include Jeffares, Pastels & Pastellists; Burns, *Invention of Pastel Painting*; Baetjer and Shelley, *Pastel Portraits*; Salmon, *Pastels in the Musée du Louvre*.

9. Burns, *Invention of Pastel Painting*, 89–94.

10. For the unique optical properties of the medium, see especially Burns, "Matte Surfaces."

11. Baillet de Saint-Julien, *Peinture*, 12–13.

12. For the links between financiers and pastel, see especially Jeffares, "Parlementaires in Pastel."

13. Barbier, *Journal historique*, 3:262; Jeffares, *Maurice-Quentin de La Tour*, 121.

14. Letter to Devaux, November 7, 1745. Graffigny, *Correspondance*, 6:577.

15. La Font de Saint-Yenne, *Reflexions sur quelques causes*, 119, 28.

16. Burns, *Invention of Pastel Painting*, 6–8; Jeffares, "Prolegomena," 22–25.

17. Leonardo used the term "pastello" in his Codex Madrid in the last decade of the fifteenth century, supplying a diagram of a mold "per far pastelli." Leonardo da Vinci, *Madrid Codices*, fol. 191r. For the link with the language of apothecaries, see Burns, *Invention of Pastel Painting*, 7.

18. The most comprehensive study to date of pastel's early use in Italy is Laura Da Rin Bettina's dissertation: Da Rin Bettina, "Disegno a pastello." See also Nova, "Pietre naturali, gessi colorati, pastelli"; Bambach, *Leonardo da Vinci Rediscovered*, 1:472–81 and 3:533–44; Bambach, "Leonardo's Notes on Pastel Drawing."

19. Burns (*Invention of Pastel Painting*) and Jeffares ("Prolegomena") both provide compelling narratives of artistic innovation as the driving force in pastel's development.

20. B. Brejon de Lavergnée, "Some New Pastels."

21. Félibien, *Entretiens*, 4:83.

22. Pader, *Peinture parlante*, n.p.

23. On the diverse forms of entertainment in salons of the late seventeenth century, see Lilti, *Monde des salons*, 225–72. This chapter was excluded from the English translation of Lilti's book.

24. Tempesti, "Conseils de R. Nanteuil," 249. On the relation of Nanteuil's portraits to the literary culture of gallantry, see Spica, "Une Madeleine au chevalet."

25. Adamczak, *Robert Nanteuil*, 98–107.

26. Montaiglon, *Procès-verbaux de l'Académie royale*, 3:236.

27. Lacombe, *Dictionnaire portatif des beaux-arts*, 689.

28. On the importance of the Salon as a proving ground for pastel, see Adamczak, "Présence du pastel au Salon."

29. Le Comte, *Cabinet des singularitez*, 3:219.

30. *Mercure de France*, December 1734, 2901. See also Börsch-Supan, "Joseph Vivien als Hofmaler der Wittelsbacher."

31. West, "Gender and Internationalism," 50; Oberer, *Life and Work of Rosalba Carriera*, 103.

32. West, "Gender and Internationalism," esp. 63–64.

33. Krellig, "Rosalba Carriera," 96–100.

34. On the social composition of Carriera's French buyers and their financial ties, see Ziskin, *Sheltering Art*, 151–56; Jeffares, "Rosalba Carriera"; Haskell, *Patrons and Painters*, 285.

35. Jeffares, "Rosalba's Portrait of John Law."

36. Ménard, *Le Français qui possédait l'Amérique*.

37. On Crozat's position within this new class of collectors, see especially Ziskin, *Sheltering Art*, 69–91.

38. De Marchi and Van Miegroet, "Ingenuity, Preference."

39. See especially Krellig, "Rosalba Carriera," 94.

40. Mariette to Carriera, February 12, 1722, in Carriera, *Lettere, diari, frammenti*, 1:416–17.

41. Dezallier d'Argenville, *Abrégé de la vie*, 1:315.

42. In addition to West ("Gender and Internationalism"), see Johns, "'An Ornament of Italy'"; Nicholson, "Having the Last Word."

43. See especially the letters she received from Crozat, which frame her visits to Paris in terms of "le plaisir de jouir de votre conversation" and "amitié." Carriera, *Lettere, diari, frammenti*, 2:468, 482.

44. Letter from Crozat to Carriera, October 28, 1718 (ibid., 1:339–40).

45. Ibid.

46. Letter from Crozat to Carriera, January 20, 1720 (ibid., 1:401). Crozat later advised her to transport her works without the glass in place. Letter from Crozat to Carriera, August 11, 1721 (ibid., 1:401).

47. See Xavier Salomon's ongoing research on the subject, outlined in Salomon, "Artistic Achievements of Rosalba Carriera." Salomon is preparing a longer publication on the topic. See also Jeffares, "Rosalba Carriera," 2.

48. All three terms are important to, for example, the abbé Maroulle's celebration of the reception piece that Carriera submitted to the Academy, published in *Le Mercure*, February 1722, 115.

49. Jeffares and Carriera, "Rosalba Carriera's Journal," 9–11.

50. The Salon *livret* described the portrait as hanging "sur la face à droite de l'escalier." Guiffrey, *Collection des livrets*, 4:33.

51. Hoisington, "Maurice-Quentin de la Tour," 80–82; on La Tour's notoriously competitive behavior, see Williams, *Académie Royale*, 275–80.

52. Documentation of La Tour's early life is scant. For an overview of the known facts, see Jeffares, *Maurice-Quentin de La Tour*, 22–24; Marandet, "Apprenticeship of Maurice-Quentin de La Tour."

53. We get a sense of the spaces that pastels occupied from the estate inventories of the period. See Wildenstein, *Inventaires après décès*.

54. Aïssé, *Lettres de Mademoiselle Aïssé*, 176.

55. Mariette, *Abecedario*, 3:69.

56. For the circumstances of the commission, see Cabezas, "Voltaire, ses portraits," 175–82.

57. Voltaire, "Le Mondain," 303.

58. Ibid., 302.

59. For the history of champagne and Voltaire's veneration of it, see Mervaud, "Du nectar pour Voltaire"; Cronk, "Epicurean Spirit."

60. Voltaire, "Le Mondain," 303.

61. Lilti, *World of the Salons*, 83–84.

62. Rowlands, *Financial Decline*, 8.

63. On the Bernard family and the slave trade, see Saint Germain, *Samuel Bernard*, 101–19. On the predatory lending practices of the Bernard family, see Rowlands, *Dangerous and Dishonest Men*, 144–65.

64. Letter to Devaux, December 24, 1745. Graffigny, *Correspondance*, 7:159.

65. Anne Lafont has suggested that the man belonged to Rieux, but no evidence for a link has been found (provenance records tie the work, instead, to the Caylus family). Lafont, *L'art et la race*, 147. For the provenance, see Jeffares, *Maurice-Quentin de La Tour*, 248–49. For a more detailed analysis of the work, see Wunsch, "Discriminating Taste."

66. On the mutually constitutive relation between refined taste and human exploitation in eighteenth-century Europe, see especially Gikandi, *Slavery and the Culture of Taste*; Kriz, *Slavery, Sugar*.

67. *Lettre à Monsieur de Poiresson-Chamarande*, 15.

68. Hoisington, "Maurice-Quentin de la Tour," 119.

69. Wine, "Review of *Paris: Life & Luxury*," 645.

70. Jeffares, "La Tour, *Le président de Rieux*," 4. See also Kerber, "Perfectibility and Its Foreign Causes," 75.

71. *Lettre à Monsieur de Poiresson-Chamarande*, 14.

72. *Mercure de France*, October 1741, 2293.

73. This point is made especially forcefully in Russo, *Styles of Enlightenment*, 1–15.

74. Voltaire, *Correspondence*, 7:11–12.

75. Bonnet, *Naissance du Panthéon*, 36.

76. Russo, *Styles of Enlightenment*, 41–43; J. Jones, *Sexing La Mode*, 116–20.

77. La Font de Saint-Yenne, *Reflexions sur quelques causes*, 118.

78. Ibid., 28.

79. Ibid., 104.

80. Ibid., 21–23.

81. Ibid., 22.

82. Voltaire, *Correspondence*, 11:120.

83. Brumfitt, *Voltaire, Historian*.

84. D'Alembert, in his eulogy for Montesquieu, describes La Tour's overtures. D'Alembert, "Eloge," 112–13.

85. See especially Jessica Fripp's examination of La Tour's 1753 Salon submissions as a response to critical attacks on portraiture. Fripp, *Portraiture and Friendship*, 35–54.

86. Caylus, "Exposition des ouvrages," 162.

87. La Font de Saint-Yenne, *Sentimens sur quelques ouvrages*, 140, 160.

88. Fripp, *Portraiture and Friendship*, 78. For the few comments that these portraits elicited, see Fend, "Gathering Likenesses," 157–58.

89. La Font de Saint-Yenne, *Sentimens sur quelques ouvrages*, 141.

90. Goodman, *Portraits of Madame de Pompadour*, 118–37; Hoisington, "Maurice-Quentin de La Tour," 218–53; Méjanès, *Maurice-Quentin Delatour*, 48–61; Jeffares, "La Tour, *Mme de Pompadour*," 9–11.

91. Léoffroy de Saint-Yves, *Observations sur les arts*, 103–4.

92. Gombaud et al., "Maurice-Quentin de La Tour and Jean Valade Pastels." See also the discussion of the issue in Jeffares, "Prolegomena," 30n116.

93. *Mercure de France*, September 1745, 135.

94. Bachaumont, "Liste des meilleurs peintres," 424.

95. On Loriot's background and various activities, see Jeffares, "Loriot, Pellechet, Jurine."

96. "La sècheresse détache à la longue le pastel; l'humidité occasionne des moisissures dans plusieurs de ces couleurs; en y plaçant la glace bien jointe, le pastel d'ordinaire s'y contre-épreuve ce qui enlève la fleur et altère le tableau, le mouvement dans les transports en fait tomber une partie au bas de la bordure; ce qui arrive même étant placé à demeure dans les appartements par le seul

ébranlement occasionné par les voitures; enfin les couleurs paraissent perdre insensiblement de leur éclat, de sorte qu'aucun peintre ne saurait se flatter que ses tableaux puissent passer à la postérité." "Rapports sur diverses inventions, lus à l'Académie de peinture. École des Beaux-Arts. Ms. 237," n.d., 1–2, Institut national d'histoire de l'art, Paris, Ms. 1023.

97. Ibid. The declared pension was for 1000 livres.

98. Loriot advertised his services at prices from 4 to 20 livres, depending on the size of the pastel to be fixed. Meusnier de Querlon, *Affiches, annonces, et avis divers*, 1763, 23.

99. For the initial publicity, see, for example, Meusnier de Querlon, *Annonces, affiches et avis divers*, 1753, 158; and *Mercure de France*, December 1753, 162–63. For continued speculation, see *Journal œconomique*, February 1758, 63–65.

100. Mariette, *Abecedario*, 3:71.

101. Ibid.

102. Renou, *Secret de fixer le pastel*. The secret was, in fact, revealed before Loriot's death. By 1779, he indicated to Jean-Baptiste Marie Pierre that he was willing to make it public. Jean-Baptiste Marie Pierre to Charles Claude de La Billarderie, comte d'Angiviller, November 26, 1779, Archives nationales, Paris, O1 1915. The secret was soon announced in various journals, such as the *Journal de physique*: Renou, "Secret de fixer le pastel."

103. The presence of fish glue in eighteenth-century fixatives has been confirmed through recent laboratory analysis: Schultz and Petersen, "Antibody-Based Techniques."

104. For a technical examination of La Tour's experiments, see especially Burns, *Invention of Pastel Painting*, 145–52.

105. *Lettre sur l'exposition . . . au Sallon du Louvre 1769*, 22–23.

106. Diderot, *Salon de 1767*, 173.

107. Grimm, *Correspondance littéraire*, 2:427 [November 15, 1754].

108. Chaperon, *Traité de la peinture au pastel*, 10–11.

CHAPTER 3

1. For initial reports, see *Gazette*, 1754, 546–50; *Le Courrier*, 1754, 383; Grimm, *Correspondance littéraire*, 2:427–28 [November 15, 1754]; *Mercure de France*, December 1754, 152–55; Meusnier de Querlon, *Annonces, affiches et avis divers*, 1754, 195–96.

2. Caylus presented Vien's painting to the Academy of Inscriptions on November 12, 1754. The published records of the Academy provide an overview of Caylus's research on the subject in the preceding years: *Histoire de l'Académie royale des inscriptions*, 25:5–7.

3. Ibid., 25:7.

4. For an instructive contemporary chronicle, see Fréron, "L'histoire & le secret."

5. Diderot, *L'histoire et le secret*, 1755.

6. For an overview of the three main categories of wax-based painting, see Rice, "Fire of the Ancients," 5–7.

7. Guiffrey, *Collection des livrets*, 18:15–28.

8. Grimm, *Correspondance littéraire*, 3:94 [September 15, 1755].

9. The most comprehensive study remains Danielle Rice's dissertation, which provides an excellent overview of the different techniques and the key players involved. Rice, "Fire of the Ancients." See also Gaehtgens, *Joseph-Marie Vien*, 24–25 and 74–78; Carofano, "Dibattito Caylus-Diderot."

10. Crow, *Painters and Public Life*, 113–18.

11. On Caylus's antiquarian activities, see Guillerme, "Caylus technologue"; Medvedkova, "Comte de Caylus"; Pomian, *Collectors and Curiosities*, 169–84; Parente, "Caylus et

l'archéologie"; Aghion and Avisseau, *Caylus, mécène du roi*; Reyes, "Drawing and History"; Pagano, "Caylus e le pitture ercolanesi"; Gaehtgens, "Archaeology and Enlightenment"; Ortona and Modolo, *Caylus e la riscoperta*.

12. Diderot divulged the price, explaining that the painting had been acquired by La Live de Jully. Diderot, *L'histoire et le secret*, 14.

13. Bachelier's now-lost painting *Le fable du cheval et du loup*, for example, apparently showed signs of cracking as early as 1755: "On craint que le tableau de M. Bachelier ne s'écaille." Fréron, "Exposition des tableaux," 57.

14. Roche and Doucet, "Propriétés mécaniques"; Nevjestic, "L'encaustique et la peinture."

15. For an overview of the discipline and its methods, see Huhtamo and Parikka, *Media Archaeology*; Parikka, *What Is Media Archaeology?*

16. See especially Kluitenberg, "On the Archaeology of Imaginary Media," 48.

17. His infatuation with Carriera's work lasted to the end of his life. In a letter from 1765, he wrote: "J'aime beaucoup les ouvrages de cette célèbre fille: j'ai une vingtaine de morceaux de sa main qui font le plaisir de mes yeux." Caylus, *Correspondance inédite*, 2:139. He owned more than a dozen of Carriera's works at the time of his death. See nos. 29–38 and 40–44 in the inventory transcribed in Hattori, "Comte de Caylus d'après les archives," 64.

18. Russo, *Styles of Enlightenment*, 94–95; Hyde, *Making Up the Rococo*, 56–58; Wunsch, "Diderot and the Materiality of Posterity."

19. Caylus, "D'une des trois manières de peindre en encaustique" (n.d.), 97, Ms. 522, Bibliothèque de l'École nationale supérieure des beaux-arts, Paris.

20. "Elle fournit plus de facilité que la pratique de l'huile . . . les années ne lui doivent causer aucune altération." Ibid., 99.

21. Diderot, *L'histoire et le secret*, 88–89.

22. Much has been made of the antipathy between Diderot and Caylus, which stemmed, in large part, from Diderot's disdain for what he regarded as Caylus's small-minded antiquarianism. In their efforts to wed sensual pleasure with a program of artistic reform, however, the men had much in common. On the conflict between them, see Seznec, "Singe antiquaire"; Masseau, "Caylus, Diderot et les philosophes."

23. The painting was submitted to the Academy on March 30, 1754. For the documentation surrounding the painting, see Gaehtgens, *Joseph-Marie Vien*, 150–51.

24. Gaehtgens has called attention to Vien's unusual interpretation of the subject in relation to the existing iconography of Daedalus and Icarus. Ibid., 75.

25. I am not the first to point out the allusion. See Faroult, Leribault, and Scherf, *Antiquité rêvée*, 146–47; Gaehtgens, *Joseph-Marie Vien*, 75.

26. Fréron, "Exposition des tableaux," 52.

27. The lecture was delivered on October 4, 1755. Caylus, "De la légèreté d'outil," 438–47.

28. Ibid., 443.

29. Ibid., 444.

30. Bell, "Unbearable Lightness of Being French."

31. Perrin, *Henriette de Marconne*, 80–81.

32. Bell, "Unbearable Lightness of Being French," 1128–29; Bell, *Cult of the Nation*, 147–48.

33. Caylus, "De la légèreté d'outil," 445.

34. Ibid., 446.

35. Ibid.

36. On misogynistic and sexualized metaphors of overconsumption, see especially

J. Jones, "Coquettes and Grisettes"; Crowston, *Credit, Fashion, Sex*, 87–95.

37. Virgil, *Virgil*, 233.

38. Bambeck, "Cire vierge"; Lawrence, "Sacred Bee."

39. Caylus and Majault, *Mémoire*, 44.

40. Gaehtgens, *Joseph-Marie Vien*, 151–56, cat. nos. 108, 109, 115, 116. I include in this count the two "priestesses" that Vien exhibited at the 1755 Salon, whose medium was unspecified in the Salon livret but were identified as encaustics by a contemporary critic: Baillet de Saint-Julien, "Lettre à un partisan," 14–15. Eighteenth-century antiquarians commonly associated priestesses with chastity. See, for example, Montfaucon's comments on the moral qualifications of priests and priestesses in Montfaucon, *Supplément au livre de l'antiquité expliquée*, 4–6.

41. In addition to the many such paintings by Vien and Van Loo that I discuss, we find comparable listings for encaustics by Louis-Joseph Le Lorrain and Dominique Lefèvre-Desforges. For Le Lorrain, see Remy, *Catalogue raisonné... après le décès de M. de Jullienne* (1767), 113, no. 297. For Lefèvre-Desforges, see Paillet, *Catalogue de tableaux des meilleurs maitres* (1775), 19, no. 60.

42. Nicholson, "Ideology of Feminine 'Virtue.'"

43. Paillet, *Catalogue de tableaux des meilleurs maitres* (1775), 17, no. 53. Remy, *Cabinet de feu Son Altesse Sérénissime Monseigneur le prince de Conti* (1777), 215, no. 713. Basan and Joullain, *Cabinet de feu M. le marquis de Ménars* (1782), 39–40, no. 128. Paillet and Chariot, *Cabinet de M. B*** [Benoit]* (1786), 16, no. 36 (the catalog specifies that the painting was acquired from the "Marquis de Ménard" [sic], meaning that it is likely the same painting as the one from the Ménars sale). Paillet, *Tableaux des trois écoles* (1788), 8, no. 10. Paillet, *Cabinet de M. de Castelmore* (1791), 12, no. 23. I base the total count on the available records in the Getty Provenance Index.

44. Fend, *Fleshing Out Surfaces*, 145.

45. For Raphael, see especially Nicolas Mignard's lecture on *La Grande Sainte Famille* from September 3, 1667, and Jean Nocret's lecture on *La belle jardinière* from April 6, 1669: Lichtenstein and Michel, *Conférences de l'Académie royale*, 1:144 and 314. For Parmigianino, see Dezallier d'Argenville, *Abrégé de la vie*, 1:222.

46. Hyde, *Making Up the Rococo*, 45–72.

47. La Font de Saint-Yenne, *Sentimens sur quelques ouvrages*, 33.

48. Hyde, *Making Up the Rococo*, 52.

49. Ibid., 83–106.

50. Grenaille, *L'honneste fille*, 3:314. The issue is explored in greater detail in Lanoë, *La poudre et le fard*, 29.

51. For eighteenth-century debates about the desirability of sheen, see Étienne, "Fenêtre ou miroir?"

52. Diderot, *L'histoire et le secret*, 92.

53. Letter from Caylus to Paciaudi, December 1758. Caylus, *Correspondance inédite*, 1:19.

54. Letter from Caylus to Paciaudi, September 15, 1760. Ibid., 1:203.

55. For Jullienne, see Remy, *Catalogue raisonné... après le décès de M. de Jullienne* (1767), 113, no. 297. For La Live, see La Live de Jully, *Catalogue historique* (1764), 38; Remy, *Cabinet de M. de Lalive de Jully* (1769), 50, no. 102.

56. Gaehtgens, *Joseph-Marie Vien*, 154.

57. On Geoffrin as a tastemaker, see Ziskin, *Private Salons*, 153–296. The relationship of Geoffrin's artistic patronage with her social status is also highlighted in Lilti, *World of the Salons*, 95; Guichard, *Amateurs d'art*, 222–23.

58. "C'est là qu'il acquit un jugement sûr et que, malgré lui, il épura son goût." Dufort

de Cheverny, *Règnes de Louis XV et Louis XVI*, 1:117.

59. Salmon, *Madame de Pompadour et les arts*, 200–202.

60. Wager, "The Fast and the Fugitive."

61. Diderot, "Regrets," 55.

62. Social scientists now use the term "Diderot effect" to describe a version of this pattern. For the coining of the term, see McCracken, *Culture and Consumption*, 118–29.

63. For a foundational account, with emphasis on the decorative arts, see Eriksen, *Early Neo-Classicism in France*, esp. 48–51. A growing body of scholarship has explored the relation between Neoclassicism and sartorial fashions. See, for example, Rauser, *Age of Undress*; Cage, "Sartorial Self."

64. Letter to Paciaudi, September 26, 1763, in Caylus, *Correspondance inédite*, 1:355.

65. La Live de Jully, *Catalogue historique* (1764), 110.

66. Boudier de Villemert and Meusnier de Querlon, *Avant-coureur*, 1760, 234; Boudier de Villemert and Meusnier de Querlon, *Avant-coureur*, 1764, 423; Meusnier de Querlon, *Affiches, annonces et avis divers*, 1764, 124. On the invocation of antiquity to promote cosmetics in particular, see M. Martin, *Selling Beauty*, 68.

67. Vigny, "Dissertation sur l'architecture," 69.

68. In this respect, the *goût grecque* of the mid-eighteenth century disrupted one of the central assumptions behind the "quarrel of the ancients and moderns." Partisans of antiquity had traditionally argued that Classicism transcended fashion because it had stood the test of time. Boileau, *Œuvres diverses du sieur D****, 189–91.

69. Rouquet, *Art nouveau*. For an analysis of Rouquet's text in the context of parodic literary devices from the period, see Lavezzi, "Tableau qui brûle."

70. Rouquet, *Art nouveau*, 11.

71. Ibid., 11.

72. Cochin, "Avis aux Dames."

73. Ibid., 127.

74. Ibid., 128.

75. Ibid., 129.

76. Vien, Bachelier, Hallé, Roslin, and Le Lorrain all exhibited works in encaustic. Guiffrey, *Collection des livrets*, 18:15–28.

77. *Lettre sur le Salon de 1755*, 27.

78. *Journal œconomique*, December 1755, 89–90.

79. "Lettre d'un particulier à un de ses parents," 644.

80. *Réponse à une lettre adressée à un partisan du bon goût*, 22.

81. The sale price of Vien's *Tête de vierge*, for example, declined by 72 percent between 1755 and 1770. Gaehtgens, *Joseph-Marie Vien*, 154.

82. For England, see Mayer and Myers, "Painting with Wax"; Dubois, "'Use a Little Wax'"; Hunter, *Painting with Fire*, 89–130. For Italy, see Liberati, "Requeno, Lorgna, Gerli e Reiffenstein"; Carofano, "Fortuna dell'encausto nel Settecento"; Calbi, "Dell'Era pittore a encausto"; Nenci, "Encausto tra teoria ed empiria." For more recent encaustic revivals, see Duffy, "Contemporary Encaustic Techniques."

83. *Mercure de France*, August 1755, 262. The invention was reviewed and approved by the Académie royale d'architecture: *Mercure de France*, June 1757, 143–44. On Odiot's purchase of Bachelier's secret, see Fréron, "L'histoire & le secret," 159–60. On the competitive market for interior wall paint during this time, see Scott, *Rococo Interior*, 22.

84. *Mercure de France*, June 1757, 167–71.

85. Fréron, "Nouvelle manière." See also a similar invention announced a year later by a certain Gadifer: Boudier de Villemert, *Feuille necessaire*, 152–53.

86. Reiffenstein, "Pensées"; Meusnier de Querlon, *Annonces, affiches, et avis divers*, 1757, 30. For more on Reiffenstein, see Hagen, "Johann Friedrich Reiffenstein."

87. The details of Montpetit's invention, which I summarily sketch here, have been more extensively documented in Massing, "Arnaud Vincent de Montpetit"; see also Justus, "Fractured Mirror."

88. Montpetit, "Peinture éludorique," 333.

89. Montpetit, "Essais sur les moyens de conserver les portraits peints à l'huile," Archives de l'Académie des sciences, Paris, pochette de séance, April 29, 1775. Montpetit also published a short summary of his methods along with a copy of the official approbation he received from the Academy: see Montpetit, *Note intéressante*. He contacted the royal arts administration about his invention the following year: Montpetit to Charles Claude de La Billarderie, comte d'Angiviller, February 28, 1776, Archives nationales, Paris, O1 1913.

90. For this reason, Montpetit went on to argue that all old oil paintings ought to be sealed behind a layer of glass to prevent further deterioration. Montpetit, "Mémoire sur le nettoyage des tableaux peints à l'huile, et leur conservation à la postérité, sans altération" (June 17, 1775), Archives nationales, Pierrefitte-sur-Seine, 20144790/126. See also Montpetit, "Essais sur les moyens de conserver les portraits," Archives de l'Académie des sciences, Paris, pochette de séance, April 29, 1775, 25; Arnaud Vincent de Montpetit to Charles Claude de La Billarderie, comte d'Angiviller, July 31, 1780, Archives nationales, Paris, O1 1913.

91. Montpetit, *Note intéressante*, 14.

92. The portrait of Louis XV has suffered moderate discoloration of the adhesive between the paint and glass, and it exhibits several small areas of paint loss. Neuner, "Étude préalable à la restauration; Vincent de Montpetit: Portrait de Louis XV," Centre de recherche et de restauration des musées de France, Versailles, no. 22792. On the instability of Montpetit's paintings more broadly, see Massing, "Arnaud Vincent de Montpetit," 363.

93. The painting underwent conservation treatment in 2005. See Langlois, Le Hô, and Eveno, "Armand Vincent Montpetit (1713–1800); Portrait d'alexis Piron (1757) L635," Centre de recherche et de restauration des musées de France, Paris, no. 6766.

94. "Soit paresse, soit intérêt, on aime à faire beaucoup en peu de temps; on ébauche, on verni, on glace, on barbouille d'huile . . . et voilà un tableaux qui fait de l'effet, qui séduit pour le moment, mais qui dans peu de temps se détruit et n'offre plus à la vue que des touches dures et désagréables. Cette manière prompte est attrayante pour ceux qui n'en connaissent pas les conséquences: c'est ainsi que les tableaux peuvent se multiplier à l'infini sans qu'il en passe beaucoup avec avantage à la postérité." Montpetit, "Essais sur les moyens de conserver les portraits peints à l'huile," Archives de l'Académie des sciences, Paris, pochette de séance, April 29, 1775, 19.

95. "On ne marchande pas l'immortalité." Guyton de Morveau, "Recherches pour perfectionner la préparation des couleurs employées dans la peinture," in "Rapports sur diverses inventions, lus à l'Académie de peinture. École des Beaux-Arts. Ms. 237," n.d., 41, Institut national d'histoire de l'art, Paris, Ms. 1023.

96. *Journal de Paris*, May 4, 1782, 494; Guyton de Morveau, "Blanc de zinc," 155. Guyton's contemporaries complained of his commercial exploits, but the details of his trade agreements with his assistant, Jean-Baptiste Courtois, remain murky. Georges Bouchard, in his foundational biography of Guyton, suggests that Courtois was

the more profit-minded of the two. Bouchard, *Guyton-Morveau, chimiste et conventionnel*, 100.

97. Montpetit, for example, came from a far more modest background than his name would suggest. The honorific "de Montpetit" likely derived from the affectionate "mon petit" that his friends used to address him; it also may have been a way to distinguish him from the painter André Vincent. Pradère, "Notice sur Vincent de Montpetit," 282. Guyton adopted the appellation "de Morveau" after a fief purchased by his father, but the family was far from rich. Bouchard, *Guyton-Morveau, chimiste et conventionnel*, 37–38.

CHAPTER 4

1. It is first recorded in the collection of Jacques-Onésyme Bergeret, though no documentation has been found indicating that he owned a bird named Fifi. See Folliot, Regnault-Delalande, and Julliot, *Cabinet de feu M. Bergeret* (1786), 105, no. 361; Poulet and Scherf, *Clodion, 1738–1814*, 301–3. Another version exists in a private collection, suggesting that the work had an appeal that extended beyond Fifi's owner. Bellanger, Dolin-Dolcy, and Spadotto, *Regard sur la sculpture*, 42.

2. Gaehtgens and Wedekind, *Culte des grands hommes*; Bonnet, *Naissance du Panthéon*.

3. Erika Naginski, in her study of eighteenth-century sculpture, has gone so far as to argue that there was "no mismatch between philosophically driven theories of posterity and actual artistic practices." Naginski, *Sculpture and Enlightenment*, 19. Aline Magnien's study of eighteenth-century sculpture treats the phenomenon in more dialectical terms, seeing the rhetoric of Classical endurance as counterbalanced by an appreciation for the accidental and contingent forms of nature. See especially her chapter "Entre le permanent et l'accidentel," in Magnien, *La nature et l'antique*, 87–121.

4. A brief but compelling overview of this market can be found in Scherf, "Collections et collectionneurs." The 2015 exhibition of sculpture at Sèvres organized by Guilhem Scherf and Tamara Préaud also provides ample documentation of the market for small-scale sculpture in porcelain. Préaud and Scherf, *Manufacture des Lumières*.

5. Poulet and Scherf, *Clodion, 1738–1814*, 303.

6. As Michael Levey has pointed out, Houdon's travels to America and Falconet's work for Catherine the Great can be attributed to the paucity of large-scale opportunities for sculptors in France under Louis XVI. Levey, *Painting and Sculpture in France*, 235.

7. Before the Seven Years' War, the treasury spent roughly 30 percent of its revenues on its debts; after the war, debt payments accounted for 60 percent of revenues. Riley, *Seven Years War*, 231.

8. On the preponderance of financiers among Clodion's patrons, see Scherf, "Collections et collectionneurs," 155; Poulet and Scherf, *Clodion, 1738–1814*, 291. On Clodion's ties to the world of real estate speculation, see Pinon, "Maison d'artiste."

9. On access to credit, see Hoffman, *Priceless Markets*, 156–57. On real estate speculation, see Pinon, "Lotissement spéculatifs." On the Paris stock exchange, see Taylor, "Paris Bourse."

10. Joullain, *Réflexions sur la peinture et la gravure*, 114.

11. Michael Levey first used these words to sum up Clodion's art in 1972,

subsequently republished in Levey, *Painting and Sculpture in France*, 235. More recent scholarship, most notably the 1992 exhibition organized by Guilhem Scherf and Anne Poulet, has given us a much more fine-grained understanding of the artist's work while largely affirming Levey's assessment. Scherf elegiacally describes Clodion as a sculptor of "le rêve immatériel d'un paradis perdu." Poulet and Scherf, *Clodion, 1738–1814*, 50. Scherf also borrowed Levey's phrase for an essay published concurrently with his exhibition: Scherf, "Clodion, sculpteur de la douceur de vivre."

12. On anti-luxury discourse in the second half of the eighteenth century, see Shovlin, *Political Economy of Virtue*. On the image-consciousness of collectors, see especially Bailey, *Patriotic Taste*.

13. Clodion and Fragonard have frequently been compared. See Villars, *Notes sur Clodion*, 5; Mantz, "Musée rétrospectif," 341; M. Levey, *Painting and Sculpture in France*, 238. On Fragonard's strategy of sidestepping the Salon to sell work directly to collectors, see especially P. Michel, *Peinture et plaisir*, 264–67.

14. The technical definition and properties of the medium have been examined thoroughly in Hubbard and Motture, "Making of Terracotta Sculpture"; Fisher, "Terracotta"; Scherf, *Playing with Fire*, 14–69; Sigel, "Visual Glossary."

15. Sigel, "Visual Glossary," 92.

16. Gaskell and Lie, "Sketches in Clay." After Bernini's death, one of his assistants apparently supported himself by selling the master's *bozzetti* to collectors. Bernini, *Vita del cavalier Gio. Lorenzo Bernino*, 161–62.

17. Scherf, *Playing with Fire*, 2–7.

18. La Live de Jully, *Catalogue historique*, vi–vii.

19. See, for example, the recognition of "le feu & la vivacité" of terracotta models in Watelet and Levesque, "Modèle," in *Encyclopédie méthodique*, 1:523.

20. On the gendered associations of fire in artistic creation during this period, see Sheriff, *Moved by Love*, 175–78.

21. On the metaphors of fiery genius more broadly, see McMahon, *Divine Fury*, 88.

22. For an excellent guide to the different forms of damage that the medium can exhibit, see Sigel, "Visual Glossary," 92–93.

23. Hubbard and Motture, "Making of Terracotta Sculpture," 87; Sigel, "Clay Modeling Techniques," 67.

24. Hubbard and Motture, "Making of Terracotta Sculpture," 91.

25. Berson et al., "Restauration des sculptures," 52.

26. Guiffrey, "Scellés et inventaires d'artistes," 284.

27. Lebrun, *Cabinet de M. M *** [Morel]* (1786), 128, no. 455.

28. Élie and Destouches, *Cabinet de feu J. B. Guyot* (1809), 98, no. 331.

29. Sale catalogs commonly specify this fact. Examples are too numerous to mention comprehensively. See, for instance, Feuillet, *Cabinet de feu M. Carpentier* (1774), 23, no. 109; Paillet, *Cabinet de M. Ch*** [Chariot]* (1788), 43–44, nos. 193–97.

30. One sale catalog stated explicitly that Clodion's works were covered with glass "pour les garantir de la poussière." Paillet and Chariot, *Cabinet de M. B. de B*** [Billard de Bélisard]* (1785), 64, no. 127.

31. See, for example, the description of a vase by Clodion as "sous sa cage de verre qui est cassée." Lebrun and Paillet, *Catalogue des objets précieux* (1793), 135, no. 515.

32. The comments served as a preamble to a series of seven lectures on seventeenth-century sculptors. Caylus, "Vie de Jacques Sarazin," 271.

33. Ibid.

34. On the importance of the term "magot" in xenophobic arguments about the debasement of taste, see Khelissa, "Menace sur le 'grand' art"; Préaud and Scherf, *Manufacture des Lumières*, 92.

35. Mariette, *Cabinet de feu M. Crozat* (1750), n.p.

36. Ibid.

37. The present location of the drawing is unknown. See Ananoff, *François Boucher*, no. 574. The vase appears in at least two of Boucher's paintings: *La Bergère prévoyante* and *Vertumne et Pomone*. Poulet and Scherf, *Clodion, 1738–1814*, 83; see also Priore, "François Boucher's Designs," 21–25; Poulet, "Neoclassical Vase by Clodion," 143.

38. *Catalogue raisonné des tableaux, desseins, estampes, bronzes . . . & autres curiosités, qui composent le cabinet de feu M. Boucher* (1771), 32–33, nos. 147–48.

39. The inventory taken at his death lists "trois tableaux de Boucher, représentant Jeux d'enfants, peints sur bois, prisés ensemble 3 francs." Guiffrey, "Sculpteur Claude Michel, dit Clodion," 414. For the intimate relation between the artists and numerous examples of Clodion's borrowings from Boucher, see Poulet and Scherf, *Clodion, 1738–1814*, 39, 83, 195, 198, 217–20, and 307.

40. On Boucher's critics, see especially Hyde, *Making Up the Rococo*. For the declining value of his work, see P. Michel, *Peinture et plaisir*, 251–54.

41. La Font de Saint-Yenne, *Reflexions sur quelques causes*, 132.

42. On the similarities between Diderot and La Font in their admiration for the sketch, see Boch, "L'art et la matière," 105, 117.

43. Diderot, *Salon de 1765*, 301.

44. See the almost verbatim repetition: "Le marbre, comme on sait, n'est que la copie de la terre cuite" (ibid., 286); "Le marbre n'est jamais qu'une copie" (ibid., 300–301).

45. "Le travail en marbre n'est qu'une copie." Watelet and Levesque, "Modèle," in *Encyclopédie méthodique*, 1:521; Magnien, *La nature et l'antique*, 319.

46. As Katie Scott has observed, La Font's fixation on the dangers of mirrors encapsulates this anxiety about mimicry's capacity to empty signs of meaning. Scott, *Rococo Interior*, 254–58.

47. Hyde, *Making Up the Rococo*, 83–106.

48. P. Michel, *Peinture et plaisir*, 34–38.

49. See the provenance notes in Poulet and Scherf, *Clodion, 1738–1814*, 78. Given that Clodion often sold copies of his own work, we cannot say definitively that all ten sales represent the same object. A linked chain of five sales, however, can be established between 1775 and 1783 (see sale catalogs of Mariette, Conti, Trouard, Tronchin, and Lebouf, which all include provenance notes), meaning that this same object sold, on average, more than once every two years.

50. Technical evidence for Clodion's use of this practice has been surveyed in Peiffer, "Statuaire céramique," 503–20. For a general overview of the molding techniques, see Fisher, "Terracotta," 39–40.

51. Scherf notes that Berruer, Pajou, and Houdon all sold reproductions of their own work. Poulet and Scherf, *Clodion, 1738–1814*, 262. For a description of Houdon's practices, see Poulet, *Jean-Antoine Houdon*, 26n53.

52. Poulet and Scherf, *Clodion, 1738–1814*, 252–59; Browne, "Sculpting the *Pittoresque*."

53. Other differences between the statues may be attributable to the work of restorers. The Mortemart version shows some evidence of restoration, such as the reconstruction of lost fingers. See the condition note in *Collections des ducs de Mortemart*, cat. 113.

54. Scherf, "Autour de Clodion," 56.

55. Ibid., 59n94.

56. Note the listing of "deux torses de femmes, de plâtre, et un lot de bras, pieds et mains, aussi en plâtre." Guiffrey, "Sculpteur Claude Michel, dit Clodion," 415–16.

57. Blanc, *Traité de la contrefaçon*, 551; Beausire, "Techniques et matériaux: Le Marcottage," 95–106.

58. Poulet and Scherf, *Clodion, 1738–1814*, 46.

59. *Mercure de France*, October 1773, 184.

60. Mariette, *Abecedario*, 1:377.

61. Basan, *Cabinet de feu M. Mariette* (1775), 11–12, no. 61; Lebrun, *Cabinet de M. Boyer-de-Fons-Colombe* (1790), 61, no. 306.

62. On the autographic trace as a means of enhancing an object's commercial value, see Guichard, *Griffe du peintre*, 77–114.

63. Dingé, *Notice sur M. Clodion*, 1–2.

64. Scott, "Reproduction and Reputation," 107–9.

65. For this longer tradition, which extends at least as far back as Donatello, see Dempsey, *Inventing the Renaissance Putto*.

66. Diderot's backhanded recognition of Boucher's "fécondité qui ne s'épuise point" is, in this respect, consistent with his condemnation of the painter's work as effeminate and oversexed. Diderot, *Salon de 1765*, 56. On the fraught eighteenth-century attitudes toward the female reproductive system as a metaphor of artistic creation, see Lajer-Burcharth, *Painter's Touch*, 191–98.

67. Shovlin, *Political Economy of Virtue*, 49–79; Kwass, "'Le superflu, chose très nécessaire.'"

68. The first such listing, as far as I am aware, appears in 1774: "Un petit Groupe de Bacchantes & Faunes, sous verre, encadré dans une bordure dorée, par M. Chandion [*sic*]: hauteur 9 pouces, largeur 8 pouces." Feuillet, *Cabinet de feu M. Carpentier*, 23, no. 109.

69. I base this count on Guilhem Scherf's survey of works by Clodion in Parisian sale catalogs from 1767 to 1820. Fifty-six works depicting bacchantes and/or satyrs can be identified from these sources. I have excluded from this count listings with nearly identical descriptions that may be resales of the same object, though this method of counting is complicated by the fact that Clodion often produced multiple versions of his work. The total number of distinct objects may therefore be higher. Scherf, "Répertoire thématique."

70. Remy, *Cabinet de feu m. Randon de Boisset* (1777), 85–86, no. 165. Patrick Michel notes that for the period from 1762 to 1778, twenty out of the thirty recorded sales of Poussin's paintings were for under 1,000 livres. Michel, *Peinture et plaisir*, 225.

71. P. Michel, *Peinture et plaisir*, 223–29.

72. Blunt, "Heroic and Ideal Landscape," 166–67.

73. In addition to Blunt, see Dempsey, "Classical Perception of Nature"; D. Panofsky, "Narcissus and Echo."

74. During his training at the French Academy in Rome, Clodion himself sometimes borrowed explicitly from antiquarian prints in his sculptures, capitalizing on the antiquarian interests of French collectors who passed through the city. Poulet, "Années romaines de Clodion."

75. The literature on agronomy, Physiocracy, and economic reform in eighteenth-century France is vast and can only be referenced selectively here. For agronomy, see especially Bourde, *Agronomie et agronomes en France*. For a critical assessment of the extensive literature on Physiocracy, see Charles and Théré, "Physiocratic Movement." For the relation between agronomy, Physiocracy, and anti-luxury sentiment, see Shovlin, *Political Economy of Virtue*, 49–79.

76. For example: "Les idées religieuses servirent ici la politique. On fit entendre

au peuple que les dieux s'intéressaient aux travaux de la campagne; qu'ils présidaient aux diverses opérations des cultivateurs, et aux différentes productions de la terre.... On rendit un culte public à ces divinités champêtres." Arcère, *De l'état de l'agriculture*, 9–12. "Cérès, Diane & Bacchus appelaient, dans les premiers temps, l'homme à la semence & à la récolte, aux soins de troupeaux & à la culture des vignes." Bedos de Celles, *Négociant patriote*, 168.

77. Mirabeau, *Ami des hommes*, 135.

78. Ibid.

79. Court de Gébelin, *Monde primitif*, 4:541–71. On Court de Gébelin's involvement in the Physiocratic movement, see Vardi, *Physiocrats*, 228–32; Charles and Théré, "Physiocratic Movement," 47.

80. Court de Gébelin, *Monde primitif*, 4:541–42.

81. For documentation of their shared membership, see Le Bihan, *Francs-maçons parisiens*, 130, 140. Scherf notes that Bouret de Vézelay, Baudard de Saint-James, and Laborde were all members. Poulet and Scherf, *Clodion, 1738–1814*, 291.

82. For related versions, see Poulet and Scherf, *Clodion, 1738–1814*, 323–26.

83. For Senneville's Bacchantes, see Paillet, *Cabinet de M*** [Le Roy de Senneville]* (1780), 86–87, nos. 268 and 267. For Chaulnes, see *Catalogue des différens cabinets ... de M. ci-devant duc de Chaulnes* (1790), 37, no. 26.

84. Shovlin, *Political Economy of Virtue*, 81.

85. In addition to Shovlin, see Charles and Théré, "Physiocratic Movement"; Kwass, "Consumption."

86. Shovlin, *Political Economy of Virtue*, 110.

87. Diderot, *Salon de 1767*, 166.

88. Shovlin, *Political Economy of Virtue*, 121–22; Mattick, "Art and Money," 31–33.

89. Shovlin, *Political Economy of Virtue*, 110–11.

90. For an overview of the key events, see Gillespie, "Ballooning in France and Britain." More recent studies include Kim, *Imagined Empire*; Thébaud-Sorger, *Aérostation au temps des Lumières*; Lynn, *Sublime Invention*.

91. *Journal de Paris*, November 22, 1783, 1340–41.

92. The financing strategies behind these projects have been examined most extensively in Thébaud-Sorger, *Aérostation au temps des Lumières*, 117–44.

93. Keen, *Literature, Commerce*, 40–77; Lynn, *Sublime Invention*, 143–62.

94. Kim, *Imagined Empire*, 53–75.

95. Furcy-Raynaud, "Correspondance de M. d'Angiviller avec Pierre," 40.

96. Ibid.

97. "Il me paraît évident que vous vous êtes laissé entraîner par autres objets puisque votre modèle ne fait que être terminé." Letter from d'Angiviller to Clodion, April 20, 1779, Archives nationales, Paris, O1 1172. Quoted in Scherf, "Autour de Clodion," 56.

98. Du Pont de Nemours, "Lettres sur les Salons," 115–16; *Mémoires secrets*, 13:269 [September 28, 1779].

99. *Mémoires secrets*, 13:269. For the period definition of *colifichet*, see *Dictionnaire de l'Académie françoise* (1762), 1:329.

100. For the invited artists, see "Notices concernant diverses expériences," 490; Furcy-Raynaud, "Correspondance de M. d'Angiviller avec Pierre," 158. See also the discussion of whether to compensate the uninvited participants: Joseph-Marie Vien to Charles Claude de La Billarderie, comte d'Angiviller, April 7, 1791, Archives nationales, Paris, O1 1148.

101. Clodion's clients could presumably see the model in his studio before he submitted it to the Academy for consideration. A proposed plan to exhibit the models at the

Salon never came to fruition after d'Angiviller deemed the entries unsuitable for display. Clodion's model was likely returned to him sometime between 1792 and 1793. Furcy-Raynaud, "Inventaire des sculptures exécutées," 418–21.

102. Furcy-Raynaud, "Correspondance de M. d'Angiviller avec Pierre," 40. For a discussion of the need for neutrality in the competition between balloon types, see Abbé de Ramatuelle, "Projet d'une piramide élevé pour la découverte des globes aërostatiques et à la gloire des voyageurs aëriens," January 17, 1784, Archives nationales, Paris, O1 1917. According to the *Mémoires secrets*, the competition was initially conceived as a means of honoring the hydrogen balloon launched by Jacques Charles before it was officially presented as a tribute to the balloon in general. *Mémoires secrets*, 24:100–101 [December 21, 1783].

103. The photograph and documentation surrounding the smaller sculpture are published in Tissandier, "Curiosités aérostatiques," 20–22; see also Poulet and Scherf, *Clodion, 1738–1814*, 62.

104. For the conclusion that the figures were molded, see Draper, "French Terracottas," 22.

105. On the structural limits of marble, see Penny, *Materials of Sculpture*, 75–79. Bronze would have afforded Clodion greater flexibility than marble, but he had virtually no experience with the medium. For the few exceptions, see Poulet and Scherf, *Clodion, 1738–1814*, 146.

106. Remington, "Monument Honoring the Invention," 246. The interpretation was subsequently endorsed in Draper, "French Terracottas," 22. Helen Rosenau offers an alternative hypothesis, suggesting that d'Angiviller may simply have found all of the submissions unsatisfactory. Rosenau, "Sphere as an Element," 65.

107. Kim, *Imagined Empire*, 173–93.

108. Tickets were sold for 3 and 6 livres. Estimates of the total ticket revenue ranged between 15,000 and 18,000 livres. Luzac, *Nouvelles extraordinaires de divers endroits*, no. 58 (July 20, 1784): n.p.

109. "L'Abbé Miolan ou Ballon abimé," 1784.

110. The sculpture passed through various private collections before being acquired by the Metropolitan Museum of Art in 1944. For the full provenance, see Wardropper, *European Sculpture*, 200, no. 69. Edmond de Goncourt describes his ravishment upon encountering the sculpture for sale twice during the nineteenth century, its price, each time, far beyond his reach. Goncourt, *Maison d'un artiste*, 184–85.

111. C. Michel, *Académie Royale*, 307–10.

112. D'Angiviller to Vien, February 18, 1790, in Furcy-Raynaud, "Correspondance de M. d'Angiviller avec Pierre," 277.

113. Ibid.

114. Dingé, "Notice sur M. Clodion," 248.

EPILOGUE

1. Tino Sehgal, untitled statement in Hantelmann and Jongbloed, *I Promise It's Political*, 96.

2. Kreuzer and van den Valentyn, *Der flexible Plan*; Lupton, "Modern Curve"; Wilson, "Post-Colonial Rococo."

3. For Sehgal's admiration of Watteau, see Luke and Sehgal, "Brush with . . . Tino Sehgal."

4. Quoted in Confino, "Tino Sehgal's Tate Modern Exhibition."

5. Simonini, "Immaterial Guy," 31.

6. Sayej, "Terms and Conditions."

7. Lescaze, "How Does a Museum Buy."

8. Luke and Sehgal, "Brush with . . . Tino Sehgal."

9. On the temporal definition of subjectivity in empirical philosophy, see Lajer-Burcharth, "Drawing Time," 24–26; Yahav, *Feeling Time*, 23–49.

10. Quoted in Guichard, *Amateurs d'art*, 177.

11. On Sehgal's relationship with the experience economy, see especially Lütticken, "Progressive Striptease"; Bishop, "Black Box." On the concept of the experience economy more broadly, see Pine and Gilmore, *Experience Economy*.

12. Hantelmann, "Experiential Turn."

13. Crary, *Suspensions of Perception*; Crary, *Techniques of the Observer*.

14. Clark, "Painting in the Year 2"; Taws, *Politics of the Provisional*.

15. See, for example, the critical comments in Pernety, *Dictionnaire portatif de peinture*, 114. On the growing reliance of artists on pre-prepared materials, see especially Labreuche, *Paris, capitale de la toile à peindre*; Roth-Meyer, "Marchands de couleurs à Paris."

16. Callen, *Art of Impressionism*, esp. 98–110 and 141–46. For Impressionist attitudes toward chemically unstable color, see also Kalba, *Color in the Age of Impressionism*, 69–119.

17. Vibert, *Science de la peinture*, 11.

18. Ibid.

19. Moreau-Vauthier, *Technique of Painting*, 62.

20. Mainardi, *End of the Salon*, 9–36 and 135–36.

21. Moreau-Vauthier, *Technique of Painting*, 65.

22. See, most recently, the effort to conserve Delacroix's murals at Saint-Sulpice: Moskalik-Detalle et al., "Conservation of Murals by Eugène Delacroix"; Assoun and Moskalik-Detalle, "Chapelle des Saints-Anges."

23. See, for example, Barton, "Capitalism for the Long Term"; Klein, *This Changes Everything*.

24. See, for example, Slawinski et al., "Role of Short-Termism"; Paulson, "Short-Termism."

25. The CEO of Duke Energy, James Rogers, called for a return to "cathedral thinking" in a 2007 interview on clean energy. Zakaria, "'Cathedral Thinking,'" 48. Greta Thunberg brought new attention to the term in her 2019 speech to the European Parliament. Thunberg, "Statement to the European Parliament."

26. Sehgal and Cattelan, "Tino Sehgal," 91.

27. Ibid.

28. Sehgal, "In Conversation."

29. Confino, "Tino Sehgal's Tate Modern Exhibition."

Bibliography

ARCHIVES

Archives de l'Académie des sciences, Paris
    Pochettes de séance
Archives nationales, Paris
    Correspondance et mémoires relatifs aux Beaux-arts, aux salons, aux expositions, aux musées, aux commandes d'œuvres d'art, 1660–1792, Series O1 1907–22 B
    Lettres du directeur général, Bâtiments du Roi, Series O1 1099–1148
Archives nationales, Pierrefitte-sur-Seine
    Archives des musées nationaux, département des peintures du musée du Louvre, 1788–1974 (Series P) 20144790/1–20144790/210
Bibliothèque de l'École nationale supérieure des beaux-arts, Paris
    Papiers divers du comte de Caylus, Mss. 522–23
Centre de recherche et de restauration des musées de France, Paris and Versailles
    Langlois, Juliette, Anne Solenn Le Hô, and Myriam Eveno. "Armand Vincent Montpetit (1713–1800) Portrait d'Alexis Piron (1757) L635." May 26, 2005, no. 6766
    Lepavec, Geneviève. "Rapport d'intervention de conservation-restauration." September 1987, no. 9533
    Neuner, Monika. "Étude préalable à la restauration; Vincent de Montpetit: Portrait de Louis XV." April 6, 2011, no. 22792
    "Procès-verbaux des commissions de restauration." January 28, 1986, no. 9530
Institut national d'histoire de l'art, Paris
    "Rapports sur diverses inventions, lus à l'Académie de peinture. École des Beaux-Arts. Ms. 237." N.d., Ms. 1023

PRIMARY AND SECONDARY SOURCES

"L'Abbé Miolan ou Ballon abimé." In *Recueil. Histoire des ballons*, 1784. Bibliothèque nationale de France, Paris, IB-2-FOL. https://gallica.bnf.fr/ark:/12148/btv1b85093234.

Adamczak, Audrey. "Présence du pastel au Salon: Étude sur l'émergence d'un art." In *Le Salon de l'Académie royale de peinture et sculpture: Archéologie d'une institution*, edited by Isabelle Pichet, 172–94. Paris: Hermann, 2014.

———. *Robert Nanteuil, ca. 1623–1678*. Paris: Arthena, 2011.

Adhémar, Hélène. *Watteau: Sa vie, son œuvre*. Paris: P. Tisné, 1950.

Aghion, Irène, and Mathilde Avisseau, eds. *Caylus, mécène du roi: Collectionner les antiquités au XVIIIe siècle*. Paris: Institut national d'histoire de l'art, 2002.

Aïssé, Charlotte Elisabeth, and Charles Augustin Sainte-Beuve. *Lettres de Mademoiselle Aïssé à Madame Calandrini*. Paris: Gerdès, 1846.

Alberti, Leon Battista. *On Painting and On Sculpture: The Latin Texts of "De Pictura" and "De Statua."* Translated by Cecil Grayson. London: Phaidon, 1972.

Ananoff, Alexandre. *François Boucher*. Lausanne: La Bibliothèque des arts, 1976.

Arcère, Louis-Étienne. *De l'état de l'agriculture chez les Romains depuis le commencement de la République jusqu'au siècle de Jules César*. Paris: A. M. Lottin l'aîné, 1777.

Assoun, Julien, and Alina Moskalik-Detalle. "La chapelle des Saints-Anges: Delacroix à l'œuvre." In *Une lutte moderne, de Delacroix à nos jours*, edited by Dominique de Font-Réaulx and Marie Monfort, 28–43. Paris: Louvre, 2018.

Bachaumont, Louis Petit de. "Liste des meilleurs peintres, sculpteurs, graveurs et architectes des Académies royales de Peinture, Sculpture et Architecture, suivant leurs rangs à l'Académie, en 1750." *Revue universelle des arts* 5 (1857): 418–27.

Baetjer, Katharine, and Marjorie Shelley. *Pastel Portraits: Images of 18th-Century Europe*. New York: Metropolitan Museum of Art, 2011.

Bailey, Colin B. *Patriotic Taste: Collecting Modern Art in Pre-Revolutionary Paris*. New Haven: Yale University Press, 2002.

———. "'Toute seule elle peut remplir et satisfaire l'attention': The Early Appreciation and Marketing of Watteau's Drawings." In *Watteau and His World: French Drawing from 1700 to 1750*, edited by Alan Wintermute, 68–92. New York: The Frick Collection, 1999.

Baillet de Saint-Julien, Louis-Guillaume. "Lettre à un partisan du bon goût sur l'exposition des tableaux faite dans le grand Sallon du Louvre." N.p., 1755. https://gallica.bnf.fr/ark:/12148/btv1b84429672.

———. *La peinture: Ode de Milord Telliab*. London: n.p., 1753. https://gallica.bnf.fr/ark:/12148/btv1b8442925q.

Bambach, Carmen C. *Leonardo da Vinci Rediscovered*. 4 vols. New Haven: Yale University Press, 2019.

———. "Leonardo's Notes on Pastel Drawing." *Mitteilungen des Kunsthistorischen Institutes in Florenz* 52, no. 2/3 (2008): 176–204.

Bambeck, Manfred. "Cire vierge (Rosenroman, V. 19490). Jean de Meun und die mittelalterliche Deutungstradition eines christlichen Symbols." *Romanistisches Jahrbuch* 33 (1982): 97–110.

Banks, Oliver T. *Watteau and the North: Studies in the Dutch and Flemish Baroque Influence on French Rococo Painting*. New York: Garland, 1977.

Barbier, Edmond-Jean-François. *Journal historique et anecdotique du règne de Louis XV*. Edited by Arthur de La Villegille. Vol. 3. Paris: Jules Renouard, 1851.

Barcilon, Pinin Brambilla, and Pietro C. Marani. *Leonardo: The Last Supper*. Translated by Harlow Tighe. Chicago: University of Chicago Press, 2001.

Barton, Dominic. "Capitalism for the Long Term." *Harvard Business Review* 89, no. 3 (2011): 84–91.

Basan, Pierre-François. *Catalogue raisonné des différens objets de curiosités dans les sciences et arts qui composoient le cabinet de feu M. Mariette*. Paris: G. Desprez, 1775.

Basan, Pierre-François, and François Charles Joullain. *Catalogue des différens objets de curiosités dans les sciences et arts qui composoient le Cabinet de feu M. le marquis de Ménars, commandeur des ordres du Roi, conseiller d'état ordinaire d'épée, lieutenant-général des provinces de Beauce & d'Orléanois, directeur & ordonnateur-général des bâtimens du Roi, jardins, arts, académies, & manufactures royales, capitaine-gouverneur* du château & de la ville de Blois*. Paris: Basan, Joullain, & Prault, 1782.

Baumer, Ursula, Johann Koller, and Irene Fiedler. "Fette Öle, trocknende Öle und Trockenöle: Die Bindemittel bei Watteau, Pater und Lancret." In *Französische Gemälde*, edited by Christoph Martin Vogtherr, 51–59. Berlin: Akademie Verlag, 2011.

Beausire, Alain. "Techniques et matériaux: Le Marcottage." In *La sculpture française au XIXᵉ siècle*, 95–106. Paris: Galeries Nationales du Grand Palais, 1986.

Bedos de Celles, François. *Le négociant patriote, contenant un tableau qui réunit les avantages du commerce, la connoissance des spéculations de chaque nation; & quelques vues particulieres sur le commerce avec la Russie, sur celui du Levant, & de l'Amérique Angloise. Ouvrage utile aux négocians, armateurs, fabriquans & agricoles*. Paris: Royez, 1784.

Bell, David A. *The Cult of the Nation in France: Inventing Nationalism, 1680–1800*. Cambridge, MA: Harvard University Press, 2001.

———. "The Unbearable Lightness of Being French: Law, Republicanism and National Identity at the End of the Old Regime." *American Historical Review* 106, no. 4 (2001): 1215–35.

Bellanger, Patrice, Catherine Dolin-Dolcy, and Karine Spadotto. *Regard sur la sculpture: "Morceaux choisis" d'une collection, 1650–1800*. Paris: Galerie Patrice Bellanger, 2003.

Bergeon, Ségolène. "Quelques points de technique picturale." In *Antoine Watteau (1684–1721): Le peintre, son temps et sa légende*, edited by François Moureau and Margaret Morgan Grasselli, 135–39. Paris: Champion-Slatkine, 1987.

Bergeon, Ségolène, and Lola Faillant-Dumas. "The Restoration of the *Pilgrimage to the Island of Cythera*." In *Watteau, 1684–1721*, edited by Margaret Morgan Grasselli and Pierre Rosenberg, 460–64. Washington, DC: National Gallery of Art, 1984.

Bergeon, Ségolène, and Élisabeth Martin. "Fragonard: Restauration et technique picturale au Louvre." *Science et technologie de la conservation et de la restauration des œuvres d'art et du patrimoine*, no. 1 (1988): 9–40.

Bernini, Domenico. *Vita del cavalier Gio. Lorenzo Bernino*. Rome: Rocco Bernabò, 1713.

Berson, Frédérique, Catherine Lepeltier, Véronique Milande, and Mélanie Parmentier. "La restauration des sculptures: Un chantier d'ampleur à Sèvres." In *La manufacture des Lumières: La sculpture à Sèvres de Louis XV à la Révolution*, edited by Tamara Préaud and Guilhem Scherf, 49–57. Dijon: Éditions Faton, 2015.

Besnard, Paul Albert, and Georges Wildenstein. *La Tour: La vie et l'œuvre de l'artiste*. Paris: Les Beaux-Arts, Edition d'études et de documents, 1928.

Bishop, Claire. "Black Box, White Cube, Gray Zone: Dance Exhibitions and Audience Attention." *TDR/The Drama Review* 62, no. 2 (2018): 22–42.

Blanc, Étienne. *Traité de la contrefaçon et de sa poursuite en justice*. Paris: Raymond, 1838.

Blunt, Anthony. "The Heroic and the Ideal Landscape in the Work of Nicolas Poussin." *Journal of the Warburg and Courtauld Institutes* 7 (1944): 154–68.

Boch, Julie. "L'art et la matière: Diderot et La Font de Saint-Yenne." In *Aux limites de l'imitation: L'ut pictura poesis à l'épreuve de la matière (XVIᵉ–XVIIIᵉ* siècles), edited by Ralph Dekoninck, Agnès Guiderdoni-Bruslé, and Nathalie Kremer, 103–20. Amsterdam: Rodopi, 2009.

Boileau, Nicolas. *Œuvres diverses du sieur D*** avec le Traité du sublime ou du merveilleux dans le discours, traduit du grec de Longin*. Paris: Barbin, 1694.

Bonnet, Jean-Claude. *Naissance du Panthéon: Essai sur le culte des grands hommes*. Paris: Fayard, 1998.

Börsch-Supan, Helmut. "Joseph Vivien als Hofmaler der Wittelsbacher." *Münchner Jahrbuch der bildenden Kunst* 14 (1963): 129–212.

Bouchard, Georges. *Guyton-Morveau, chimiste et conventionnel: 1737–1816*. Paris: Librairie académique Perrin, 1938.

Boudier de Villemert, Pierre-Joseph, ed. *La feuille nécessaire*. Paris: Michel Lambert, 1759.

Boudier de Villemert, Pierre-Joseph, and Anne-Gabriel Meusnier de Querlon, eds. *L'avant-coureur*. Paris: Michel Lambert, 1760–73.

Bouhours, Dominique. *Les entretiens d'Ariste et d'Eugène*. Paris: Sebastien Mabre-Cramoisy, 1671.

———. *La manière de bien penser dans les ouvrages d'esprit: Dialogues*. Amsterdam: Wolfgang, 1688.

Bourde, André J. *Agronomie et agronomes en France au XVIIIe siècle*. Paris: SEVPEN, 1967.

Bourdieu, Pierre. *Distinction: A Social Critique of the Judgement of Taste*. Translated by Richard Nice. Cambridge, MA: Harvard University Press, 1984.

Braudel, Fernand. *The Wheels of Commerce*. Translated by Siân Reynolds. Vol. 2. New York: Harper & Row, 1982.

Brejon de Lavergnée, Arnauld. *L'inventaire Le Brun de 1683: La collection des tableaux de Louis XIV*. Paris: Réunion des musées nationaux, 1987.

Brejon de Lavergnée, Barbara. "Some New Pastels by Simon Vouet: Portraits of the Court of Louis XIII." *Burlington Magazine* 124, no. 956 (1982): 689–93.

Browne, Elizabeth Saari. "Sculpting the *Pittoresque*: Clodion's *Erigone*." *French Porcelain Society Journal* 8 (2020): 119–37.

Brumfitt, J. H. *Voltaire, Historian*. Oxford: Oxford University Press, 1958.

Bryson, Norman. *Word and Image: French Painting of the Ancien Régime*. Cambridge: Cambridge University Press, 1981.

Bucklow, Spike. "The Description and Classification of Craquelure." *Studies in Conservation* 44, no. 4 (1999): 233–44.

———. "The Description of Craquelure Patterns." *Studies in Conservation* 42, no. 3 (1997): 129–40.

Burns, Thea. *The Invention of Pastel Painting*. London: Archetype, 2007.

———. "Matte Surfaces: Meaning for Audiences of 18th-Century Pastel Portraits and the Implications for Their Care Today." *Kermes*, no. 101–2 (2018): 19–25.

———. "The Political Construction of Fragility and French Arts Policy Around 1750." *Studies in Conservation* 43, suppl. 1 (1998): 190–93.

Bury, Adrian. *Maurice-Quentin de La Tour: The Greatest Pastel Portraitist*. London: Skilton, 1971.

Cabezas, Hervé. "Voltaire, ses portraits, par Maurice-Quentin de La Tour et Joseph Rosset, et leur reproduction, au Musée Antoine Lécuyer de Saint-Quentin." *Bulletin de la Société de l'histoire de l'art français,* année 2009 (2011): 175–202.

Cage, E. Claire. "The Sartorial Self: Neoclassical Fashion and Gender Identity in France, 1797–1804."

Eighteenth-Century Studies 42, no. 2 (2009): 193–215.

Cailleux, Jean. "A Strange Monument and Other Watteau Studies." *Burlington Magazine* 117, no. 865 (1975): 246–49.

Calbi, Emilia. "Dell'Era pittore a encausto." In *Giovan Battista Dell'Era (1765–1799): Un artista lombardo nella Roma neoclassica*, 96–105. Milan: Mazzotta, 2000.

Callen, Anthea. *The Art of Impressionism: Painting Technique and the Making of Modernity*. New Haven: Yale University Press, 2000.

Camesasca, Ettore. *Tout l'œuvre peint de Watteau*. Paris: Flammarion, 1982.

Carofano, Pierluigi. "Il dibattito Caylus-Diderot e il primato della riscoperta dell'encausto." *Bulletin de l'Association des historiens de l'art italien* 13 (2007): 82–95.

———. "Fortuna dell'encausto nel Settecento: I 'Saggi sul ristabilimento dell'antica arte de' greci e romani pittori' di Vincenzo Requeño." *Anales de historia del arte*, 2013, 177–92.

Carriera, Rosalba. *Rosalba Carriera: Lettere, diari, frammenti*. Edited by Bernardina Sani. 2 vols. Florence: Leo S. Olschki, 1985.

Catalogue des différens cabinets qui composent la riche collection de M. ci-devant duc de Chaulnes. Paris: Gaillard, Dumotiez, Paillet, Regnault, & Jaluseau, 1790.

Catalogue raisonné des tableaux, desseins, estampes, bronzes . . . & autres curiosités, qui composent le cabinet de feu M. Boucher. Paris: Musier, Père, 1771.

Caviglia, Susanna. *History, Painting, and the Seriousness of Pleasure in the Age of Louis XV*. Oxford: Voltaire Foundation, 2020.

Caylus, Anne-Claude-Philippe, comte de. *Correspondance inédite du comte de Caylus avec le P. Paciaudi, théatin (1757–1765): Suivie de celles de l'abbé Barthélemy et de P. Mariette avec le même*. Edited by Charles Nisard. 2 vols. Paris: Imprimerie nationale, 1877.

———. "De la légèreté d'outil." In Lichtenstein and Michel, *Conférences de l'Académie royale*, 6:438–47.

———. "Exposition des ouvrages de l'Académie Royale de Peinture & de Sculpture, faite dans une sale du Louvre le 25 Août 1753." *Mercure de France*, October 1753, 158–65.

———. "Vie d'Antoine Watteau." In Lichtenstein and Michel, *Conférences de l'Académie royale*, 5:81–103.

———. "Vie de Jacques Sarazin." In Lichtenstein and Michel, *Conférences de l'Académie royale*, 5:268–83.

Caylus, Anne-Claude-Philippe, comte de, and Michel-Joseph Majault. *Mémoire sur la peinture à l'encaustique et sur la peinture à la cire*. Geneva: Pissot libraire, 1755.

Chaperon, Paul Romain. *Traité de la peinture au pastel: Du secret d'en composer les crayons, & des moyens de le fixer; avec l'indication d'un grand nombre de nouvelles substances propres à la peinture à l'huile, & les moyens de prévenir l'altération des couleurs*. Paris: Defer de Maisonneuve, 1788.

Charles, Loïc, and Christine Théré. "The Physiocratic Movement: A Revision." In *The Economic Turn: Recasting Political Economy in Enlightenment Europe*, edited by Sophus Reinert and Steven Kaplan, 35–70. London: Anthem Press, 2019.

Chu, John. "High Art and High Stakes: The 3rd Duke of Dorset's Gamble on Reynolds." *British Art Studies*, no. 2 (2016). https://doi.org/10.17658/issn.2058-5462/issue-02/jchu.

Clark, T. J. "Painting in the Year 2." In *Farewell to an Idea: Episodes from a History of Modernism*, 14–53. New Haven: Yale University Press, 1999.

Claverías, Belén Moreno. "L'inégalité comme norme: Modèles de consommation dans l'Espagne préindustrielle." In *Consommateurs et consommation, XVIIe–XXIe siècle: Regards franco-espagnols*, edited by Nicolas Marty and Antonio Escudero, 15–46. Perpignan: Presses universitaires de Perpignan, 2015.

Clements, Candace. "Noble Liberality and Speculative Industry in Early Eighteenth-Century Paris: Charles Coypel." *Eighteenth-Century Studies* 29, no. 2 (1995): 213–18.

Cochin, Charles-Nicolas. "Avis aux Dames." *Mercure de France*, May 1755, 126–31.

Collections des ducs de Mortemart, Château du Réveillon. Paris: Sotheby's, 2015.

Confino, Jo. "Tino Sehgal's Tate Modern Exhibition Metaphor for Dematerialisation." *Guardian*, October 5, 2012, sec. Guardian Sustainable Business. https://www.theguardian.com/sustainable-business/tino-sehgal-tate-modern-exhibition-metaphor-dematerialisation.

Coquery, Natacha. *L'hôtel aristocratique: Le marché du luxe à Paris au XVIIIe siècle*. Paris: Publications de la Sorbonne, 1998.

———. *Tenir boutique à Paris au XVIIIe siècle: Luxe et demi-luxe*. Paris: Comité des travaux historiques et scientifiques, 2011.

Le Courrier. Avignon: Alexandre Giroud, 1754.

Court de Gébelin, Antoine. *Monde primitif analysé et comparé avec le monde moderne considéré dans son génie allégorique et dans les allégories auxquelles conduisit ce génie*. Vol. 4. Paris: n.p., 1776.

Coypel, Antoine. "Commentaire de l'Épitre à son fils: Le coloris et le pinceau." In Lichtenstein and Michel, *Conférences de l'Académie royale*, 4:72–89.

———. "Commentaire de l'Épitre à son fils: Les anciens et les modernes." In Lichtenstein and Michel, *Conférences de l'Académie royale*, 4:115–25.

Crary, Jonathan. *Suspensions of Perception: Attention, Spectacle, and Modern Culture*. Cambridge, MA: MIT Press, 2001.

———. *Techniques of the Observer: On Vision and Modernity in the 19th Century*. Cambridge, MA: MIT Press, 1992.

Cronk, Nicholas. "The Epicurean Spirit: Champagne and the Defence of Poetry in Voltaire's 'Le Mondain.'" *Studies on Voltaire and the Eighteenth Century*, no. 371 (1999): 53–80.

Crow, Thomas. *Painters and Public Life in Eighteenth-Century Paris*. New Haven: Yale University Press, 1987.

Crowston, Clare Haru. *Credit, Fashion, Sex: Economies of Regard in Old Regime France*. Durham: Duke University Press, 2013.

D'Alembert, Jean Le Rond. "Eloge de M. le président de Montesquieu." *Mercure de France*, November 1755, 77–124.

Da Rin Bettina, Laura. "Il disegno a pastello in Italia nel XVI secolo: Un problema critico." Ph.D. diss., Università di Parma, 2016.

Debrie, Christine, and Xavier Salmon. *Maurice-Quentin de La Tour: Prince des pastellistes*. Paris: Somogy, 2000.

Delcourt, André. *La France et les établissements français au Sénégal entre 1713 et 1763*. Dakar: Institut français d'Afrique noire, 1952.

De Marchi, Neil, and Hans J. Van Miegroet. "Ingenuity, Preference, and the Pricing of Pictures: The Smith-Reynolds

Connection." *History of Political Economy* 31 (1999): 379–412.

———. "Transforming the Paris Art Market, 1718–1750." In *Mapping Markets for Paintings in Europe, 1450–1750*, 383–404. Turnhout: Brepols Publishers, 2006.

Démoris, René. "Le comte de Caylus et la peinture: Pour une théorie de l'inachevé." *Revue de l'art*, no. 142 (2003): 31–43.

Dempsey, Charles. "The Classical Perception of Nature in Poussin's Earlier Works." *Journal of the Warburg and Courtauld Institutes* 29 (1966): 219–49.

———. *Inventing the Renaissance Putto*. Chapel Hill: University of North Carolina Press, 2001.

De Piles, Roger. *Cours de peinture par principes*. Paris: Jacques Estienne, 1708.

———. *Les premiers élémens de la peinture pratique*. Paris: Langlois, 1684.

Dermigny, Louis. *La Chine et l'Occident: Le commerce à Canton au 18ᵉ siècle, 1719–1833*. Paris: SEVPEN, 1964.

Desfontaines, Pierre-François Guyot. *Apologie du caractère des Anglois et des François, ou Observations sur le livre intitulé, Lettres sur les Anglois et les François, et sur les voyages*. Paris: Briasson, 1726.

Dezallier d'Argenville, Antoine-Joseph. *Abrégé de la vie des plus fameux peintres*. 3 vols. Paris: De Bure, 1745.

Dictionnaire de l'Académie françoise. Vol. 1. Paris: J. B. Coignard, 1694.

Dictionnaire de l'Académie françoise. Vol. 1. Paris: Veuve de Bernard Brunet, 1762.

Dictionnaire universel françois et latin, contenant la signification et la définition tant des mots de l'une et de l'autre langue. Vol. 1. Paris: Veuve Delaune, 1743.

Diderot, Denis. *L'histoire et le secret de la peinture en cire*. N.p., 1755.

———. "Le pour et le contre." In *Œuvres complètes*, edited by Emita Hill, Roland Mortier, and Raymond Trousson, vol. 15. Paris: Hermann, 1986.

———. "Regrets sur ma vieille robe de chambre." In *Œuvres complètes*, edited by Jean Varloot, 18:41–60. Paris: Hermann, 1984.

———. *Ruines et paysages: Salon de 1767*. Edited by Else Marie Bukdahl, Annette Lorenceau, and Michel Delon. Paris: Hermann, 1995.

———. *Salon de 1765*. Edited by Else Marie Bukdahl and Annette Lorenceau. Paris: Hermann, 1984.

Dingé, Antoine. "Notice sur M. Clodion." *Journal des arts, des sciences, et de littérature* 18 (1814): 244–49.

———. *Notice sur M. Clodion*. Paris: A. Clo, 1814.

Draper, James David. "French Terracottas." *Metropolitan Museum of Art Bulletin* 49, no. 3 (1991): 1–56.

Dryden, John. *Fables Ancient and Modern*. London: Jacob Tonson, 1700.

———. *The Satires of D. J. Juvenalis Translated into English Verse*. London: J. Tonson, 1697.

Dubin, Nina L. *Futures and Ruins: Eighteenth-Century Paris and the Art of Hubert Robert*. Los Angeles: Getty Research Institute, 2010.

Dubois, Hélène. "'Use a Little Wax in Your Colours, but Don't Tell Anybody': Sir Joshua Reynolds's Painting Experiments with Wax and His Sources." *Hamilton Kerr Institute Bulletin* 3 (2000): 97–106.

Duffy, Michael. "Contemporary Encaustic Techniques—Johns, Marden, Thek." *Postprints: American Institute for Conservation of Historic and Artistic Works, Paintings Specialty Group* 18 (2006): 84–93.

Dufort de Cheverny, Jean-Nicolas. *Mémoires sur les règnes de Louis XV et Louis XVI et sur la Révolution*. Edited by Robert de Crèvecœur. Vol. 1. Paris: E. Plon, Nourrit et Cie, 1886.

Du Pont de Nemours, Pierre-Samuel. "Lettres sur les Salons de 1773, 1777 et 1779 adressées par Du Pont de Nemours à la Margrave Caroline-Louise de Bade." *Archives de l'art français,* new period, 2 (1908): 1–123.

Edwards, JoLynn. *Alexandre-Joseph Paillet: Expert et marchand de tableaux à la fin du XVIIIᵉ siècle*. Paris: Arthena, 1996.

Eidelberg, Martin. "Watteau's Drawings: Their Use and Significance." Ph.D. diss., Princeton University, 1977.

Elias, Norbert. *The Civilizing Process: Sociogenetic and Psychogenetic Investigations*. Translated by Edmund Jephcott. Oxford: Blackwell, 1994.

———. *The Court Society*. Translated by Edmund Jephcott. New York: Pantheon, 1983.

Élie, Charles, and F. Destouches. *Catalogue d'une riche collection de tableaux par les meilleurs maîtres des trois écoles: Figures, bustes, bas-reliefs et vases en marbre, terres cuites, bronzes, porcelaine, meubles des cabinets en laque, très-belle pendule et jeu de flûte, tour à guillocher, etc., composant le cabinet de feu J. B. Guyot, ancien Chanoine et Prévôt de l'abbaye de Saint-Martin de Tours*. Paris: Fournier & Petit-Quenot, 1809.

Elkins, James. *Why Are Our Pictures Puzzles? On the Modern Origins of Pictorial Complexity*. London: Routledge, 1999.

Eriksen, Svend. *Early Neo-Classicism in France: The Creation of the Louis Seize Style in Architectural Decoration, Furniture and Ormolu, Gold and Silver, and Sèvres Porcelain in the Mid-Eighteenth Century*. London: Faber, 1974.

Étienne, Noémie. "Fenêtre ou miroir? Quand le vernis définit le tableau (1750–1800)." In *La restauration des peintures et des sculptures: Connaissance et reconnaissance de l'œuvre*, edited by Pierre-Yves Kairis, Béatrice Sarrazin, and François Trémolières, 43–52. Paris: Armand Colin, 2012.

———. *The Restoration of Paintings in Paris, 1750–1815: Practice, Discourse, Materiality*. Translated by Sharon Grevet. Los Angeles: Getty Conservation Institute, 2017.

Fairchilds, Cissie. "The Production and Marketing of Populuxe Goods in Eighteenth-Century Paris." In *Consumption and the World of Goods*, edited by John Brewer and Roy Porter, 228–48. London: Routledge, 1993.

Faroult, Guillaume, Christophe Leribault, and Guilhem Scherf, eds. *L'Antiquité rêvée: Innovations et résistances au XVIIIᵉ siècle*. Paris: Gallimard, 2010.

Félibien, André. *Entretiens sur les vies et sur les ouvrages des plus excellens peintres anciens et modernes*. 5 vols. Paris: Le Petit, 1666–88.

———. *Recueil de descriptions de peintures et d'autres ouvrages faits pour le Roy*. Paris: Veuve de S. Mabre-Cramoisy, 1689.

———. *Tableaux du Cabinet du roy: Statues et bustes antiques des maisons royales*. Vol. 1. Paris: Imprimerie royale, 1677.

Fend, Mechthild. *Fleshing Out Surfaces: Skin in French Art and Medicine, 1650–1850*. Manchester: Manchester University Press, 2017.

———. "Gathering Likenesses: Quentin de La Tour at the Salon of 1753." In *L'art de l'Ancien Régime: Sortir du rang!*, edited by Thomas Kirchner, Sophie Raux, and Marlen Schneider, 147–68. Paris: Deutsches Forum für Kunstgeschichte, 2022.

Ferré, Jean. *Watteau*. Madrid: Éditions artistiques Athena, 1972.

Feuillet, Jean-Baptiste. *Catalogue des tableaux, desseins, bronzes, plâtres bronzés & porcelaines du cabinet de feu M. Carpentier, architecte du Roi & de ses académies, membre de l'Académie des Inscriptions & Belles-Lettres de Rouen*. Paris: Prault, 1774.

Fisher, Wendy. "Terracotta." In *The Making of Sculpture: The Materials and Techniques of European Sculpture*, 35–48. London: V&A Publications, 2007.

Folliot, J., François-Léandre Regnault-Delalande, and Philippe-François Julliot. *Catalogue des tableaux des trois écoles, gouaches, miniatures, pastels, dessins et estampes, bustes, vases, colonnes et tables de marbre, figures de bronze, terres cuites, porcelaines, meubles d'acajou, feux, bras et girandoles en bronze doré, bijoux, camées, figures moulées sur l'antique, & autres effets précieux, qui composoient le Cabinet de feu M. Bergeret, commandeur, trésorier-honoraire de l'ordre royal & militaire de Saint-Louis, receveur-général des finances*. Paris: Folliot, Delalande, & Julliot, 1786.

Frederick, Shane, George Loewenstein, and Ted O'Donoghue. "Time Discounting and Time Preference: A Critical Review." *Journal of Economic Literature* 40, no. 2 (2002): 351–401.

Fréron, Élie-Catherine. "Exposition des tableaux." *L'année littéraire*, 1755, vol. 6, letter 3 (September 19, 1755): 49–72.

———. "L'histoire & le secret de la peinture en cire." *L'année littéraire*, 1755, vol. 3, letter 7 (May 19, 1755): 145–71.

———. "Nouvelle manière de dorer sur le bois." *L'année littéraire*, 1758, vol. 1, letter 14 (February 16, 1758): 335–39.

Fripp, Jessica L. *Portraiture and Friendship in Enlightenment France*. Newark: University of Delaware Press, 2020.

Furcy-Raynaud, Marc, ed. "Correspondance de M. d'Angiviller avec Pierre." *Nouvelles archives de l'art français*, 3rd ser., 22 (1906; pub. 1907).

———. "Inventaire des sculptures exécutées au XVIIIe siècle pour la Direction des bâtiments du roi." *Archives de l'art français*, new period, 14 (1925–26; pub. 1927).

Furetière, Antoine. *Dictionnaire universel contenant généralement tous les mots françois tant vieux que modernes et les termes de toutes les sciences et des arts*. Vol. 1. The Hague: Arnout et Reinier Leers, 1690.

Gaehtgens, Thomas W. "Archaeology and Enlightenment: The Comte de Caylus and French Neo-Classicism." In *The First Painters of the King: French Royal Taste from Louis XIV to the Revolution*, edited by Colin B. Bailey, 37–45. New York: Stair Sainty Matthiesen, 1985.

———. *Joseph-Marie Vien, peintre du roi (1716–1809)*. Paris: Arthena, 1988.

Gaehtgens, Thomas W., and Gregor Wedekind, eds. *Le culte des grands hommes, 1750–1850*. Paris: Éditions de la Maison des sciences de l'homme, 2009.

Gaskell, Ivan, and Henry Lie, eds. "Sketches in Clay for Projects by Gian Lorenzo Bernini: Theoretical, Technical, and Case Studies." *Harvard University Art Museums Bulletin* 6, no. 3 (1999): 1–179.

Gazette. Paris: Bureau d'adresse, 1631–1765.

Gersaint, Edme-François. *Catalogue raisonné des bijoux, porcelaines, bronzes, lacqs, lustres de cristal de roche et de porcelaine, pendules de goût & autres meubles curieux ou composés; tableaux, desseins, estampes, coquilles & autres effets de curiosité, provenans de la succession* de M. Angran, vicomte de Fonspertuis. Paris: Pierre Prault & Jacques Barrois, 1747.

———. *Catalogue raisonné des diverses curiosités du cabinet de feu M. Quentin de Lorangère*. Paris: Jacques Barois, 1744.

Gibson-Wood, Carol. *Studies in the Theory of Connoisseurship from Vasari to Morelli*. New York: Garland, 1988.

Gikandi, Simon. *Slavery and the Culture of Taste*. Princeton: Princeton University Press, 2011.

Gillespie, Richard. "Ballooning in France and Britain, 1783–1786: Aerostation and Adventurism." *Isis* 75, no. 2 (1984): 249–68.

Glorieux, Guillaume. *À l'enseigne de Gersaint: Edme-François Gersaint, marchand d'art sur le Pont Notre-Dame, 1694–1750*. Paris: Presses universitaires de France, 2002.

———. *Watteau*. Paris: Citadelles & Mazenod, 2011.

Gombaud, Cécile, Julia Schultz, David Buti, Kaj Thuresson, and Magnus Mårtensson. "Maurice-Quentin de La Tour and Jean Valade Pastels: History, Materials and Studio Practice." *ICOM Committee for Conservation 18th Triennial Meeting*, 2017, 1–10. https://www.icom-cc-publications-online.org/1722/Maurice-Quentin-de-La-Tour-and-Jean-Valade-pastels--History-materials-and-studio-practice.

Goncourt, Edmond de. *Catalogue raisonné de l'œuvre peint, dessiné et gravé d'Antoine Watteau*. Paris: Rapilly, 1875.

———. *La maison d'un artiste*. Paris: G. Charpentier, 1881.

Goodman, Elise. *The Portraits of Madame de Pompadour: Celebrating the Femme Savante*. Berkeley: University of California Press, 2000.

Graffigny, Françoise de. *Correspondance de Madame de Graffigny*. Edited by J. A. Dainard. 15 vols. Oxford: Voltaire Foundation, 1985–2016.

Grasselli, Margaret Morgan, and Pierre Rosenberg. *Watteau, 1684–1721*. Washington, DC: National Gallery of Art, 1984.

Grenaille, François de. *L'honneste fille*. Vol. 3. Paris: J. Paslé, 1639.

Grimm, Friedrich Melchior. *Correspondance littéraire*. Edited by Maurice Tourneux. 16 vols. Paris: Garnier frères, 1877–82.

Guérin, Nicolas. *Description de l'Académie royale des arts, de peinture et de sculpture: Par feu M. Guérin, secrétaire perpétuel de ladite Académie*. Paris: Jacques Collombat, 1715.

Guichard, Charlotte. *Les amateurs d'art à Paris au XVIIIe siècle*. Seyssel: Champ Vallon, 2008.

———. *La griffe du peintre*. Paris: Seuil, 2018.

Guicharnaud, Hélène. "*Le progrès des arts du dessin sous le règne de Louis XIV*, par Nicolas Loir (1624–1679)." *L'Estampille* 401 (2005): 19–20.

Guiffrey, Jules, ed. *Collection des livrets des anciennes expositions depuis 1673 jusqu'en 1800*. 42 vols. Paris: Liepmannssohn et Dufour, 1869–1872.

———. "Histoire de l'Académie de Saint-Luc." *Archives de l'art français*, new period, 9 (1915).

———. "Scellés et inventaires d'artistes: 1741–1770." *Nouvelles archives de l'art français*, 2nd ser., 5 (1884).

———. "Le sculpteur Claude Michel, dit Clodion (1738–1814)." *Gazette des beaux-arts* 9 (1893): 392–417.

Guillerme, Jacques. "Caylus technologue: Note sur les commencements problématiques d'une discipline." *Revue de l'art*, no. 60 (1983): 47–50.

———. *L'atelier du temps: Essai sur l'altération des peintures*. Paris: Hermann, 1964.

Guyton de Morveau, Louis-Bernard. "Blanc de zinc pour la peinture." *Observations sur la physique*, August 1782, 155.

Hagen, August. "Johann Friedrich Reiffenstein." *Altpreußische Monatsschrift* 2 (1865): 506–36.

Hantelmann, Dorothea von. "The Experiential Turn." In *Living Collections Catalogue*. Minneapolis: Walker Art Center, 2014. http://walkerart.org/collections/publications/performativity/experiential-turn/.

Hantelmann, Dorothea von, and Marjorie Jongbloed, eds. *I Promise It's Political: Performativität in der Kunst*. Cologne: Museum Ludwig, 2002.

Haskell, Francis. *Patrons and Painters: A Study in the Relations Between Italian Art and Society in the Age of the Baroque*. New Haven: Yale University Press, 1980.

———. *Rediscoveries in Art: Some Aspects of Taste, Fashion, and Collecting in England and France*. Oxford: Phaidon, 1980.

Hattori, Cordélia. "Le comte de Caylus d'après les archives: Première partie." *Les cahiers d'histoire de l'art*, no. 5 (2007): 54–70.

Haudrère, Philippe. "L'origine du personnel de direction générale de la Compagnie française des Indes, 1719–1794." *Revue française d'histoire d'outre-mer* 67, no. 248 (1980): 339–71.

Heinich, Nathalie. *Du peintre à l'artiste: Artisans et académiciens à l'Age classique*. Paris: Éditions de Minuit, 1993.

Herrenschmidt, Florence. "Le prêt des pastels du musée Antoine Lécuyer à Saint-Quentin en 2004." *Support tracé*, no. 9 (2009): 17–23.

Histoire de l'Académie royale des inscriptions et belles-lettres. Vol. 25. Paris: Imprimerie royale, 1759.

Hoffman, Philip T. *Priceless Markets: The Political Economy of Credit in Paris, 1660–1870*. Chicago: University of Chicago Press, 2000.

Hoisington, Rena. "Maurice-Quentin de la Tour and the Triumph of Pastel Painting in Eighteenth-Century France." Ph.D. diss., New York University, Institute of Fine Arts, 2006.

Hubbard, Charlotte, and Peta Motture. "The Making of Terracotta Sculpture: Techniques and Observations." In *Earth and Fire: Italian Terracotta Sculpture from Donatello to Canova*, edited by Bruce Boucher, 83–95. New Haven: Yale University Press, 2001.

Huguet, Edmond. *Dictionnaire de la langue française du seizième siècle*. Vol. 2. Paris: Librairie ancienne Honoré Champion, 1932.

Huhtamo, Erkki, and Jussi Parikka, eds. *Media Archaeology: Approaches, Applications, and Implications*. Berkeley: University of California Press, 2011.

Hunter, Matthew C. "Joshua Reynolds's 'Nice Chymistry': Action and Accident in the 1770s." *Art Bulletin* 97, no. 1 (2015): 58–76.

———. *Painting with Fire: Sir Joshua Reynolds, Photography, and the Temporally Evolving Chemical Object*. Chicago: University of Chicago Press, 2019.

Hyde, Melissa Lee. *Making Up the Rococo: François Boucher and His Critics*. Los Angeles: Getty Research Institute, 2006.

Jeffares, Neil. *Dictionary of Pastellists Before 1800*. London: Unicorn Press, 2006.

———. "La Tour, *Le président de Rieux*." Pastels & Pastellists. 2021. http://www.pastellists.com/essays/latour_rieux.pdf.

———. "La Tour, *Mme de Pompadour*." Pastels & Pastellists. 2022. http://www.pastellists.com/Essays/LaTour_Pompadour.pdf.

———. "Loriot, Pellechet, Jurine: The Secrets of Pastel." Pastels & Pastellists. 2022. http://www.pastellists.com/Essays/Loriot.pdf.

———. *Maurice-Quentin de La Tour*. Pastels & Pastellists. 2021. http://www.pastellists.com/Misc/Jeffares_LaTour_2021ed.pdf.

———. "Parlementaires in Pastel." In *Regards nouveaux sur les institutions représentatives de l'Ancien Régime, la cour, la diplomatie, la guerre et la littérature: Essais en hommage à John Rogister*, edited by Bertrand Augé, 85–112. Paris: Éditions Pedone, 2017.

———. "Prolegomena." Pastels & Pastellists. 2016. http://www.pastellists.com/Misc/Prolegomena.pdf.

———. "Rosalba Carriera." Pastels & Pastellists. 2022. http://www.pastellists.com/articles/carriera.pdf.

———. "Rosalba's Portrait of John Law." *Neil Jeffares* (blog), October 29, 2020. https://neiljeffares.wordpress.com/2020/10/29/rosalbas-portrait-of-john-law/.

Jeffares, Neil, and Rosalba Carriera. "Rosalba Carriera's Journal." Pastels & Pastellists. 2022. http://www.pastellists.com/Essays/Carriera_journal.pdf.

Johns, Christopher M. S. "'An Ornament of Italy and the Premier Female Painter of Europe': Rosalba Carriera and the Roman Academy." In *Women, Art and the Politics of Identity in Eighteenth-Century Europe*, edited by Melissa Lee Hyde and Jennifer Dawn Milam, 20–45. Burlington, VT: Ashgate, 2003.

Jones, Jennifer. "Coquettes and Grisettes: Women Buying and Selling in Ancien Régime Paris." In *The Sex of Things: Gender and Consumption in Historical Perspective*, edited by Victoria de Grazia and Ellen Furlough, 25–53. Berkeley: University of California Press, 1996.

———. *Sexing La Mode: Gender, Fashion and Commercial Culture in Old Regime France*. Oxford: Berg, 2004.

Jones, Rica. "Introduction." In *Paint and Purpose: A Study of Technique in British Art*, edited by Stephen Hackney, Rica Jones, and Joyce Townsend, 9–16. London: Tate, 1999.

Joullain, François Charles. *Réflexions sur la peinture et la gravure, accompagnées d'une courte dissertation sur le commerce de la curiosité et les ventes en général*. Metz: Claude Lamort, 1786.

Journal de Paris. Paris: Quillau, 1777–1827.

Journal œconomique, ou Mémoires, notes et avis sur les arts, l'agriculture, le commerce et tout ce qui peut y avoir rapport, ainsi qu'à la conservation et à l'augmentation des biens de familles. Paris: Antoine Boudet, 1751–72.

Justus, Kevin L. "A Fractured Mirror: Vincent de Montpetit's 1774 Portrait on Glass of Louis XV." *Source: Notes in the History of Art* 26, no. 4 (2007): 33–38.

Kalba, Laura Anne. *Color in the Age of Impressionism: Commerce, Technology, and Art*. University Park: Penn State University Press, 2017.

Kavanagh, Thomas M. *Esthetics of the Moment: Literature and Art in the French Enlightenment*. Philadelphia: University of Pennsylvania Press, 1996.

Keen, Paul. *Literature, Commerce, and the Spectacle of Modernity, 1750–1800*. Cambridge: Cambridge University Press, 2012.

Kerber, Peter Björn. "Perfectibility and Its Foreign Causes: Reading for Self-Improvement in Eighteenth-Century Paris." In *Paris: Life & Luxury in the Eighteenth Century*, edited by Charissa Bremer-David, 75–89. Los Angeles: J. Paul Getty Museum, 2011.

Khelissa, Anne Perrin. "Menace sur le 'grand' art: Le peuple des magots et des statuettes en porcelaine au siècle des Lumières." In *Penser le "petit" de l'Antiquité au premier XXe siècle*, edited by Anne Perrin Khelissa, 88–98. Lyon: Fage, 2017.

Kim, Mi Gyung. *The Imagined Empire: Balloon Enlightenments in Revolutionary Europe*. Pittsburgh: University of Pittsburgh Press, 2016.

Kimball, Fiske. *The Creation of the Rococo*. Philadelphia: Philadelphia Museum of Art, 1943.

Klein, Naomi. *This Changes Everything: Capitalism vs. the Climate*. New York: Simon & Schuster, 2014.

Klinka-Ballesteros, Isabelle. *Les Pastels*. Orléans: Musée des beaux-arts, 2005.

Kluitenberg, Eric. "On the Archaeology of Imaginary Media." In *Media Archaeology: Approaches, Applications, and Implications*, edited by Erkki Huhtamo and Jussi Parikka, 48–69. Berkeley: University of California Press, 2011.

Kosek, Joanna M. "The Heyday of Pastels in the Eighteenth Century." *Paper Conservator* 22, no. 1 (1998): 1–9.

Kraatz, Anne. *Catalogue des dentelles*. Paris: Réunion des musées nationaux, 1992.

Krellig, Heiner. "Rosalba Carriera: Neue Quellen und Erkenntnisse zu den Lebensumständen der 'ersten Malerin Europas.'" In *Künstlerinnen: neue Perspektiven auf ein Forschungsfeld der Vormoderne*, edited by Birgit Ulrike Münch, Andreas Tacke, Markwart Herzog, and Sylvia Heudecker, 89–110. Petersberg: Michael Imhof Verlag, 2017.

Kreuzer, Stefanie, and Heike van den Valentyn. *Der flexible Plan: Das Rokoko in der Gegenwartskunst*. Dortmund: Verlag Kettler, 2018.

Kriz, Kay Dian. *Slavery, Sugar, and the Culture of Refinement: Picturing the British West Indies, 1700–1840*. New Haven: Yale University Press, 2008.

Kwass, Michael. "Big Hair: A Wig History of Consumption in Eighteenth-Century France." *American Historical Review* 111, no. 3 (2006): 631–59.

———. *The Consumer Revolution, 1650–1800*. Cambridge: Cambridge University Press, 2022.

———. "Consumption and the World of Ideas: Consumer Revolution and the Moral Economy of the Marquis de Mirabeau." *Eighteenth-Century Studies* 37, no. 2 (2004): 187–213.

———. "'Le superflu, chose très nécessaire': Physiocracy and Its Discontents in the Eighteenth-Century Luxury Debate." In *The Economic Turn: Recasting Political Economy in Enlightenment Europe*, edited by Sophus Reinert and Steven Kaplan, 117–37. London: Anthem Press, 2019.

Labreuche, Pascal. *Paris, capitale de la toile à peindre: XVIIIe–XIXe siècle*. Paris: CTHS/INHA, 2011.

Lacombe, Jacques. *Dictionnaire portatif des beaux-arts, ou Abrégé de ce qui concerne l'architecture, la sculpture, la peinture, la gravure, la poésie et la musique*. Paris: La Veuve Estienne et fils et J.-T. Hérissant, 1752.

La Fevrerie. "En quoy consiste l'Air du Monde, & la veritable politesse."

Extraordinaire du Mercure galant, July 1681, 47–102.

Lafont, Anne. *L'art et la race: L'Africain (tout) contre l'œil des Lumières*. Dijon: Les presses du réel, 2019.

La Font de Saint-Yenne, Étienne. *Reflexions sur quelques causes de l'état présent de la peinture en France: Avec un examen des principaux ouvrages exposés au Louvre le mois d'août 1746*. The Hague: Jean Neaulme, 1747.

———. *Sentimens sur quelques ouvrages de peinture, sculpture et gravure*. N.p., 1754. https://gallica.bnf.fr/ark:/12148/btv1b84429620.

Lajer-Burcharth, Ewa. "Drawing Time." *October*, no. 151 (2015): 3–42.

———. *The Painter's Touch: Boucher, Chardin, Fragonard*. Princeton: Princeton University Press, 2018.

La Live de Jully, Ange-Laurent de. *Catalogue historique du cabinet de peinture et sculpture françoise, de M. de Lalive*. Paris: P. Al. Le Prieur, 1764.

Lanoë, Catherine. *La poudre et le fard: Une histoire des cosmétiques de la Renaissance aux Lumières*. Paris: Champ Vallon, 2008.

Lavezzi, Elisabeth. "Le tableau qui brûle: La peinture à l'encaustique en débat et en parodie au milieu du XVIIIᵉ siècle." In *Séries parodiques au siècle des Lumières*, edited by Sylvain Menant and Dominique Quéro, 377–91. Paris: Presses de l'Université Paris-Sorbonne, 2005.

Lawrence, Elizabeth Atwood. "The Sacred Bee, the Filthy Pig, and the Bat out of Hell: Animal Symbolism as Cognitive Biophilia." In *The Biophilia Hypothesis*, edited by Stephen R. Kellert and Edward O. Wilson, 301–44. Washington, DC: Island Press, 1993.

Le Bihan, Alain. *Francs-maçons parisiens du Grand Orient de France (fin du XVIIIᵉ siècle)*. Paris: Bibliothèque nationale, 1966.

Lebrun, Jean-Baptiste-Pierre. *Catalogue d'une belle collection des tableaux des écoles d'Italie, de Flandre, de Hollande et de France: d'une superbe collection de dessins des mêmes écoles: gouaches, aquarelles, figures en marbre & en bronze: porcelaines du Japon, de la Chine: vases de marbre: meubles & autres objets, venans du cabinet de M. M*** [Morel]. Paris: Lebrun, 1786.

———. *Catalogue d'une collection de tableaux d'Italie, de Flandre, de Hollande et de France, dessins en feuilles des trois écoles, gouache, miniatures, recueils d'estampes dont les œuvres de Salvator Rosa, de Poilly, Vandermeulen, Dietricy, Wille, Chodowiecki, Bernard Derode de Berlin, le cabinet du Roi, superbes épreuves, &c. &c. &c., et autres belles estampes rares en feuilles, terres cuites, figures en bas-relief, en marbre & bronze, pierres antiques, gravées en relief & en creux, montées en bagues, émaux du célèbre Petitot, coupe de porphyre, d'Agate, boëte d'or & de jaspe, bijoux, meubles & autres objets curieux formant le cabinet de M. Boyer-de-Fons-Colombe, d'Aix en Provence*. Paris: Prault, 1790.

Lebrun, Jean-Baptiste-Pierre, and Alexandre-Joseph Paillet. *Catalogue des objets précieux trouvés après le décès du citoyen Vincent Donjeux, ancien négociant de tableaux et curiosités*. Paris: Lebrun, Paillet, & Jalusau, 1793.

Le Carpentier, Charles-Louis-François. *Galerie des peintres célèbres, avec des remarques sur le genre de chaque maître*. Vol. 2. Paris: Treuttel et Wurtz, 1821.

Le Comte, Florent. *Cabinet des singularitez d'architecture, peinture, sculpture et gravure ou Introduction à la connoissance des plus beaux arts, figurés sous les tableaux, les statues & les estampes*. Brussels: Lambert Marchant, 1702.

Le Noble, Eustache. *L'école du monde*. Vol. 6. Paris: Martin Jouvenel, 1702.

Léoffroy de Saint-Yves, Charles. *Observations sur les arts: et sur quelques morceaux de peinture & de sculpture exposés au Louvre en 1748: où il est parlé de l'utilité des embellissemens dans les villes*. Leiden: Elias Luzac, 1748. https://gallica.bnf.fr/ark:/12148/btv1b8442814k.

Leonardo da Vinci. *The Madrid Codices*. Edited by Ladislao Reti. New York: McGraw-Hill, 1974.

Lescaze, Zoë. "How Does a Museum Buy an Artwork That Doesn't Physically Exist?" *New York Times*, November 8, 2018, *T Magazine*. https://www.nytimes.com/2018/11/08/t-magazine/tino-sehgal-hirshhorn-museum-art.html.

Lespinasse, René de. *Les métiers et corporations de la ville de Paris*. Vol. 2. Paris: Imprimerie nationale, 1892.

Lettre à Monsieur de Poiresson-Chamarande, Lieutenant-General au Bailliage & Siege Présidial de Chaumont en Bassigny. N.p., 1741. https://gallica.bnf.fr/ark:/12148/btv1b8442781n.

"Lettre d'un particulier à un de ses parents, peintre en province sur le salon." N.p., 1755. https://gallica.bnf.fr/ark:/12148/btv1b10546621w.

Lettre sur l'exposition des ouvrages de peinture & de sculpture au Sallon du Louvre 1769. Paris: Vente, 1769. https://gallica.bnf.fr/ark:/12148/btv1b8443018s.

Lettre sur le Salon de 1755, adressée à ceux qui la liront. Amsterdam: Arkstée et Merkus, 1755. https://gallica.bnf.fr/ark:/12148/btv1b8442964t.

Levey, Michael. *Painting and Sculpture in France, 1700–1789*. New Haven: Yale University Press, 1993.

Levey, Santina M. *Lace: A History*. London: Victoria & Albert Museum, 1983.

Lévy, Claude Frédéric. *Capitalistes et pouvoir au siècle des lumières*. Vol. 2. Paris: Mouton, 1979.

Liberati, Alessandro. "Requeno, Lorgna, Gerli e Reiffenstein: Fonti e trattatistica per una storia materiale dell'encausto." In *Contemporanea: Scritti di storia dell'arte per Jolanda Nigro Covre*, edited by Ilaria Schiaffini and Claudio Zambianchi, 21–32. Rome: Campisano Editore, 2013.

Lichtenstein, Jacqueline, and Christian Michel, eds. *Conférences de l'Académie royale de peinture et de sculpture*. 6 vols. Paris: École nationale supérieure des beaux-arts, 2007–15.

Lilti, Antoine. *Le monde des salons: Sociabilité et mondanité à Paris au XVIIIᵉ siècle*. Paris: Fayard, 2005.

———. *The World of the Salons: Sociability and Worldliness in Eighteenth-Century Paris*. Translated by Lydia G. Cochrane. Oxford: Oxford University Press, 2015.

"Louvre Plan/Information." Musée du Louvre / Technigraphic, 2008.

Luhmann, Niklas. *Love as Passion: The Codification of Intimacy*. Cambridge, MA: Harvard University Press, 1986.

Luke, Ben, and Tino Sehgal. "A Brush with . . . Tino Sehgal." *A Brush With . . .* (podcast), produced by Julia Michalska, Aimee Dawson, David Clack, Henrietta Bentall, and Kabir Jhala, August 4, 2021. https://www.theartnewspaper.com/2021/08/04/a-brush-with-tino-sehgal.

Lupton, Ellen. "The Modern Curve: Form, Structure, and Image in the Twentieth Century and Beyond." In *Rococo: The*

Continuing Curve, 1730–2008, edited by Sarah D. Coffin, Gail S. Davidson, Ellen Lupton, and Penelope Hunter-Stiebel, 218–45. New York: Cooper-Hewitt, National Design Museum, 2008.

Lütticken, Sven. "Progressive Striptease: Performance Ideology Past and Present." In *Secret Publicity: Essays on Contemporary Art*, 165–80. Rotterdam: NAi Publishers, 2006.

Luzac, Jean, ed. *Nouvelles extraordinaires de divers endroits*. Leyden: Jean & Étienne Luzac, 1784.

Lynn, Michael R. *The Sublime Invention: Ballooning in Europe, 1783–1820*. London: Pickering & Chatto, 2010.

Magnien, Aline. *La nature et l'antique, la chair et le contour: Essai sur la sculpture française du XVIIIe siècle*. Oxford: Voltaire Foundation, 2004.

Mainardi, Patricia. *The End of the Salon: Art and the State in the Early Third Republic*. Cambridge: Cambridge University Press, 1993.

Mantz, Paul. "Musée rétrospectif; La Renaissance et les Temps modernes." *Gazette des beaux-arts*, 1865, 326–49.

Marandet, François. "The Apprenticeship of Maurice-Quentin de La Tour (1704–88)." *Burlington Magazine* 144, no. 1193 (2002): 502–5.

Marcel, Pierre. "Les peintres et le public en France au XVIIIe siècle." In *Mélanges Bertaux: Recueil de travaux dédié à la mémoire d'Émile Bertaux*, 205–13. Paris: E. de Boccard, 1924.

———. *La peinture française au début du dix-huitième siècle: 1690–1721*. Paris: G. Baranger Fils, 1906.

Mariette, Pierre-Jean. *Abecedario de P. J. Mariette: et autres notes inédites de cet amateur sur les arts et les artistes*. Edited by P. de Chennevièvres and A. de Montaiglon. 6 vols. Paris: J.-B. Dumoulin, 1851–60.

———. *Description sommaire des statues, figures, bustes, vases et autres morceaux de sculpture, tant en marbre qu'en bronze, & des modèles en terre cuite, porcelaines et fayences d'Urbin, provenans du cabinet de feu M. Crozat dont la vente se fera le 14 décembre 1750 & jours suivans, en l'Hôtel où est décédé M. le Marquis du Châtel, rue de Richelieu*. Paris: Louis-François Delatour, 1750.

Marin, Louis. *Portrait of the King*. Minneapolis: University of Minnesota Press, 1988.

Marsy, François Marie de. *Dictionnaire abrégé de peinture et d'architecture*. 2 vols. Paris: Nyon & Barrois, 1746.

Martin, Elisabeth, and Claudia Sindaco-Domas. "La technique picturale des peintres de fêtes galantes dans le contexte du XVIIIe siècle." *Technè*, no. 30–31 (2009): 25–36.

Martin, Morag. *Selling Beauty: Cosmetics, Commerce, and French Society, 1750–1830*. Baltimore: Johns Hopkins University Press, 2009.

Martin, W. "The Life of a Dutch Artist. Part VI—How the Painter Sold His Work." *Burlington Magazine for Connoisseurs* 11, no. 54 (1907): 357–69.

Masseau, Didier. "Caylus, Diderot et les philosophes." In *Le comte de Caylus: Les arts et les lettres*, edited by Nicholas Cronk and Kris Peeters, 45–57. Amsterdam: Rodopi, 2004.

Massing, Ann. "Arnaud Vincent de Montpetit and Eludoric Painting." *Zeitschrift für Kunsttechnologie und Konservierung* 7, no. 2 (1993): 359–68.

———. "French Painting Technique in the Seventeenth and Early Eighteenth Centuries and De La Fontaine's *Académie de la peinture* (Paris 1679)." In *Looking*

Through Paintings: The Study of Painting Techniques and Materials in Support of Art Historical Research, edited by Erma Hermens, 319–90. London: Archetype Publications, 1998.

———. "Painting Materials and Techniques: Toward a Bibliography of the French Literature Before 1800." In *Die Kunst und ihre Erhaltung: Rolf E. Straub zum 70. Geburtstag gewidmet*, edited by K. W. Bachman, W. Koch, and U. Schiessl, 57–96. Worms: Wernersche Verlagsgesellschaft, 1990.

———. *Painting Restoration Before La Restauration: The Origins of the Profession in France*. Cambridge: Hamilton Kerr Institute, 2012.

Mattick, Paul. "Art and Money." In *Art in Its Time: Theories and Practices of Modern Aesthetics*. London: Routledge, 2003.

Mayer, Lance, and Gay Myers. "Painting with Wax in Britain and America During the Eighteenth and Early Nineteenth Centuries." *Postprints: American Institute for Conservation of Historic and Artistic Works, Paintings Specialty Group* 18 (2006): 53–66.

McClellan, Andrew. *Inventing the Louvre: Art, Politics, and the Origins of the Modern Museum in Eighteenth-Century Paris*. Berkeley: University of California Press, 1994.

———. "Watteau's Dealer: Gersaint and the Marketing of Art in Eighteenth-Century Paris." *Art Bulletin* 78, no. 3 (1996): 439–53.

McCracken, Grant David. *Culture and Consumption: New Approaches to the Symbolic Character of Consumer Goods and Activities*. Bloomington: Indiana University Press, 1988.

McMahon, Darrin M. *Divine Fury: A History of Genius*. New York: Basic Books, 2013.

Medvedkova, Olga. "Le comte de Caylus entre les antiquaires, les amateurs et les artistes." In *Réseaux de l'esprit en Europe: Des lumières au XIXᵉ siècle*, edited by Wladimir Bérélowitch and Michel Porret, 125–47. Geneva: Droz, 2009.

Méjanès, Jean-François. *Maurice-Quentin Delatour: La marquise de Pompadour*. Paris: Réunion des musées nationaux, 2002.

Mémoires secrets. 36 vols. London: John Adamson, 1783–89.

Ménard, Pierre. *Le Français qui possédait l'Amérique: La vie extraordinaire d'Antoine Crozat, milliardaire sous Louis XIV*. Paris: Cherche midi, 2017.

Menu, Michel, ed. *Leonardo da Vinci's Technical Practice: Paintings, Drawings and Influence*. Paris: Hermann, 2014.

Le Mercure. Paris: Cavelier, Cavelier fils, & Cailleau, 1721–23.

Mercure de France. Paris, 1724–91.

Merrifield, Mary Philadelphia. *Original Treatises: Dating from the XIIth to XVIIIth Centuries on the Arts of Painting, in Oil, Miniature, Mosaic, and on Glass; of Gilding, Dyeing, and the Preparation of Colours and Artificial Gems; Preceded by a General Introduction; with Translations, Prefaces, and Notes*. Vol. 2. London: J. Murray, 1849.

Mervaud, Christiane. "Du nectar pour Voltaire." *Dix-huitième siècle* 29, no. 1 (1997): 137–45.

Meusnier de Querlon, Anne-Gabriel, ed. *Affiches, annonces et avis divers*. Paris: Bureau d'adresse, 1761–84.

———, ed. *Annonces, affiches et avis divers*. Paris: Bureau d'adresse, 1751–60.

Michel, Christian. *The Académie Royale de Peinture et de Sculpture: The Birth of the French School, 1648–1793*. Translated by Chris Miller. Los Angeles: Getty Research Institute, 2018.

———. *Le célèbre Watteau*. Geneva: Droz, 2008.

Michel, Patrick. *Le commerce du tableau à Paris dans la seconde moitié du XVIIIe siècle: Acteurs et pratiques*. Villeneuve d'Ascq: Presses universitaires du Septentrion, 2007.

———. *Peinture et plaisir: Les goûts picturaux des collectionneurs Parisiens au XVIIIe siècle*. Rennes: Presses universitaires de Rennes, 2010.

Mirabeau, Victor Riqueti, marquis de. *L'ami des hommes ou traité de la population*. Avignon: n.p., 1756.

Montaiglon, Anatole de, ed. *Procès-verbaux de l'Académie royale de peinture et de sculpture, 1697–1793*. Vol. 3. Paris: J. Baur, 1880.

Montfaucon, Bernard de. *Supplément au livre de l'antiquité expliquée et représentée en figures*. Vol. 2. Paris: La Veuve Delaulne, 1724.

Montias, J. Michael. "Cost and Value in Seventeenth-Century Dutch Art." *Art History* 10, no. 4 (1987): 455–66.

Montpetit, Arnaud Vincent de. *Note intéressante sur les moyens de conserver les portraits peints à huile et de les faire passer sans altération à la postérité*. Paris: M. de Montpetit, 1775.

———. "La peinture éludorique, nouvelle façon de peindre en miniature, par M. Vincent de Montpetit." 1759. https://gallica.bnf.fr/ark:/12148/btv1b10542994w.

Moreau-Vauthier, Charles. *The Technique of Painting*. London: W. Heinemann, 1912.

Moskalik-Detalle, Alina, Julien Assoun, Marie-Laure Martiny, and Marie Monfort. "Conservation of Murals by Eugène Delacroix at Saint Sulpice." In *Gels in the Conservation of Art*, edited by Lora V. Angelova, Bronwyn Ormsby, Joyce H. Townsend, and Richard Wolbers, 200–208. London: Archetype, 2017.

Nagel, Alexander. *Medieval Modern: Art out of Time*, 196–209. London: Thames & Hudson, 2012.

Nagel, Alexander, and Christopher Wood. *Anachronic Renaissance*. New York: Zone Books, 2010.

Naginski, Erika. *Sculpture and Enlightenment*. Los Angeles: Getty Research Institute, 2009.

Nenci, Chiara. "L'encausto tra teoria ed empiria nell'Italia tardo settecentesca." In *Artisti lombardi e centri di produzione italiani nel Settecento*, edited by Gianni Carlo Sciolla and Valerio Terraroli, 213–19. Bergamo: Bolis, 1995.

Neuman, Robert. "Watteau's *L'Enseigne de Gersaint* and Baroque Emblematic Tradition." *Gazette des beaux-arts*, no. 104 (1984): 153–64.

Nevjestic, Virgil. "L'encaustique et la peinture à la cire." *Conservation restauration* 3 (1985): 17–19.

Nicholson, Kathleen. "Having the Last Word: Rosalba Carriera and the Académie Royale de Peinture et de Sculpture." *Eighteenth-Century Studies* 52, no. 2 (2019): 173–77.

———. "The Ideology of Feminine 'Virtue': The Vestal Virgin in French Eighteenth-Century Allegorical Portraiture." In *Portraiture: Facing the Subject*, edited by Joanna Woodall, 52–72. Manchester: Manchester University Press, 1997.

Nicot, Jean, ed. *Thresor de la langue françoyse tant ancienne que moderne*. Paris: David Douceur, 1606.

"Notices concernant diverses expériences des globes aérostatiques." *Journal encyclopédique*, February 1784, 483–90.

Nova, Alessandro. "Pietre naturali, gessi colorati, pastelli e il problema del ritratto." *Mitteilungen des Kunsthistorischen Institutes in Florenz* 52, no. 2/3 (2008): 158–75.

Oberer, Angela. *The Life and Work of Rosalba Carriera (1673–1757): The Queen of Pastel*. Amsterdam: Amsterdam University Press, 2020.

Orain, Arnaud. *La politique du merveilleux: une histoire culturelle du système de Law (1695–1795)*. Paris: Fayard, 2018.

Ortona, Erminia Gentile, and Mirco Modolo. *Caylus e la riscoperta della pittura antica: Attraverso gli acquarelli di Pietro Santi Bartoli per Luigi XIV: Genesi del primo libro di storia dell'arte a colori*. Rome: De Luca editori d'arte, 2016.

Oudry, Jean-Baptiste. "Sur la pratique de peindre." In Lichtenstein and Michel, *Conférences de l'Académie royale*, 6:49–80.

Oxford Latin Dictionary. Oxford: Clarendon Press, 1968.

Pader, Hilaire. *La peinture parlante*. Toulouse: Arnaud Colomiez, 1653.

Padiyar, Satish. *Fragonard: Painting out of Time*. London: Reaktion Books, 2020.

Pagano, Enrica. "Caylus e le pitture ercolanesi." *Anabases*, no. 6 (2007): 113–34.

Paillet, Alexandre-Joseph. *Catalogue de tableaux des meilleurs maitres Hollandois, Flamands & François: peintures à gouasse, dessins & estampes montés & en feuilles, porcelaine de Sève, vases de marbre, sculpture en ivoire, & autres objets de curiosité*. Paris: Paillet, 1775.

———. *Catalogue de tableaux des trois écoles, dessins et estampes, sous verres, porcelaines, bijoux, meubles, et autres objets curieux, composant le cabinet de M. de Castelmore*. Paris: Paillet & Boileau, 1791.

———. *Catalogue d'une belle collection de tableaux originaux des meilleurs maîtres françois et hollandois, figures en bronze, porcelaine ancienne, & autre, pendules à répétition, & divers objets curieux, qui composent le Cabinet de M.*** [Leroy de Senneville]*. Paris: Prault, 1780.

———. *Catalogue d'une collection choisie de tableaux originaux et dessins précieux des trois écoles, grouppes & figures de terre cuite, bustes en marbre, bronzes d'un beau choix, vases de porphyre, & porcelaines richement garnies en bronze doré, meubles et autres objets curieux, du cabinet de M. Ch*** [Chariot]*. Paris: Paillet, 1788.

———. *Tableaux des trois écoles, dont plusieurs sont originaux de Paul Véronèse, Luc Jordans, Stella, Carle Vanloo, Restout, Dietricci, Rooz, Brakemburg Franck, Paul Brill, Ostade, Loutherbourg & autres bons maîtres*. Paris: Paillet & Girardin, 1788.

Paillet, Alexandre-Joseph, and Antoine-Claude Chariot. *Catalogue des tableaux des trois écoles, quelques morceaux à gouaches & dessins de bons maîtres, belle pendule de la Paute, & autres, secrétaire à cilindre bien conditionné, & divers autres objets, du Cabinet de M. B*** [Benoit]*. Paris: Paillet & Chariot, 1786.

———. *Catalogue d'une collection de tableaux des meilleurs maîtres des trois écoles, peintures à gouaches, bustes en marbre, terres cuites, bronzes, vases de porphyre & marbres rares, meubles de Boule, dessins de grands maîtres, recueil d'estampes concernant les productions des peintres d'histoire & d'architecture, un beau clavecin & divers objets curieux qui composent le Cabinet de M. B. de B****

[Billard de Bélisard], sous la direction de A. J. Paillet, peintre, dont la vente se fera au plus offrant, le mardi 15 mars 1785, & jours suivans, en la grande salle de l'hôtel de Bullion, rue Plâtrière. Paris: Paillet & Chariot, 1785.

Palacios-Huerta, Ignacio. "Time-Inconsistent Preferences in Adam Smith and David Hume." *History of Political Economy* 35, no. 2 (2003): 241–68.

Panofsky, Dora. "Narcissus and Echo; Notes on Poussin's *Birth of Bacchus* in the Fogg Museum of Art." *Art Bulletin* 31, no. 2 (1949): 112–20.

Panofsky, Erwin. "Et in Arcadia Ego: On the Conception of Transience in Poussin and Watteau." In *Philosophy and History: Essays Presented to Ernst Cassirer*, 223–52. Oxford: Clarendon Press, 1963.

Parente, Anna Rita. "Caylus et l'archéologie en Italie au XVIIIᵉ siècle." *Les nouvelles de l'archéologie*, no. 110 (2007): 17–23.

Parikka, Jussi. *What Is Media Archaeology?* Malden, MA: Polity Press, 2012.

Paulson, Henry M. "Short-Termism and the Threat from Climate Change." McKinsey & Company, April 1, 2015. https://www.mckinsey.com/business-functions/strategy-and-corporate-finance/our-insights/short-termism-and-the-threat-from-climate-change.

Peiffer, Jacques G. "La statuaire céramique et ses pratiques d'atelier au XVIIIᵉ siècle, œuvres originales, tirages originaux, éditions en terre cuite: Critères d'identification." In *Clodion et la sculpture française de la fin du XVIIIᵉ siècle*, edited by Guilhem Scherf, 503–20. Paris: La Documentation française, 1993.

Penny, Nicholas. *The Materials of Sculpture*. New Haven: Yale University Press, 1993.

Pernety, Antoine-Joseph. *Dictionnaire portatif de peinture, sculpture et gravure*. Paris: Bauche, 1757.

Perrin, Jacques-Antoine-René. *Henriette de Marconne, ou Mémoires du chevalier de Présac*. Amsterdam: n.p., 1763.

Pevsner, Nikolaus. *Academies of Art, Past and Present*. Cambridge: Cambridge University Press, 1940.

Pine, B. Joseph, and James H. Gilmore. *The Experience Economy*. Boston: Harvard Business Press, 2011.

Pinon, Pierre. "Lotissement spéculatifs, formes urbaines et architectes à la fin de l'Ancien Régime." In *Soufflot et l'architecture des lumières*, 178–91. Paris: École nationale supérieure des beaux-arts, 1986.

———. "Une maison d'artiste: Clodion à la Chaussée d'Antin." In *Clodion et la sculpture française de la fin du XVIIIᵉ siècle*, edited by Guilhem Scherf, 401–20. Paris: La Documentation française, 1993.

Plax, Julie Anne. *Watteau and the Cultural Politics of Eighteenth-Century France*. Cambridge: Cambridge University Press, 2000.

Plutarch. *Moralia*. Translated by Frank Cole Babbitt. Vol. 2. Cambridge, MA: Harvard University Press, 1928.

Pomian, Krzysztof. *Collectors and Curiosities: Paris and Venice, 1500–1800*. Cambridge: Polity Press, 1990.

Pommier, Édouard. *Théories du portrait: De la Renaissance aux Lumières*. Paris: Gallimard, 1998.

Posner, Donald. "Concerning the 'Mechanical' Parts of Painting and the Artistic Culture of Seventeenth-Century France." *Art Bulletin* 75, no. 4 (1993): 583–98.

———. "Mme. de Pompadour as a Patron of the Visual Arts." *Art Bulletin* 72, no. 1 (1990): 74.

———. "*Watteau* by Jean Ferré." *Art Bulletin* 57, no. 2 (1975): 292–93.

———. "Watteau mélancolique: La formation d'un mythe." *Bulletin de la Société de l'histoire de l'art français*, 1973 (pub. 1974), 346–61.

Poulet, Anne L. "Les années romaines de Clodion." In *Clodion, 1738–1814*, by Anne L. Poulet and Guilhem Scherf, 15–34. Paris: Réunion des musées nationaux, 1992.

———. *Jean-Antoine Houdon: Sculptor of the Enlightenment*. Washington, DC: National Gallery of Art, 2003.

———. "A Neoclassical Vase by Clodion." *Art Institute of Chicago Museum Studies* 15, no. 2 (1989): 139–80.

Poulet, Anne L., and Guilhem Scherf. *Clodion, 1738–1814*. Paris: Réunion des musées nationaux, 1992.

Pradère, Onésime. "Notice sur Vincent de Montpetit." *Bulletin de la Société académique de Brest* 2 (1874–75): 261–303.

Préaud, Tamara, and Guilhem Scherf, eds. *La manufacture des Lumières: La sculpture à Sèvres de Louis XV à la Révolution*. Dijon: Éditions Faton, 2015.

Priore, Alicia M. "François Boucher's Designs for Vases and Mounts." *Studies in the Decorative Arts* 3, no. 2 (1996): 2–51.

Rauser, Amelia. *The Age of Undress: Art, Fashion, and the Classical Ideal in the 1790s*. New Haven: Yale University Press, 2020.

Reiffenstein, Johann Friedrich. "Pensées de M. Reifstein sur la peinture, avec l'exposé d'une nouvelle façon de peindre en pastel." *Journal étranger*, February 1757, 100–106.

Remington, Preston. "A Monument Honoring the Invention of the Balloon." *Metropolitan Museum of Art Bulletin* 2, no. 8 (1944): 241–48.

Remy, Pierre. *Catalogue des tableaux & desseins précieux des maîtres célebres des trois écoles, figures de marbres, de bronze & de terre cuite, estampes en feuilles & autres objets du cabinet de feu m. Randon de Boisset, Receveur géneral des finances*. Paris: Musier, 1777.

———. *Catalogue d'une riche collection de tableaux des maîtres les plus célèbres des trois écoles, dessins aussi des plus grands maîtres, sous verre & en feuilles, bronzes, marbres, terre cuite du Quesnoi, de Bouchardon, &c., pierres gravées antiques, pendules, montres, & bijoux, & autres objets curieux qui composent le cabinet de feu Son Altesse Sérénissime Monseigneur le prince de Conti, prince du sang, & grand prieur de France*. Paris: Muzier, 1777.

———. *Catalogue raisonné des tableaux, dessins et estampes, et autres effets curieux, après le décès de M. de Jullienne*. Paris: Vente, 1767.

———. *Catalogue raisonné des tableaux de différentes écoles, des figures & bustes de marbre, des figures, groupes & bas-reliefs de terre cuite, des morceaux en ivoire, des desseins & estampes, des meubles précieux par Boule & Philippe Cassieri, des coquilles univalves & bivalves, choisies, & d'autres objets qui composent le cabinet de M. de Lalive de Jully*. Paris: Vente, 1769.

Renou, Antoine. *Secret de fixer le pastel, inventé par M. Loriot, et publié par l'Académie royale de peinture et sculpture, en 1780*. Paris: Veuve Hérissant, 1780.

———. "Secret de fixer le pastel, inventé par M. Loriot, & publié par l'Académie royale de peinture & sculpture, en 1780." *Journal de physique, de chimie, d'histoire naturelle et des arts* 15 (June 1780): 448–52.

Réponse à une lettre adressée à un partisan du bon goût, sur l'exposition des tableaux faite dans le grand Salon du Louvre, le 28 août 1755. N.p., 1755. https://gallica.bnf.fr/ark:/12148/btv1b8443008d.

Rétif de La Bretonne, Nicolas-Edme. *Monsieur Nicolas; ou Le cœur-humain dévoilé*. Vol. 8. Paris: Veuve Marion-R, 1797.

Reyes, Hector. "Drawing and History in the Comte de Caylus' *Recueil d'antiquités*." *Studies in Eighteenth-Century Culture* 42, no. 1 (2013): 171–89.

Rice, Danielle. "The Fire of the Ancients: The Encaustic Painting Revival 1755 to 1812." Ph.D. diss., Yale University, 1979.

Richelet, Pierre. *Dictionnaire françois*. Geneva: J. H. Widerhold, 1680.

Riley, James C. *The Seven Years War and the Old Regime in France: The Economic and Financial Toll*. Princeton: Princeton University Press, 1986.

Roche, Alain, and Stéphanie Doucet. "Propriétés mécaniques des peintures à la cire et à l'encaustique." *Technè*, no. 23 (2006): 20–27.

Roche, Daniel. *The Culture of Clothing: Dress and Fashion in the Ancien Régime*. Translated by Jean Birrell. Cambridge: Cambridge University Press, 1994.

———. *France in the Enlightenment*. Translated by Arthur Goldhammer. Cambridge, MA: Harvard University Press, 1998.

Roland Michel, Marianne. *Watteau, an Artist of the Eighteenth Century*. Translated by Richard Wrigley. London: Trefoil Books, 1984.

Rosenau, Helen. "The Sphere as an Element in the Montgolfier Monuments." *Art Bulletin* 50, no. 1 (1968): 65–66.

Rosenberg, Pierre, ed. *Vies anciennes de Watteau*. Paris: Hermann, 1984.

Roth-Meyer, Clothide. "Les marchands de couleurs à Paris au XIXe siècle." Ph.D. diss., Université Paris IV Sorbonne, 2004.

Rouquet, Jean André. *L'Art nouveau de la peinture en fromage, ou en ramequin, inventée pour suivre le louable projet de trouver graduellement des façons de peindre inférieures à celles qui existent*. Paris: Marolles, 1755.

Rowlands, Guy. *Dangerous and Dishonest Men: The International Bankers of Louis XIV's France*. London: Palgrave Macmillan, 2015.

———. *The Financial Decline of a Great Power: War, Influence, and Money in Louis XIV's France*. Oxford: Oxford University Press, 2012.

Russo, Elena. *Styles of Enlightenment: Taste, Politics, and Authorship in Eighteenth-Century France*. Baltimore: Johns Hopkins University Press, 2007.

Saint Germain, Jacques. *Samuel Bernard, le banquier des rois; d'après de nombreux documents inédits*. Paris: Hachette, 1960.

Salmon, Xavier. *Madame de Pompadour et les arts*. Paris: Réunion des musées nationaux, 2002.

———. *Pastels in the Musée du Louvre: 17th and 18th Centuries*. Paris: Louvre éditions, 2018.

———. *Le voleur d'âmes: Maurice Quentin de La Tour*. Versailles: Artlys, 2004.

Salomon, Xavier F. "The Artistic Achievements of Rosalba Carriera." Art Herstory, April 15, 2021. https://artherstory.net/rosalba-carriera-at-the-frick-collection/.

Sargentson, Carolyn. *Merchants and Luxury Markets: The Marchands Merciers of*

Eighteenth-Century Paris. London: Victoria & Albert Museum, 1996.

Sauvage, Leïla. "'De poudre et de papier': Conservation et restauration des œuvres au trace pulverulent." M.A. thesis, Université Paris 1 Panthéon-Sorbonne, 2010.

Sauvage, Leila, W. (Bill) Wei, and Marcias Martinez. "When Conservation Meets Engineering: Predicting the Damaging Effects of Vibrations on Pastel Paintings." *Studies in Conservation* 63, suppl. 1 (2018): 418–20.

Sayej, Nadja. "Terms and Conditions: Selling Tino Sehgal." *ArtUS*, no. 15 (October 2006): 20–23.

Scherf, Guilhem. "Autour de Clodion: Variations, répétitions, imitations." *Revue de l'art* 91, no. 1 (1991): 47–59.

———. "Clodion, sculpteur de la douceur de vivre." *L'Estampille*, no. 256 (March 1992): 66–73.

———. "Collections et collectionneurs de sculptures modernes: Un nouveau champ d'étude." In *L'art et les normes sociales au XVIIIe siècle*, edited by Thomas W. Gaehtgens, Christian Michel, and Martin Schieder, 147–64. Paris: Éditions de la Maison des sciences de l'homme, 2001.

———. *Playing with Fire: European Terracotta Models, 1740–1840*. New Haven: Yale University Press, 2003.

———. "Répertoire thématique des œuvres de Clodion d'après les catalogues de ventes parisiennes entre 1767 et 1820." In *Clodion, 1738–1814*, by Anne L. Poulet and Guilhem Scherf, 421–48. Paris: Réunion des musées nationaux, 1992.

Schieder, Martin. *Jenseits der Aufklärung. Die religiöse Malerei im ausgehenden Ancien régime*. Berlin: Gebr. Mann, 1997.

Schnapper, Antoine. *Jean Jouvenet, 1644–1717: et la peinture d'histoire à Paris*. Paris: Arthena, 2010.

———. *Le métier de peintre au Grand Siècle*. Paris: Gallimard, 2004.

Scholar, Richard. *The Je-Ne-Sais-Quoi in Early Modern Europe: Encounters with a Certain Something*. Oxford: Oxford University Press, 2005.

Schultz, Julia, and Karin Petersen. "Antibody-Based Techniques to Distinguish Proteins and Identify Sturgeon Glue in Works of Art." *Proceedings of CCI-ICC Symposium: Adhesives and Consolidants for Conservation*, 2011, 1–13.

Scott, Katie. "Reproduction and Reputation: 'François Boucher' and the Formation of Artistic Identities." In *Rethinking Boucher*, edited by Melissa Lee Hyde and Mark Ledbury, 91–132. Los Angeles: Getty Research Institute, 2006.

———. *The Rococo Interior: Decoration and Social Spaces in Early Eighteenth-Century Paris*. New Haven: Yale University Press, 1995.

Sehgal, Tino. "In Conversation: GCC Talks to Tino Sehgal and Louise Hojer." Gallery Climate Coalition, September 8, 2021. https://galleryclimatecoalition.org/news/58-in-conversation-gcc-talks-to-tino-sehgal-and/.

Sehgal, Tino, and Maurizio Cattelan. "Tino Sehgal: Economics of Progress." *Flash Art International* 42, no. 264 (2009): 90–91.

Seidel, Paul. "Friedrich der Grosse als Sammler. Fortsetzung und Nachtrag." *Jahrbuch der Königlich Preussischen Kunstsammlungen* 15 (1894): 48–57.

———. *Les collections d'œuvres d'art français du XVIIIe siècle appartenant à sa majesté* *l'Empereur d'Allemagne, roi de Prusse.* Berlin: Giesecke & Devrient, 1900.

Sewell, William H. *Capitalism and the Emergence of Civic Equality in Eighteenth-Century France.* Chicago: University of Chicago Press, 2021.

———. "The Empire of Fashion and the Rise of Capitalism in Eighteenth-Century France." *Past & Present*, no. 206 (2010): 81–120.

Seznec, Jean. "Le singe antiquaire." In *Essais sur Diderot et l'Antiquité*, 79–96. 1955. Oxford: Clarendon Press, 1957.

Shammas, Carole. "Changes in English and Anglo-American Consumption from 1550 to 1800." In *Consumption and the World of Goods*, edited by John Brewer and Roy Porter, 177–205. London: Routledge, 1993.

Shell, Marc. *Art and Money.* Chicago: University of Chicago Press, 1995.

Shelley, Marjorie. "Pastelists at Work: Two Portraits at the Metropolitan Museum by Maurice Quentin de La Tour and Jean Baptiste Perronneau." *Metropolitan Museum Journal* 40 (2005): 105–13.

Sheriff, Mary D. *Fragonard: Art and Eroticism.* Chicago: University of Chicago Press, 1990.

———. *Moved by Love: Inspired Artists and Deviant Women in Eighteenth-Century France.* Chicago: University of Chicago Press, 2004.

Shovlin, John. *The Political Economy of Virtue: Luxury, Patriotism, and the Origins of the French Revolution.* Ithaca: Cornell University Press, 2006.

Sigel, Anthony B. "The Clay Modeling Techniques of Gian Lorenzo Bernini." *Harvard University Art Museums Bulletin* 6, no. 3 (1999): 48–72.

———. "Visual Glossary." In *Bernini: Sculpting in Clay*, edited by Claude Douglas Dickerson III, Anthony Sigel, and Ian Wardropper, 87–107. New York: Metropolitan Museum of Art, 2012.

Simonini, Ross. "Immaterial Guy." *Psychology Today* 4, no. 4 (2011): 30–31.

Slawinski, Natalie, Jonatan Pinkse, Timo Busch, and Subhabrata Bobby Banerjee. "The Role of Short-Termism and Uncertainty Avoidance in Organizational Inaction on Climate Change: A Multi-Level Framework." *Business and Society* 56, no. 2 (2017): 253–82.

Smentek, Kristel. *Mariette and the Science of the Connoisseur in Eighteenth-Century Europe.* Burlington, VT: Ashgate, 2014.

Sorel, Charles. *De la prudence, ou des bonnes reigles de la vie pour l'acquisition, la conservation & l'usage legitime des biens du corps & de la fortune, et des biens de l'ame où l'on void ce qu'il est dans la bienseance du monde, et ce qui peut rendre un homme accomply.* Paris: André Pralard, 1673.

Spica, Anne-Elisabeth. "Une Madeleine au chevalet: Mademoiselle de Scudéry et les peintres." *Œuvres et critiques* 29 (2004): 11–29.

Taws, Richard. *The Politics of the Provisional: Art and Ephemera in Revolutionary France.* University Park: Penn State University Press, 2013.

Taylor, George V. "The Paris Bourse on the Eve of the Revolution, 1781–1789." *American Historical Review* 67, no. 4 (1962): 951–77.

Tempesti, Domenico Marchi. "Conseils de R. Nanteuil pour l'exécution des portraits au pastel." In *Le cabinet de l'amateur*, edited by Eugène Piot, 247–50. Paris: Firmin Didot, 1863.

Thébaud-Sorger, Marie. *L'aérostation au temps des Lumières.* Rennes: Presses universitaires de Rennes, 2009.

Thunberg, Greta. "Statement to the European Parliament." European Parliament,

April 16, 2019. https://www.europarl.europa.eu/resources/library/media/20190416RES41665/20190416RES41665.pdf.

Tillerot, Isabelle. *Jean de Jullienne et les collectionneurs de son temps: Un regard singulier sur le tableau.* Paris: Éditions de la Maison des sciences d'l'homme, 2010.

Tissandier, Gaston. "Curiosités aérostatiques de l'origine des ballons, collection Tissandier." *Le Bulletin des Beaux-Arts* 3 (1885–86): 17–32.

van Eikema Hommes, Margriet. "Methods Used by Painters to Prevent Color Changes Described in 16th to Early 18th Century Sources on Oil Painting Techniques." In *Changing Pictures: Discoloration in 15th–17th-Century Oil Paintings*, 17–50. London: Archetype, 2004.

Vardi, Liana. *The Physiocrats and the World of the Enlightenment.* Cambridge: Cambridge University Press, 2012.

Viala, Alain. *La France galante: Essai historique sur une catégorie culturelle, de ses origines jusqu'à la Révolution.* Paris: Presses universitaires de France, 2008.

Vibert, Jehan Georges. *La science de la peinture.* Paris: P. Ollendorff, 1891.

Vidal, Mary. *Watteau's Painted Conversations: Art, Literature, and Talk in Seventeenth- and Eighteenth-Century France.* New Haven: Yale University Press, 1992.

Vigée Le Brun, Louise-Élisabeth. *Souvenirs de Mme Louise-Élisabeth Vigée-Lebrun.* 2 vols. Paris: H. Fournier, 1835.

Vigny, Pierre Vigné de. "Dissertation sur l'architecture." *Journal œconomique, ou Mémoires, notes et avis sur les arts, l'agriculture, le commerce et tout ce qui peut y avoir rapport, ainsi qu'à la conservation et à l'augmentation des biens de familles,* March 1752, 68–107.

Villars, Franz de. *Notes sur Clodion, statuaire, à propos du cabinet d'un amateur.* Paris: Veuve Jules Renouard, 1862.

Virgil. *Virgil.* Loeb Classical Library 63. Cambridge, MA: Harvard University Press, 1999.

Vogtherr, Christoph Martin. *Französische Gemälde.* Berlin: Akademie Verlag, 2011.

Vogtherr, Christoph Martin, and Eva Wenders de Calisse. "Watteau's 'Shop-sign': The Long Creation of a Masterpiece." *Burlington Magazine* 149, no. 1250 (2007): 296–304.

Volle, Nathalie. "Les restaurations des tableaux de Watteau: Une histoire à écrire." *Technè,* no. 30–31 (2009/2010): 97–106.

Voltaire. *Correspondence.* Edited by Theodore Besterman. 51 vols. Oxford: Voltaire Foundation, 1968–77.

———. "Le Mondain." In *Œuvres complètes de Voltaire*, edited by H. T. Mason, 16:273–313. Oxford: Voltaire Foundation, 2003.

Voßkamp, Friederike. "Preservation of Pastels: A Comparative Study on Museum Preservation Practice in France, Germany and Austria." *Restaurator. International Journal for the Preservation of Library and Archival Material* 34, no. 1 (2013): 45–66.

Wager, Susan M. "The Fast and the Fugitive: Pompadour's Curatorial Self/Portrait at Versailles." *Journal18: A Journal of Eighteenth-Century Art and Culture,* no. 8 (Fall 2018). http://www.journal18.org/issue8/the-fast-and-the-fugitive-pompadours-curatorial-self-portrait-at-versailles/.

Wardropper, Ian. *European Sculpture, 1400–1900, in the Metropolitan Museum of Art.* New York: Metropolitan Museum of Art, 2011.

Watelet, Claude-Henri, and Pierre-Charles Levesque. *Encyclopédie méthodique. Beaux-arts*. Vol. 1. Paris: Panckoucke, 1788.

Wenders de Calisse, Eva. "Zur Maltechnik von Antoine Watteau." In *Französische Gemälde*, edited by Christoph Martin Vogtherr, 63–80. Berlin: Akademie Verlag, 2011.

West, Shearer. "Gender and Internationalism: The Case of Rosalba Carriera." In *Italian Culture in Northern Europe in the Eighteenth Century*, 46–66. Cambridge: Cambridge University Press, 1999.

Wildenstein, Daniel. *Inventaires après décès d'artistes et de collectionneurs français du XVIIIe siècle*. Paris: Les Beaux-Arts, Éditions d'études et de documents, 1967.

Wile, Aaron. "Watteau, Reverie, and Selfhood." *Art Bulletin* 96, no. 3 (2014): 319–37.

Williams, Hannah. *Académie Royale: A History in Portraits*. Burlington, VT: Ashgate, 2015.

Wilson, Sarah. "Post-Colonial Rococo: Yinka Shonibare MBE Plays Fragonard." In *Rococo Echo: Art, History and Historiography from Cochin to Coppola*, edited by Melissa Lee Hyde and Katie Scott, 313–28. Oxford: Voltaire Foundation, 2014.

Wine, Humphrey. "Review of *Paris: Life & Luxury in the Eighteenth Century*, by Charissa Bremer-David." *Burlington Magazine* 154, no. 1314 (2012): 644–45.

Wood, Christopher. *A History of Art History*. Princeton: Princeton University Press, 2019.

Wunsch, Oliver. "Diderot and the Materiality of Posterity." *Early Modern French Studies* 40, no. 1 (2018): 63–78.

———. "Discriminating Taste: Skin Color and Connoisseurship in Eighteenth-Century France." *H-France Salon* 14, no. 8 (2022): 1–12. https://h-france.net/Salon/SalonVol14no08.2.Wunsch.pdf.

Yahav, Amit S. *Feeling Time: Duration, the Novel, and Eighteenth-Century Sensibility*. Philadelphia: University of Pennsylvania Press, 2018.

Zakaria, Fareed. "'Cathedral Thinking'; Energy's Future: Until We Solve Climate Change, Says James E. Rogers, We Need Even the Dirtiest Fuel." *Newsweek*, August 20, 2007.

Ziskin, Rochelle. *Private Salons and the Art World of Enlightenment Paris*. Leiden: Brill, 2022.

———. *Sheltering Art: Collecting and Social Identity in Early Eighteenth-Century Paris*. University Park: Penn State University Press, 2012.

Index

Note: Page numbers in italics denote figures. Endnotes are referenced with "n" followed by the endnote number.

Actors at a Fair (Watteau), 13–14, *15*
"Advice for Ladies" (Cochin), 80
agronomic rhetoric, 96–103, *98, 99, 100, 102,* 140n76
Aïssé, Charlotte, 43
À la gloire des frères mongolfier (Clodion), 108, *109*
Alberti, Leon Battista, *On Painting,* 33
Alembert, Jean Le Rond d', 55, *56*
Alexis Piron (Montpetit), 82, *83*
Allegory of the Foundation of the Royal Academy of Painting and Sculpture (Loir), 27, *28*
ami des hommes, L' (Mirabeau), 98–99
Amor and Psyche (Sergel), 89, *90*
Angiviller, Charles Claude de la Billarderie, comte d', 105, 112–13
antiquity
    encaustic's virtues and, 67, 68
    Neoclassicism, 78–79, 85, 103, 135n68, 137n3
anti-Rococo criticisms, 30–31, 54, 55–56, 74, 82–83, 88, 91
art
    attention economy in, 117–21
    as defined by delicacy, 1, 9–10, 52–53, 71–72, 113–14
    dematerialization of, 115–16
    as intellectual pursuit, 16
    temporality of, 5–12, 24–32, 64, 78–84, 103, 115–21
    See also encaustic; oil painting; pastel; terracotta

attention, commodification of, 117–21
austerity, rhetoric of, 97, 103, 105, 110, 112

Bacchanalian Revel Before a Term, A (Poussin), 97, *99*
Bacchante and Satyr with Young Satyr (Clodion), 97, *98*
Bacchic imagery, 96–102, *98, 99, 100, 102*
Bachelier, Jean-Jacques, 65, 79
balloon craze, 103–5, *106,* 110, 112, *113, 114*
Barocci, Federico, 36
Basan, Pierre-François, 96
bees, symbolism of, 72
Bell, David, 71
Benard, Jean-François, *Grotesque,* 6, *6*
Bernini, Gian Lorenzo, 89
Boucher, François
    artistic exchange with Clodion, 91, *92, 93,* 97, 139n39
    criticisms of, 74–75, *75,* 92
    on posterity, 5
Bouhours, Dominique, 7, 10
Bryson, Norman, 13
Buste d'un nègre (La Tour), 50, *50,* 131n65

capitalism. *See* commerce and consumption
carelessness vs. elegance, 24
Carriera, Rosalba, 36, 39–40, *40,* 41–42, *42,* 133n17
Caylus, Anne-Claude-Philippe, comte de
    animosity between Diderot and, 133n22
    as collector of pastels, 68, 133n17
    commending La Tour, 55
    criticizing Watteau, 14, 20
    encaustic painting and, 65, 68, 69, 71–72
    on fashion and desire, 79
    on sexual desire for antiquities, 75
    on terracotta's fragility, 90–91

ceramics. *See* terracotta
champagne, as emblem, 46, 48
Chaperon, Paul-Romain, 63
Charles-Louis de Secondat, baron de La Brède et de Montesquieu (Clodion), 107, *108*
chastity, 72, 134n40
Chaulnes, Marie-Joseph-Louis d'Albert d'Ailly, duc de, 101
Chéreau, J., *Embrâsement Déplorable de la Machine Aërostatique des S.rs Miolan et Janinet*, 112, *113*
class dissimulation, 8–9, 124n25
climate crisis, 119–20
Clodion
    balloon monument, *104*, 105–14, *109*, *110*, *111*, 141n101
    Bacchic imagery, 96–102, *98*, *99*, *100*, *102*, 140n69
    borrowing from François Boucher, 91, *92*, *93*, 139n39
    Erigone, 93, *94*, *95*
    fragility of work, 89–90
    market demand for sculpture and, 85–88, *86*, *87*, 137n1
    Mausoleum of Fifi, 85–87, *86*, *87*, 137n1
    Montesquieu, 105–7, *107*, *108*
    relationship with royal arts administration, 105, 107, *107*, *108*
    studio practice, 93–96, *94*, *95*, 139n49
    Vase with Putti, 91, *92*
Clodion's Montesquieu at the Salon of 1779 (Saint-Aubin), 105, *107*
Cochin, Charles-Nicolas, "Advice for Ladies," 80
Colbert, Jean-Baptiste, 26
colonialism, 8, 18, 34, 40, 50, 87, 125n26, 126n36
commerce and consumption
    agronomic rhetoric and, 96–103, *98*, *99*, *100*, *102*, 140n76
    attention economy, 117–21
    balloon craze, 103–5, *106*, 110, 112, *113*, *114*
    class dissimulation and, 8–9, 124n25
    colonialism and, 8, 34, 40
    commercial reproduction, 93–96, *94*, *95*
    co-opting permanence, 78–84, *82*, *83*
    criticisms of, 30–32, 53–54, 67, 82–83, 88, 91, 92
    decline of institutional stability, 16–17, 25, 26–30, 31, 117
    fluctuating consumer desires, 5, 18–19, 29–30, 78, 116, 135n62
    French preoccupation with delicacy and, 9–10
    permanence, durability and, 16–19, *17*
    posterity vs. economic interest, 24–26
    sexualized metaphors of consumption, 72–78, *73*, *75*, *76*, *77*, 97, 112
    small-scale sculpture, demand for, 87–88
    speculative finance, 18–19, 40–41, 87, 93
    transience, commodification of, 12, 115–16
    xenophobia and elitism in, 91
    See also encaustic; oil painting; pastel; terracotta
Court de Gébelin, Antoine, *Le monde primitif*, 99
Coypel, Antoine, 24–25
Cozette, Pierre-François, *The Vestal Tuccia*, 77, *77*
Crary, Jonathan, 117
Crow, Thomas, 31
Crozat, Antoine, 40
Crozat, Pierre, 40, 41
cultural purification, 74–75

Daedalus Attaching the Wings of Icarus (Vien), 69–71, *70*
Dandrillon (house painter), 81
Delacroix, Eugène, 119
delicacy
    as aesthetic sensibility, 10–11
    association with style, 6–7
    attaching new meaning to, 9, 12
    class dissimulation and, 8–9, 124n25
    commercial developments and, 5–6
    French preoccupation with, 9–10
    technical innovation and, 1–2, *3*, *4*, 11
    See also encaustic; oil painting; pastel; terracotta

délicatesse
    artistic genius in, 113–14
    base fragility vs., 69
    concept of, 7–8
    criticisms of, 53–54
    French preoccupation with, 9–10
    La Tour's thematization of, *45,* 45–52, *46, 47, 49, 51, 52*
    legitimized through courtliness, 71
    pastel as proxy for, 33–34, *35*
    Watteau as exemplar of, 13
    See also pastel
De Marchi, Neil, 40
Demarteau, Gilles, *The Virgin,* 76, *76*
dematerialization, 115–16
Desrais, Claude-Louis, *Vue et perspective du jardin de Mr. Réveillon,* 105, *106*
Dezallier d'Argenville, Antoine-Joseph, 41
Diderot, Denis
    animosity between Caylus and, 133n22
    on consumer desire, 30, 78
    on encaustic painting, 65, 68–69
    on overconsumption, 78, 135n62
    Physiocratic rhetoric and, 101
    on precarity of pastel, 63
    "Regrets on Parting with My Old Dressing Gown," 78
    on terracotta's virtues, 91
    on virginal honesty of encaustic, 75
digital technologies, rise of, 117
Dingé, Antoine, 96
Drawing of a Vase (Clodion), 91, *93*
Dryden, John, 10
Duval de l'Épinoy, Louis, 34, *35*

école du monde, L' (Le Noble), 8–9
economic reform, 97, 98–103, 105, 110, 112
elegance vs. carelessness, 24
elitism, 91
eludoric painting, 81–82, *82,* 136nn89–90
Embrâsement Déplorable de la Machine Aërostatique des S.rs Miolan et Janinet (Chéreau), 112, *113*

encaustic
    durability through, 68–72, *70*
    fashionable permanence of, 78–84, *82, 83*
    mid-century revival of, 65–67, *66*
    virginal subject matter and, 72–78, *73, 75, 76, 77*
environmentalism, 119–20
Erigone (Clodion), 93, *94, 95*
Esprit des loix (Montesquieu), 57, 58
"experience economy," 117

Falconet, Étienne-Maurice, 5
fashion, permanence and, 31, 78–84, *82, 83,* 118–19, 135n68
Félibien, André, 16, 37
fertility, iconography of, 96–103, *98, 99, 100, 102*
fire, terracotta sculpture and, 89, *104,* 108–9, *110*
fragility
    association with "delicacy," 7
    pastel market and, 11, 43–53, *44, 45, 46, 47, 49, 50, 51, 52*
    of terracotta, 89–91, *90*
    See also delicacy
Fragonard, Jean-Honoré, *The Warrior's Dream of Love,* 2, *3,* 4
France
    commercial forces and craftsmanship, 18
    "lightness" as virtue, 71
    preoccupation with delicacy, 9–10
François, Jean-Charles, *The Virgin,* 76, *76*
Frederick the Great, King of Prussia, 22
French Royal Academy of Painting and Sculpture
    establishment of, 16
    prioritizing posterity, 24–25
    turn against commercialism, 67

Gabriel Bernard de Rieux (La Tour), 48–52, *49, 51, 52*
gender
    in consumption discourse, 72–78, *73, 75, 76, 77,* 97, 112

gender (*continued*)
    fire and masculinity, 89
    necessitating social rituals, 41
    stereotypes around portraiture, 56–58, *57, 58*
genius, 88–91, 96, 113–14, 138n21
Geoffrin, Marie-Thérèse, 76
Gersaint, Edme-François, 13, 14, 20, 25–26, 28, 30
Gersaint's Shop Sign (Watteau), 26–30, *27, 29*, 116, 127n75
gilding, *à la grecque* technique, 81
Goncourt, Edmond de, 22
goût moderne, 6–7, 67, 74–75, 78–79
    See also Rococo
Graffigny, Françoise de, 34, 48
Grimm, Friedrich Melchior, 63
Grotesque (Benard), 6, *6*
Guyton de Morveau, Louis-Bernard, 83

Haskell, Francis, 5
Henriade (Voltaire), *57*, 58
hot air balloon craze, 103–5, *106*, 110, 112, *113, 114*
huile grasse ("fatty oil"), 20, 126n44, 126n49

imitation and copying, 91–92
Intoxication of Wine, The (Clodion), *102*

Janinet, Jean-François, 112, *113*
Jansenism, opposition to lavish decoration, 17
Jean-Jacques Rousseau (La Tour), 55, *55*
Jean Le Rond d'Alembert (La Tour), 55, *56*
Jeanne-Antoinette Poisson, Marquise de Pompadour (Boucher), 74–75, *75*
Jean Restout (La Tour), 59, *59*
John Law (Carriera), 40, *40*
John Law's System, 18, 34, 39, 43
Joullain, François Charles, 87
Jullienne, Jean de, 17–18, 76

Koons, Jeff, 115

lace, decrease in substantiality, 8, *8*
La Font de Saint-Yenne, Étienne
    on commerce and ephemerality, 30–31, 32
    criticizing contemporary painting, 9
    criticizing pastel, 36, 54
    critiquing portraiture, 55–56
    misogynistic rhetoric, 74
    on terracotta's virtues, 91
La Live de Jully, Ange-Laurent de, 76, 79, 89
La Roque, Antoine, 13
La Tour, Maurice-Quentin de
    adoption of pastel, 43–45
    attempts at stabilizing pastel, *59*, 59–64, *60, 62*
    attempts to redefine work, 36, *55*, 55–59, *56, 57, 58*
    Buste d'un nègre, 50, *50*, 131n65
    portrait of Gabriel Bernard de Rieux, 48–52, *49, 51, 52*
    portrait of Jean-Jacques Rousseau, 55, *55*
    portrait of Jean Le Rond d'Alembert, 55, *56*
    portrait of Madame de Pompadour, 56–58, *57*
    portrait of Voltaire, 45, 45–48, *46, 47*
    self-portrait for 1737 Paris Salon exhibition, 43, *44*
    strategic use of pastel, 11, 34, *35*
Law, John, 18, 34, 39, 41
Lebrun, Jean-Baptiste-Pierre, 96
Le Noble, Eustache, *L'école du monde*, 8–9
Leonardo da Vinci, 5, 36, 129n17
Le Roy de Senneville, Jean-François, 101
"lightness of touch," 71–72, 96
Loir, Nicolas, *Allegory of the Foundation of the Royal Academy of Painting and Sculpture*, 27, *28*
Loriot, Antoine-Joseph, 61–62, 132n98, 132n102
Louis Duval de L'Epinoy (La Tour), 34, *35*
Louis XIII, King of France, 37, *37*
Louis XIV, King of France, 6, 16, 25, 26–27
Louis XV (Montpetit), 82, *82*

(174) INDEX

Madame de Pompadour (La Tour), 56–58, *57*
"marcottage," 96
Mariette, Pierre-Jean, 14, 20, 41, 61, 91, 96
masculinity and fire, 89
Mausoleum of Fifi (Clodion), 85–87, *86*, *87*, 137n1
Michel, Claude. *See* Clodion
Michel, Patrick, 93
Minerva (Vien), 65, *66*, 67
Miolan, abbé, 112, *113*
Mirabeau, Victor Riqueti, marquis de, *L'ami des hommes,* 98–99
misogyny, in consumption discourse, 72–78, *73, 75, 76, 77,* 97, 112
"Mondain, Le" (Voltaire), 46, 48, 54, 97, 102–3
monde primitif, Le (Court de Gébelin), 99
Mme Le Riche de La Pouplinière, nee Françoise-Catherine-Thérèse Boutinon des Hayes (La Tour), 62
Model for a Proposed Monument to Commemorate the Invention of the Balloon (Clodion), 103, *104*, 109–10, *110, 111,* 141n101
Montesquieu, Charles-Louis de Secondat, baron de La Brède et de
    Clodion's statue of, 105–7, *107, 108*
    Esprit des loix, 57, 58
    La Tour's desire to portray, 55
Montgolfier, Jacques-Étienne, 103, 105
Montgolfier, Joseph-Michel, 103, 105
Montpetit, Arnaud Vincent de, 81–83, *82*, 136nn89–90, 137n97
monumental sculpture, 103, *104,* 105–14, *107, 108, 109, 110, 111*
Moreau-Vauthier, Charles, 118–19

Nanteuil, Robert, 36, 38, *38*
Neoclassicism, 78–79, 85, 103, 135n68, 137n3
"neo-Rococo" movement, 115
New Art of Painting in Cheese, The (Rouquet), 79–80

Odiot, Théodore, 81

oil painting
    changing studio practices, 13–15, *14, 15,* 19–24, *21, 22, 23*
    eludoric painting, 81–82, *82,* 136nn89–90
    huile grasse ("fatty oil"), 20, 126n44, 126n49
    market temporality and, 25–32, *27, 28, 29*
    pastel as alternative to, 37, 38–39
    permanence and, 16–19, *17*
On Painting (Alberti), 33
Oudry, Jean-Baptiste, 5, 20

pagan fertility gods, 97–98
painting. *See* encaustic; oil painting
paper, as emblem of fragility, 51–52, *57,* 58, *58*
pastel
    critical turn against, 34, 36, 53–59, *55, 56, 57, 58*
    development and early use, 36, 129n17
    drawbacks to, 33
    encaustic vs., 68
    fixatives, *59,* 59–64, *60, 62,* 132n102
    integrated with encaustic (*pastel en cire*), 81
    as proxy for social *délicatesse,* 33–34, *35*
    selling fragility, 11, 43–53, *44, 45, 46, 47, 49, 50, 51, 52*
    as social medium, 36–43, *37, 38, 39, 40, 42*
pastel en cire, 81
patriotism, 105, 112
permanence
    delicacy made durable, 68–72, *70*
    encaustic revival, 65–67, *66*
    as fashionable, 78–84, *82, 83*
    language of virginity and, 72–78, *73, 75, 76, 77*
Perrin, Jacques-Antoine-René, 71
Physiocracy, 98–99, 101–2, 140n76
Piles, Roger de, 24
Pilgrimage to the Isle of Cythera, The (Watteau), 13, *14,* 20, *21,* 126n52
Piron, Alexis, 82, *83*
Pleasures of the Ball, The (Watteau), 17, *17*
Pliny, the Elder, 68

Point de France lace, 8, *8*
Poisson, Abel François, 76
Pompadour, Jeanne-Antoinette Poisson, Marquise de, 56–58, *57*, 74–75, *75*, 77
porcelain vs. terracotta, 89
Portrait of Monseigneur Louis Doni d'Attichy, Bishop of Riez (Nanteuil), 38, *38*
Portrait of René Potier, duc de Tresme (Louis XIII), 37, *37*
Portrait of Voltaire (La Tour), 45–46, *47*
portraiture
    association with vanity, 54
    gender stereotypes around, 56–58, *57*, *58*
    pastel vs. oil painting, 38–39, *39*
    See also pastel
posterity
    artistic attitudes toward, 5, 24–26, 36, 81–84
    Classical tradition and, 25, 67, 85
    conflict with market, 25–32
    Enlightenment cult of, 53–56, 63–64, 85
    monuments and, 85, 103–14
    views of patrons and collectors on, 16–19, 39–43, 103–5
Poussin, Nicolas, 97–98, *99*
Preparation for the Portrait of Voltaire (La Tour), 45, *45*, *46*
Priestess Embroidering Temple Decorations (Vien), 72, *73*
Princesse de Rohan (La Tour), *58*, 59
private art market
    decline of institutional stability, 16–17, 25, 26–30, 31, 117
    public commissions vs., 88, 103, 105, 107–8, 112–13

"Regrets on Parting with My Old Dressing Gown" (Diderot), 78
Reiffenstein, Johann Friedrich, 81
reproduction, commercial, 93–96, *94*, *95*
Restout, Jean, 59, *59*
Rieux, Gabriel Bernard de, 48–52, *49*, *51*, *52*
Robert de Saint-Victor, Louis, 116

Rococo
    criticisms of, 30–31, 54, 55–56, 74, 82–83, 88, 91
    delicacy and, *6*, 6–7
    in extant scholarship, 11
    "neo-Rococo," 115
    terracotta sculpture and, 87–88
Rothschild, Henri de, 33
Rouquet, Jean André, 79–80
Rousseau, Jean-Jacques, 55, *55*

Saint-Aubin, Gabriel de, *Clodion's Montesquieu at the Salon of 1779*, 105, *107*
Saint-Pierre, Charles-Irénée Castel, abbé de, 53
Scott, Katie, 7, 31, 97
Sculptor François Girardon, The (Vivien), 38–39, *39*
sculpture, monumental, 103, *104*, 105–14, *107*, *108*, *109*, *110*, *111*
    See also terracotta
Sehgal, Tino, 12, 115–17, 120
Self-Portrait (La Tour), 60, *60*
Self-Portrait with Index Finger (La Tour), 43, *44*
sensualism, 68–69, 97–101, *98*, *99*, *100*, 133n22
Sergel, Johan Tobias, *Amor and Psyche*, 89, *90*
sexual politics, 72–78, *73*, *75*, *76*, *77*, 97, 112
Shonibare, Yinka, 115
Shovlin, John, 101
slavery, 40, 48, 50, 130n63, 131n66
social currency, pastels as, 41
Sorel, Charles, 8
speculative finance, 18–19, 40–41, 87, 93
sprezzatura (apparent effortlessness), 24

terracotta
    defined, 89
    Bacchic imagery and agronomy, 96–103, *98*, *99*, *100*, *102*

commercial potential of, 91–96, *92, 93, 94, 95*
fragility of, 89–91, *90*
market demand for, 85–88, *86, 87,* 137n1
transience, 12, 115–16
Trémolières, Pierre-Charles, 31

Unigenitus (papal bull), 17

Van Loo, Carle, 74, 77, *77*
Van Miegroet, Hans J., 40
Vase with Putti (Clodion), 91, *92*
Vestal Tuccia, The (Cozette), 77, *77*
Vibert, Jehan Georges, 118
Vien, Joseph-Marie
   Daedalus Attaching the Wings of Icarus, 69–71, *70*
   Minerva, 65, *66,* 67
   virginal subject matter, 72–74, *73,* 76, *76*
Vigny, Pierre Vigné de, 79
Village Bride, The (Watteau), 20–22, *22, 23,* 127n56
Virgin, The (François and Demarteau), 76, *76*
Virgin, The (Vien), 76, *76*
virginity, symbolism of, 72–78, *73, 75, 76, 77*
Vivien, Joseph, *The Sculptor François Girardon,* 38–39, *39*
Voltaire
   embracing philosopher identity, 54–55
   Henriade, in La Tour's *Madame de Pompadour, 57,* 58
   "Le Mondain," 46, 48
   portrait by La Tour, *45,* 45–48, *46, 47*
Votaries of Bacchus (Clodion), *100,* 101
Vouet, Simon, 37
Vue et perspective du jardin de Mr. Réveillon (Desrais), 105, *106*

Wager, Susan, 77
Warrior's Dream of Love, The (Fragonard), *2, 3,* 4
Watteau, Antoine
   Actors at a Fair, 13–14, *15*
   artistic production and circulation, *17,* 17–18, 127n57
   Gersaint's Shop Sign, 26–30, *27, 29,* 116, 127n75
   influence on Tino Sehgal, 115
   La Font's criticisms of, 30–31
   material delicacy and social *délicatesse,* 10, 32
   Pilgrimage to the Isle of Cythera, The, 13, *14,* 20, *21,* 126n52
   Pleasures of the Ball, The, 17, *17*
   Village Bride, The, 20–22, *22, 23,* 127n56
   working habits, 13–15, *14, 15,* 19–24, *21, 22, 23*
wax, virginity and, 72
   See also encaustic
wax-based wall paint, 81
women. See gender
"worldliness," 46, 48

xenophobia, 91